I Canno This Wrong

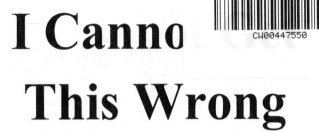

Change the way you think about anxiety

Create joy & heal collectively

Dr. Sarah Madigan
Kyra Crawford Calvert
Eliott Simpson
Naomi Preston
Faten Almregawe
Edited by and co-created with Nadia Karim

ISBN: 9798517907783

About the Structure of this Book

Part One, *Moving Towards Collective Joy,* looks at the journey this book has taken, from initially being only about my own experiences of anxiety, to blossoming into an exploration of how the stage is set for anxiety within our modern world. I explore barriers to joy and the role that discrimination can play in how we experience the world. I examine my position in the wellness world and offer a template for collective healing and responsibility.

Part Two, *My Anxiety,* zooms in on my own story. I examine the roots of my anxiety through the lens of self-compassion. I explore the role that formative experiences, societal expectations, family dynamics and trauma played in my coping mechanisms. I highlight what debilitating anxiety meant for me at that point in my life. I also invite you to the turning point where, for me, everything changed.

Part Three, *Transformations*, explores what transforming your anxiety can look and feel like within your mind, your body, and your community. I share how my feelings towards anxiety, fear, shame, guilt, and grief have been transformed beyond recognition. I explore ways to best sustain your newfound approach to seeking joy. I explain the power of telling your authentic story. I show you why supportive community is important and how to find your people.

Part Four, *Anxiety Explained and the Actions that are Always Within Your Control*, gets to the root of what anxiety is and introduces you to some ideas about brain development that might explain the origins of your own anxiety and why joy does not always feel easy to access. I share nourishing practices to address and resolve anxiety and conflict. Part Four is grounded in gratitude, surrender and celebration, offering you tangible ways to make more space in your life for joy and healing. It shows you how to move beyond coping and begin to thrive.

PART ONE

Moving Towards
Collective Joy

What If

I cannot get this wrong.

How did you read that? Read in different ways, it can mean two *very* different things.

Version One: *I must not make mistakes.*

OR

(and this is the point of my book)

Version Two: **However I act, think or feel is *not wrong*. There is no right way to do this. I cannot get this wrong.** I *allow* anxiety, I *allow* myself, I let go of fear of judgement. When I allow myself to fully be me, when I celebrate myself, in any given moment I am free. When I do this, there is nothing to fear.

When, as in Version One, I *resist* life, myself and my emotions, I *create* anxiety. In Version Two, when I release resistance and am present and focused on allowing life, on allowing myself and my emotions, I create excitement.

I cannot get this wrong.

Let that sink in.

There's self-compassion, forgiveness, and joy wrapped up in that switch from Version One, where I spent most of my life, to Version Two, where I exist now. In this book, I will outline many practices that will support this shift in mindset for you, but the initial power of telling this new story was magical. Everything changed.

2

Anxiety is just another emotion to me now, like anything. I still feel it from time to time, just as I feel excited, happy, sad, angry; but I don't focus on it anymore. It just comes and goes. As long as I am in a human body it will, and that's OK.

Anxiety isn't a *bad* thing that I need to get rid of. It just is.

Today, you could decide to give yourself a newfound grace, to allow your imperfections; to stop caring what others think.

This mantra, Version Two, is how I live my life now and it has completely transformed my anxiety (and *joy)*. A world whose edges were once harsh, cold, and terrifying has softened, opening up to become vibrant and fun.

I hope, once you've heard my story, you'll understand how you can choose to change your mindset about anxiety.

It *can* be that easy.

Hello reader,

Thank you for being here with me.

I'm Sarah. I'm writing this from a wee town in Scotland called Burntisland, which is just over the bridge from glorious Edinburgh. I am forty years old now. I still feel like a kid in many ways, though in others I do feel older and (debatably) wiser. Whales are my favourite animal. I also love elephants. I love evening light shining on buildings. A train line runs along the coast where we live and sometimes train drivers take the time to beep and wave at children on the beach. It melts my heart every time. I love it when elderly people who remind me of my grandparents dress smartly to sit at home or nip to the shops. I love it when crops blowing in the wind look like waves. I love the sound of footprints in the snow. I love live music. I love to dance.

I'm a mum to a funny and scrummy three year old, Isaac. He calls flamingos 'maflingos', hospitals 'hospibals', ambulances 'ambliances' and gives the best hugs. I'm also mum to Finlay. He would have been 6 now. He received a terminal diagnosis of spinal muscular atrophy type 1 when he was 3 months old and died in September 2015 when he was nearly 8 months old. He was an old soul, a total dreamboat. He had a little vein on his eyelid that looked like a reindeer, he had eyes that I wanted to swim in and the gentle noises he made were like a symphony to my ears. Their dad Neil, my partner, is a wonder. He is calm and gentle and adores nature; he loves sea otters, octopuses, and butterflies. He is silly and fun and we laugh a lot. We do ridiculous walks to make each other laugh and often dance in the kitchen to nineties dance music. His energy soothes me. He is accepting and encouraging of me and can also tell me when I am being unreasonable, which I love. I've never felt more safe or at ease with anyone in my life.

I am trained as a clinical psychologist and recently retrained as a transformational coach and relationship expert (which is a

4

lot more fun). I now get to do things my way, with total freedom. I host large online events, run courses and offer a small amount of one to one work. I have created a magical career and life up here in Scotland. It's marvelous and it keeps getting better, rendering me eternally grateful and in awe of the changes that have taken place in a few short years.

It wasn't always marvelous. From the age of around 21 until very recently I experienced debilitating anxiety. I spent my life trying to hide it as best I could. I was successful at doing so. It felt like a dirty secret in the world of clinical psychology; a world full of 'professionals' and high achievers. It was an environment rather non-conducive to showing vulnerability; and an environment where anxiety was viewed as a 'disorder', something we should try to help people get rid of or aim to 'fix'. I took propranolol (a drug that slows down your heart) to cope. I told a story that I was failing miserably. I succeeded in helping others overcome their anxiety but I couldn't overcome mine. I felt like a fraud. I was convinced there was something inherently wrong with me. Just to kick myself while I was down, there was, on top of the crippling anxiety, an extremely thick layer of shame. I was deeply ashamed of my seeming inability to cope with the smallest of things. I told a story that *everyone* else was coping better than me.

In the last year or so I have completely rewritten these stories about anxiety. They are just that, *stories*. I have become obsessed with creating joy, instead of being fanatic about avoiding fear. I have created a brand new world for myself. It feels so far removed from the old one full of misery and shame. Now, my world is full of fun, silliness, tenderness, love, and connection. And trust. It's full to the brim with trust.

Of course, it is also still peppered with other emotions at times such as sadness, grief, anger, and fear - but I relate to these emotions entirely differently these days, which irrevocably shifts the texture of them. Take my old nemesis Fear, for example. It's become something I accept. I take fear lightly, I feel no shame around it, I celebrate it, I laugh at it and I carry on regardless. *I embrace myself fully, with or without anxiety.* I used to resist it, fear it, think about it *all* the time, and tell so many stories about how I shouldn't feel it.

Having lost a child, I am astounded by this truth but here it is: I am without doubt the happiest I have ever been. I want to shine a light on the little accidents and non-accidents along the way that led to this; to share what has helped me so much, how I have found such solace, peace, and happiness. I want *you* to gain from the wisdom I have developed from a culmination of twenty years of being a nervous wreck! From my lifetime as an empath deeply feeling everything and witnessing the processes that occur within and around me (I've always been fascinated with emotion). From my experiences of mothering and grieving for a terminally ill child. From my career as a clinical psychologist and transformational coach and my work with hundreds and hundreds of people with anxiety. I want you to know what the evidence says about anxiety in a way that you can relate to, even when you're deep in the grip of it and finding it hard to imagine a life that isn't defined by feeling anxious.

Thousands and thousands of souls all over the world right now are experiencing debilitating anxiety. People are panicking, using substances to escape, trying all kinds of methods to numb out, even taking their own lives. Most people try to manage it alone, going untreated, not seeing a psychologist or a therapist. This is where my story comes in. All of us can vastly improve our lives with more knowledge of anxiety and how it works. My story sits at that intersection of personal experience and professional case studies and approaches from the belief, amongst others, that you need to *focus on something other than the anxiety* to overcome it. This book will help you to re-jig the kaleidoscope, find the new patterns that work best for you. It will help you to discover and tune into your new focus.

Clinical psychologists often view themselves as scientist-practitioners and may question my ability to add to the evidence base, since I am not conducting a randomised control trial (a carefully measured and controlled experiment, the gold standard in scientific research). To that, I say, '*I cannot get this wrong*'. This is my book and I'm doing it my way. I have written the book I so wish I could have read when in the depths of my own darkness and hopelessness. My goal is to spread love and healing and to help people release shame. I trust my wisdom, I trust my learned experience, I trust my ability to inspire people and light them up. I have hard evidence behind me, in terms of my completely altered emotional world, and the altered worlds of hundreds of my clients as well. I am excited to share with you *my way*. No longer do I have to triple check the strict academic reference style guidelines for the specific scientific journal to which I'm submitting. That's not to say that I take this responsibility lightly; I feel a duty to tell the stories in this book with as much truth and authenticity as possible, and as much empathy as if you were sitting across from me in a session, because I believe that's what will help you. I am celebrating the fact that I can follow my rules instead of someone else's! This freedom has made the process of writing this book a joy, a privilege, and a pleasure. A bit like my life now, I am free from my fear of fear.

For me, this freedom had a *lot* to do with *focus*.

This book is not just about me. I am beyond thrilled that, as the project evolved, four marvelous humans joined me to share their words and their hearts. I'm excited to introduce them and for you to read their stories within these pages.

Kyra Crawford Calvert is a published writer and art historian, multi-media artist, and the founding engineer/principal designer at Black Fish Gold Studios. She is a native of the historic Rondo neighbourhood in St. Paul, Minnesota and splits her time between the USA and Jamaica.

Eliott Simpson is an autistic, asexual comedian & filmmaker. He was born in Cambridge, UK. Eliott moved to Budapest when

7

he was 3 months old, then Michigan, then New Jersey. He grew up mostly in Hungary and the USA.

Naomi Preston is one of my closest friends. She is a Cognitive Behavioural Therapist working in the NHS. Born and raised in Milton Keynes, she has studied in Scotland and Japan. Now residing on Walney Island in Cumbria, UK, with her husband Mark and two children Mayumi and Micah.

Faten Almregawe is a writer and mother of two beautiful boys. She was born in Homs, Syria. The war led her and her husband and children to seek refuge, first to Jordan in 2012, and then to Cumbria, UK, in 2019.

I included these four chapters for the following reasons:

- To increase understanding of the various ways anxiety can present for different people within modern society
- To amplify voices that may not normally be heard
- To help people working directly with 'minds', and psychological, emotional well-being to start to consider their responsibility to understand all minds (I am honest about my journey with this and how it's something I've only recently begun to intentionally do)
- To help you feel connected to the guest authors, like I do
- To inspire you to reflect on how you think and talk about people who seem different to you and, if applicable, to consider how the children in your life learn about 'difference'
- To increase empathy and understanding of people whose life experiences differ to yours, because when we allow ourselves to feel other people's feelings, we empathise and connect to our shared humanity
- To prevent people from feeling excluded from the messages within the book
- As a stance against the marginalisation I have witnessed within health professions and educational settings and which I was also part of

- Because I adore the authors and was fascinated to hear their voices, as I'm sure you will be too
- So that the guest authors may inspire people who share similar experiences to either speak out their needs, develop more compassion for themselves and/or to take action to feel better
- In the same way I want you to turn towards your own pain in order to heal, I want us to turn towards other people's pain in order for them to heal too - validation is an important part of healing
- I want us to connect to 'other' people so as to stop making them 'other' people. In the same way, I want you to connect to the parts of yourself you may reject or view as unacceptable so that you can release judgement of self. To nurture a move away from separation - separation from the parts of ourselves we judge and from the part of others we judge (or don't understand, or fear) - and turn instead towards acceptance and wholeness.
- When you meet yourself exactly where you are, it is easier to meet others exactly where they are. We have been physically separated during the pandemic: we know the pain of separation. Mental and emotional separation are also painful and damaging - I want people to get closer to each other's minds and perspectives.
- I want you to empathise more deeply with your feelings and needs - not to judge them but to understand and empathise. Similarly, I want you to empathise more deeply with other people's feelings and needs (this could be your children, partner, friend, colleague or a marginalised group of people you perhaps knew less about before reading the book)
- These two processes of empathising more deeply with self and others are not unrelated. When you understand and love yourself more powerfully you are more able to do this with others too - when you stop making yourself wrong it is easier to stop making others wrong

Through the chapters, I'm going to take you on a little journey and give you the following:

- A sense that *you are not alone*
- An unwavering belief that *there is nothing wrong with you*
- Encouragement to *entirely release any shame around anxiety*
- A new way of thinking about anxiety; not viewing it as *bad,* or something you need to get rid of
- The knowledge that gratitude practice (and it is a practice) can transform your experience as a human
- A soothed soul
- Hope
- A laugh (and maybe a cry)
- An understanding of what is happening in your body when you are anxious
- Knowledge of the body's important role in transforming anxiety or trauma
- An understanding that you may have created a vicious cycle of thinking and behaving and thinking and behaving that *you can* turn around - you can gain momentum in the other direction
- A plan on how to move forward (and get lit the f up!)
- Ways to cope (to more than cope - to *thrive*)
- Ways of writing new stories about yourself and your anxiety
- The ability to stop caring what other people think
- Inspiration to start focusing on what you *do* want in life and not on what you don't want
- Ways to stop modelling shame and fear to your children or loved ones and to help them celebrate themselves and others (to celebrate and not fear differences)
- Ways instead to live your dream life
- Ways to create *freedom* of body, mind, emotions, and spirit

- A space to consider marginalised groups; and how we need to collectively take action to move forward in ways that enable everyone to create joy
- Confidence to get messy and to allow yourself to not have all the answers around sensitive topics (like I did in the process of writing the book - and will talk about!); knowing that it is better to try from a position of honesty than to say and do nothing
- Last but not least. Encouragement to simultaneously *feel it all*. To allow your messy, unpredictable, wild experience which is inevitable in a human body.

I will delve more deeply throughout the book into all of this but here are the actions, little and gigantic, that I've taken and continue to practice every day:

I left a job that wasn't aligned with my spirit; found a community of amazing people who uplift and support me; had therapy (some was helpful and some not); had transformational coaching (game changer); decided to start telling a different story about my anxiety; regularly and purposefully do things that make me fear the judgements of others; dance; meditate; fully accepted and embraced my 'too-much-ness', released shame around it and now use it as my magic in my career; feel and express joy a *lot* (joy is an incredibly vulnerable emotion and you will trigger many people when you allow yourself to fully feel it and lean into it; do it anyway)....

Key to all of the above?

I stopped caring about what other people think and I stopped living my life for others.

Of course, you don't just stop doing this altogether. I (and likely you) will work on it again and again for the rest of my life. However, these days, I pay attention to my thoughts and fears. When I realise I am drifting towards doing or not something because of what other people or society might think, I pause. Instead, I base my decisions on what is right for *me* in my soul, what my body knows is right, and it's crystal clear (when I listen).

I started listening to my body and my inner voice and trusting my inner knowing.

I started giving voice to and listening to my heart.

I use my inner system to guide me to what is right for me, not external factors or my conditioned mind.

I make decisions from a place of love not fear.

Corona times

When the inspiration came to me to write this book, I didn't even think about the global pandemic despite being slap bang in the middle of it. I was lying in the bath one evening and suddenly thought, '*I have to share what has helped me so much*'. I thought back to all the wasted times that could have been glorious had I not hated myself so much for being anxious, or had I not spent the whole time focusing on my anxiety rather than being present to the beauty of the moment. Everything slotted together like a jigsaw in my mind - the anxiety, joy, loss, learning. I started typing on my phone there and then and haven't stopped since.

But, of course, we have been experiencing such an upending and once in a lifetime (let's hope!) experience, Covid-19. No doubt it has had a significant impact on many people's anxiety levels. Thousands of amazing healthcare staff, teachers and frontline workers have had to carry on in their jobs, exposing themselves to the virus. The Health Foundation (health.org.uk) reported that 69% of people in the UK have reported feeling somewhat or very worried about the effect Covid is having in their life. The most common issues are worry about the future (63%), feeling stressed or anxious (56%) and feeling bored (49%). The IFS (Institute for Fiscal Studies) states that mental health has worsened substantially by over 8% on average as a result of the pandemic. Social isolation, jobs and financial strains, housing insecurity, domestic violence, working in frontline services, alongside reduced access to mental health services are a powerful concoction.

I hope that this book will be of help in the time during and after the global pandemic to arm people with the knowledge and skills to be able to step into the role of *empowered creator* of their life. I want you to feel powerful in the face of any adversity. Although you cannot change the current situation, avoid the restrictions or eradicate the virus, you absolutely can create beautiful experiences in your life and choose to take action to

13

feel better and to take control of your body, mind, emotions, and spirit.

I think the experience of caring for my terminally ill child - and then subsequently, you could argue, triumphing in the face of extremely deep grief - has given me such a strong and resolute belief that we can overcome more than we realise. That our mindset, and not the environment, is the most important thing. You can use the pandemic to explain negative emotions, or you can take 100% responsibility for your focus and mindset. This is not to dismiss your reality. Each of us has experienced the pandemic in starkly different ways, and it has impacted our lives to different degrees. For some, the repercussions of the pandemic will last many years beyond the lifting of lockdown. Some people have lost loved ones. Some people now find themselves in situations of chronic stress because of lack of access to the support services they previously relied upon, or with health problems aggravated by delays in treatment. Those already in situations of vulnerability may now feel completely isolated. Others may be living with long-term financial uncertainty or in unsafe relationships. If this is your experience, you may find comfort and strength in the pages of the book: the realisation that while you cannot control some aspects of your situation, you can take control of your anxieties *around* your situation and, in time, transform your experiences.

Before Finlay died, you could argue that everything was going swimmingly. Nothing major had gone wrong, I had a loving partner, great friends, and a nice home. After he died, alongside the pain and loss grew a more dynamic, beautiful, rich emotional world within me. My mindset and perspective shifted seismically, in a way that has made me feel so differently about life. I am so much less focused on the negative, so much more connected to love and trust, so much more determined to make the most of every second that is gifted to me on this planet.

I am keenly aware of the fragility of life. The odd time in the dark of night, it freaks me out. I have moments of '*I can't believe*

14

one day I will be separated from all the people that I love the most' and, *'WTAF?! What is the point in all of this?'* Most distressing for me are fears about my son Isaac's health. Thankfully, though, these madness-inducing states are always fleeting and then the other feelings resume. The ones where I am aligned with my truth and my true nature and my deep-down feelings; my soul. Then I feel like I am *supposed* to feel good. It is *supposed* to feel easy. I can deliberately create ease and joy. The positive side of this particular form of anxiety - that deep, ever-present feeling in my bones that life is fleeting - is that I focus passionately and (almost) unwaveringly on making the most of my time here. I help others do the same in my work as a transformational coach. It is my reason for being here and I am so driven and connected to this purpose.

I remember close to the start of the pandemic Rob Delaney (the actor from Catastrophe which is a fantastic British comedy) shared a post on Instagram about how caring for his son who had cancer and subsequently died (rest in peace Henry) had prepared him for Covid. My husband Neil and I knew what he meant. We had spent months in a form of isolation. We didn't ever see people who had even a whiff of a runny nose. We didn't leave the house much aside from a quick walk on the beach, dragging along with us all of the equipment needed to 'vacuum up' all of Finny's secretions from his mouth so he wouldn't choke on them. We also faced the worst. We faced Finn's definite death; we couldn't avoid it by wearing masks or washing our hands. We also survived the worst. So, when I found out that Covid affected kids a lot less than adults, I have to admit I didn't feel too anxious about it. Early on in the pandemic, too, the adults in our household - me, Neil, and our friend Jane who was living with us at the time - experienced Covid in a mild form, which likely enabled me to feel less anxious about subsequently catching it as the months progressed.

I know that, had the pandemic happened during Finn's life, I would have been beyond anxious. If you are a parent out there with a poorly child, or someone with immunodeficiency or if you

15

have vulnerable loved ones, I am sending you love and strength. If you have lost someone you love, I am sending my compassion. For some this has been an extremely stressful time and if this is you, I send you love and healing. I hope this book empowers and inspires you. Keep the faith.

When *others* tell you that you are wrong

There's an expression in the wellness world: 'Don't let anybody steal your joy.' Yes, we can all begin to form positive new mindset habits that remind us that we cannot get this wrong, and I hope you're beginning to believe that transformation is possible for you. But what about when it's not ourselves but *other people* who are telling us that we are wrong? Telling us, violently and persistently, that there is something fundamentally wrong and offensive about our existence in the world.

Often within the self-development world, mental wellbeing is framed as solely a mindset issue, to the detriment of those bodies and minds that do not fit the normative standard. It can be extremely distressing, infuriating, and fatiguing for people who exist within a societal structure that can devalue, dehumanise or hurt them (for example facing discrimination due to race, gender, sexual orientation, socio-economic status, being in care, or for any other reason) to be told that their mental wellbeing is entirely within their control. That single narrative leaves little space for truly understanding the psychological impact of unprovoked attacks, which happen without warning and can puncture an individual's joy no matter how empowered and uplifted they are feeling in the preceding seconds. I will be talking a great deal about things that you *can* do to empower yourself but this book has taken such an interesting path to becoming something *much* bigger than an individualistic guide to managing anxiety.

To begin with, the book was mainly my story, with some guidance on how to transform your experience of anxiety. But the truth is, I was too scared of getting it wrong to dive deeper into thinking about anxiety and joy for *everyone*.

There may be people reading this book thinking, 'It's not me who thinks I'm doing anything wrong; it's other people in society.' You may have experienced racism, homophobia, ableism or transphobia or more than one of those; you may have experienced a society that tells you that you are '*getting it wrong*' just by being you, just because of the colour of your skin or because of who you love. Read on. I hope you see yourself reflected in the other stories shared within these pages. I see you.

The impact of childhood trauma on anxiety and joy

There may also be people reading who did not experience loving parents in the same way I did; who may have experienced extreme abuse and neglect in childhood. You may think, 'I cannot relate to this author'. You may have received lifelong messages that there is something wrong with you. Children often assume there is something wrong with them when they have abusive parents because it is easier than the alternative, which is to think that there is something wrong with the people who they rely on; a terrifying and life threatening thought for a child. I will talk about the impact of early childhood trauma on brain development, anxiety, and joy later in the book. I have years of experience of working with young people and adults who have experienced trauma, so even if you can't relate to *my* experiences, I hope this book can still be very valuable for you.

It is absolutely my belief that whatever life has dealt you, you *can* empower yourself and you can do this by training, conditioning and reprogramming your mind. You *can* commit to viewing yourself as the powerful creator of your life whatever your experiences. You are not your past. You can choose more helpful feelings, thoughts, and emotions; you can work at releasing your limiting beliefs. I also acknowledge that this is easier for some than others, depending on how society and people may label or respond to you, and on your early childhood experiences.

This book is *both* a guide to transforming your mindset *and* an invitation to think about how we can all collectively create a society whereby people are able to create joy from a more level playing field. It is an invitation to celebrate *difference* and to help children and their generation do the same.

The journey this book took to exploring collective joy

This chapter feels vulnerable yet important to write. Like I said, this book started out as 'my story'. When I sent a copy of my first draft of this book to my editor Nadia, I hadn't included *anything* about the impact of discrimination on anxiety and joy. Worse, I had fleetingly considered doing so but felt scared of 'getting it wrong' so avoided it. I told a story that it was an autobiographical book and so I couldn't talk powerfully about these issues. It wasn't my place.

It, of course, isn't my place to talk about the direct impact of racism or other forms of discrimination that I have never experienced or which sit outside my area of expertise. It is, however, my place to consult those who have experienced this. To learn, to be open, to be honest about the anxieties that arose for me during this process - in the hope that others may feel more able to also take risks and confront, explore and reflect on discrimination - rather than avoid it, as I had been doing previously. Further, it *is* my duty as someone working with 'minds' and 'mindsets' to actively seek out information to help me deepen my understanding of all minds - not just minds similar to mine.

The truth is I made the initial decision to focus the book solely on my mind from a place of fear. Of course, the universe has a way of pulling that stuff back into focus! I waited for Nadia's initial feedback (oh my, the nerves of sending a first draft of your first book to someone for the first time... talk about fearing getting it wrong!) - and there it was. As well as some incredibly positive feedback, she admitted that the book was triggering for her as a Black woman. It was a common experience for her to finish a book about wellbeing and joy that made no acknowledgement of the fact that the system is rigged. She suggested my book could be more useful to a wider group of people if I changed it to address these issues. Later, when we spoke on the phone, Nadia admitted that it was equally difficult for her to raise these concerns. She spoke about how, in previous roles as editor, she would gloss over the fact that she didn't see herself reflected in the pages she was helping to craft. It felt different this time. Here was an opportunity not to erase the experiences of people like her, and of all minority groups. She realised that if she felt alienated, others would too. We spoke about how there was no easy way to have this conversation: it tugged at the seams of discomfort and vulnerability for both of us.

I felt shame that I hadn't already explored the impact of discrimination on anxiety and joy and feared I had got it *wrong*. Even now as I am writing this, part of me wants to hit *delete* and just pretend it was all my idea from the start but that isn't the truth. There was a great deal of valuable learning for me in this process and I believe it is important and potentially immensely helpful to share this process.

This book is about *not hiding*; it is about releasing shame, so I need to practice what I preach. It isn't about me feeling comfortable. It isn't about me 'getting it wrong'. I need to put my ego aside and be prepared to jump in and get it wrong. I am willing to leave my comfort zone and make mistakes. I am willing to be wrong, to learn and to do things differently next time.

My living in a white body, and all the benefits that come along with that, meant that I hadn't *really* deeply considered the impact of racism on joy. Even in my career as a clinical psychologist, I had never examined the role of facilitating 'collective joy'.

These uncomfortable feelings associated with the thought 'f*ck I'm getting this totally wrong' also surfaced for me in an interaction with Kyra, one of the guest chapter authors. I was hiring Kyra in the role of 'race consultant' initially to explore these issues. This, I'm thrilled, developed into the role of guest author. I messaged Kyra one day about an upcoming meeting and told her about a conversation I had read on Facebook regarding the American election. The Facebook conversation (a public conversation) I recounted to her began with the following declaration by an individual and went along the lines of this:

'Please remember that whoever becomes President there is only one person responsible for your life and your joy; that person is you.'

Some people felt upset and angry. They claimed this statement showed a total lack of understanding and empathy for Black, Indigenous and People of Colour (BIPOC). They pointed out how much support was going to a racist white supremacist ideal, and that this was frightening for people.

They called for the acknowledgement that there are external factors impacting our ability to create joy.

The comment that struck me the most, especially given that I was writing a book about the very topic, was the following:

'*Also, you can't generate joy if you are dead.*'

I had repeated this conversation to Kyra but hadn't received a response and felt increasingly concerned that I had offended her. I worried that, without knowing her well enough, I had been insensitive or careless reciting such an impactful statement. When we spoke, I learned I had not offended her and felt grateful that we were able to talk about this process. This sense of (white) people feeling like they need to 'walk on eggshells' was not new for Kyra. All of these feelings and untanglings and resolutions were helping me to learn, though. Then I could do better next time.

Of course, I could have avoided those feelings entirely by not having hired a race consultant, or by having never told Kyra about the Facebook conversation, perhaps by having logged off instead of engaging with the comments at all. I could have told myself that it was nothing to do with me, just something happening in a volatile place on the other side of an ocean. But what a missed opportunity for understanding, learning, and empathy that would have been.

This 'stress about getting it wrong' was what I had been shying away from, and maybe why I had been reticent to speak to people directly about the impact of racism on anxiety and joy. It's a dangerous stance. This is not about me or my feeling comfortable. Ego doesn't serve this situation. It's OK to get things wrong, it's OK to mess up, to get messy, to jump in, with good intentions in your heart. To get involved and get it wrong and feel shame and try again. It is *so* much better than saying and doing nothing. Avoiding.

When we avoid, we invalidate.

When we avoid, we dismiss.

When we avoid, we ignore.

When we avoid, we are complicit.

I was starting to reflect on how I had been avoiding thinking about my role in fighting for racial justice for too long, both as an individual and as a health professional. I am vigilant about focusing on positive things (as you will read in the book) but there has to be room to think about 'collective joy' - especially for people working in the areas of mental health and 'wellness'. What about collectively focusing on a world where everyone is more able to access and sustain joy?

The world of therapy needs to listen more powerfully to minority groups and to learn about *all minds* and *all emotional worlds*. I was speaking to a Black friend recently (she consented to me sharing this information) about how during Covid, she was able to speak to a Black therapist in a different part of the country on Zoom. She said it was such a relief not having to waste energy explaining to the therapist about the impact of racism on her emotional wellbeing. She talked about how freeing it was to be able to speak without constantly wondering if they believed her, whether they judged her as being 'overly sensitive', because they had a shared experience of being Black in Britain. Nadia helped me to understand how the subtexts of the impact of discrimination often never reach the surface in relationships; they remain unspoken, hidden, not taken into account, unheard, and untreated. It reminded me of how one of my closest friends, Naomi, often didn't voice her needs with regards to her deafness - how her needs often remained hidden, too. I was starting to open my eyes to the serious barriers that exist in our society and inevitably influence both anxiety and joy - the topics of my book.

When I spoke to Kyra regarding my fear of 'getting it wrong', she said that when she read my message, she felt that I 'saw her humanity'. The phrase, *'you can't create joy if you are dead'*, was exactly the kind of thing that she would say.

Here are some examples of how living in a white, heterosexual, cis-gendered, abled body have benefited me in the wellness world and in the wider world, and without doubt impacted my wellbeing and ability to create joy. I also outline ways in which various identities have been marginalised in the settings, both professional and educational, that I have been in.

- I wrote a book on anxiety and joy and didn't really think about how they were impacted by society and discrimination until someone told me about this, i.e. I had not experienced significant societal barriers to joy or stressors which regularly impacted my anxiety

- My white face is represented in nearly all the coaching circles I am exposed to and the advertising for wellness events

- I have been at events that have been attended by nearly all white people and I haven't even noticed or registered this

24

- All of my lecturers from undergrad university and during my doctorate were white

- I don't have to worry about Isaac being harassed or devalued by society because of the colour of his skin

- If Isaac chose to go backpacking when he was 18, I wouldn't have to worry about which countries were likely to be more or less racist

- In so many of the children's books that I own, Isaac's white face and his able body are represented. If I had a non-white child this would not be the case. Finlay was disabled and so I feel it even more deeply now, when I see how there are few books with representations of disabled children

- I see positive representations of white people all the time in the news and media

- During my 5 year doctoral training as a clinical psychologist I received zero training on race, or on racism. Now that I have been learning about how race and racism impact so much on physical and mental health, this seems astounding

- I do not have to worry about whether I, my family or child would be protected by the police because of skin colour

- I don't have to expend energy wondering if someone hates me or my family because of skin colour

- I have never had hateful words shouted at me from strangers, just because of the colour of my skin

- I have never had to deal with the impact of this level of discrimination on my central nervous system

25

- I have never had to question if I was welcome or if I would receive microaggressions in the wellness places I have attended: dance, yoga, coaching; all predominantly white spaces

- I don't have to answer questions all the time about where I am from because of my appearance

- I don't have to feel like I am 'representing' my race and the resultant pressure of this

- When seeing footage of police murdering a Black man, I don't have the added trauma (alongside the trauma that most humans feel when witnessing such an act) that this could happen to *my* child one day

- When I got married, I didn't have to wonder if people would shout homophobic comments at me in the street and ruin my day

- I do not experience a sense of invisibility, prejudice, discrimination or invalidation when asked to tick the box describing my gender on official forms, or any other number of daily aggressions that transgender people and non-binary people experience

- I am able to use a toilet that matches my gender without other people debating my choice

- I can access toilets and public transport without any stress because of the way they are designed for able bodies (in the town I currently live in, there is no access for wheelchair users at the train station. If you need to get off at Burntisland you must take a bus from a nearby station, thereby making the journey a lot longer and separating you from your fellow travelers)

26

- In the workplace, if I am asked if I have a boyfriend or a husband, I do not have the energy drain of deciding whether or not to explain that I am not heterosexual

- I can walk anywhere in the UK holding hands with Neil without fearing physical violence or verbal abuse

- If I get a new job, I assume people will celebrate me and assume I got the job on my own merits, I do not suspect that people are questioning if I got the job because of my race or disability

There are many more examples of how living in a white, able, cis-gendered body have privileged me. Intersectionality sits at the heart of our identities: none of us is just one thing. We are Black, white, queer, disabled, cis-gendered, northern, asexual, working class, Catholic, able-bodied... and every one of our actions and inactions, every time we choose to stand up or remain silent, has a ripple effect on those around us. Perhaps the most striking truth that hit me this year is that, like many white, university-educated, professionally qualified people of my generation (and in a profession centred around individual emotion), I made it to the age of 40 without having been required to think deeply about the impact of racism, discrimination, and systemic inequality on physical and mental health, on anxiety or joy. I used to journal about racism as a child - and my objections to it. What happened to that part of me? As an adult I continued to strongly (but pathetically in retrospect) object to racism, I challenged things people said from time to time, I watched documentaries about racism and thought about it more broadly within the political sphere, I talked to my husband and friends from time to time. But I failed to think about how it was right in front of me, in my actions or inactions, how it was something I should be studying and fighting against - as an individual and as a professional working with 'minds'. This is why Kyra's words in the next chapter touched so many nerves for me - how could I have missed this reality for so long?

27

On Blackness, Madness, and the Joy of Authenticity
By Kyra Crawford Calvert

> Negroes,
> Sweet and docile,
> Meek, humble and kind:
> Beware the day
> They change their mind!
> Wind
> In the cotton fields,
> Gentle Breeze:
> Beware the hour
> It uproots trees!
> — Langston Hughes

Of every piece of literature, verse, or music I've known —
written, live, or recorded — this 10 line poem from Langston
Hughes stays with me most inherently. It shines through my
mind as a timeless question with which I grapple daily:

How and when?

I've had it memorized from a young age and I know many
black people who can recite some version of the first sentence.

It resonates as deeply as one's own voice cutting through that
initial slice of morning — those moments of surreality between
dreaming and waking where the futures possible are endless.

I often find myself in wonder about the enduring nature of
black life, joy, and influence under incredibly egregious and
systemically damaging circumstances. I am awed that there
aren't more cracks in our cultural foundation of joy because the
shared and widely recorded realities of slavery and historic

28

robbery are often denied, undermined, and rewritten at large. It is the gaslighting of nations.

Gaslighting is psychological manipulation whereby one is caused to doubt their reality and thus their sanity. Gaslighting racism creates a heightened level of anxiety around a collective and individual **truth**. It is necessary to acknowledge and treat racism as a mental health crisis for both the sufferer and suffering. It is necessary to acknowledge and treat the denial of racism and race-based consequences as a symptom of that crisis.

How have I persisted and when will I stop doing so...joyfully?

My grandmother kept several bottles of 7-Up in both refrigerators, the one in the kitchen and the one in the guest bedroom upstairs. It was a medicinal necessity to help 'calm her stomach.'

I could never understand why her stomach was so chronically upset until I started to experience these strange and sometimes catastrophic sensations in my gut — waves of shooting pain and uneasiness, sweating, vomiting and worse. At the time, doctors attributed it, along with my every ailment, to morbid obesity. When I talked to my grandmother — a petite woman in every sense — about the episodes, she told me they were due to worry and to get some 7-Up. The doctors don't know nothing.

About a year before she died, I was joyfully ascending the stairs of my home and having a conversation with my partner who was behind me. Suddenly, my heart began to race and clench, my stomach burned, my body was shaking. I could not move further but was afraid to let myself fall. I knew if I fell I'd die of a heart attack. I didn't know it. But I knew it. I held on to the banister and leaned forward while my partner held me up.

29

'Are you okay? What is happening?!'

'I don't know, I don't know! I think I'm dying...'

'Please help me.'

And soon the wave washed over and out. I could breathe and was filled with utter gratitude to know that alive is a feeling.

When I went to the hospital there was no sign of a heart attack and since I had lost over 150 pounds it could not be attributed to my weight. Thus, it was attributed to nothing.

Over the next two months, I would have numerous episodes, each more intense than the last. I was in the hospital 6 times during this period and never received a diagnosis beyond severe abdominal pain, chest pain, cyclic vomiting.

Multiple stressors would cause me to seek cognitive behavioral therapy where I described these episodes to my therapist as being my mental and emotional breaking point. She realized that I was describing, symptom for symptom, the DSM-5 criteria for panic disorder. I found out that people with panic disorder frequently go to the emergency room (ER) with chest pain or shortness of breath, fearing that they are dying of a heart attack. They commonly report a sudden unexpected and spontaneous onset of fear or discomfort, typically reaching a peak within 10 minutes. And I wondered, after six visits to the same ER, why was this diagnosis not available or considered sooner? After I complained that multiple pain medications weren't helping, did doctors think my goal was a higher prescription or, worse, that I was creating illness?

Whenever I have an episode, which is rare these days, I grab a 7-Up and Saltine crackers. In ritual, I pour a little seltzer out for my grandmother and the systems that, perhaps, don't believe black women are entitled to joy. It is difficult not to ponder if there is a deeply embedded fabric in our nation(s) that cloak black people in pain to refrain from humanizing our existence. To acknowledge, for instance, that I feel pain is to know that so too did my commodified, whipped, and psychologically abused ancestors.

It's just a musing, but it's the sort that stems from an insidious reality and makes it more complex to manifest joy from self-determination and higher vibrational thinking. It has been important for me on my transformational journey to first remain rooted, though not beholden or enslaved, to this reality. I do not blame myself for having to overcome the anxieties of racism to live a life of joy, nor do I take on the responsibility of convincing others that my experience is real, global, and unrectified. There are numerous resources — scientific and primary — that speak to racism, the lack of reparations, and their effect on the economy, mental wellness, and societal realities of black people.

It is my sole responsibility to radically and by any means create a life of pure bliss and fulfilled desires. It is a historical debt that so many of us owe ourselves in this timeline and timelines previous.

It is not easy. It is certainly a feat, a triumph. And in wisdom and truth, it can be done. Here and now.

—-

A week before my grandmother died, I spoke with her about the stomach upsets and told her that the 7-Up had been a great help to me. I told her about my time in the hospital and that I had finally received a diagnosis from a therapist. That I had panic disorder, which basically meant my body could no longer differentiate between moments of fight or flight and produced panic attacks that mimicked heart attacks. She didn't respond immediately and I wondered if she was thinking of a way to politely tell me that therapists don't know nothing.

With an unfitting exasperation of relief, she replied,

31

'This world is not meant for us, baby. It's hard to feel safe around all this Whiteness.' —-

When my grandmother died, my cousin told me a story that made her sad. My grandmother shared with her that people in the break room at her job (she cleaned buildings and dorms for a local university) jokingly called her 'The Egg Lady'. They called her this because she ate boiled eggs everyday for lunch. She'd laugh along with them but cry to herself because eggs were all she had to eat.

I hear this and am reminded that we live in a system without much empathy around the connectedness of race, addiction, poverty and homelessness, generational wealth, access to resources, and joy.

If someone eats a boiled egg everyday for lunch, it is naive and dangerous to automatically assume the egg is a habit of joy over circumstance. The assumption of joy is steeped in historical atrocities whereby the presence of colonialism has been detrimentally deemed a necessary and saving grace.

—-

A system is defined as a set of things working together as parts of a mechanism or an interconnecting network.

Also as a set of principles or procedures according to which something is done.

An organized scheme or method.

A complex whole.

—-

Together, we and the rules we've accepted to govern each other, are a system.

32

The system is not compartmentalized. It either works as a whole or it doesn't work at all.

Our system just doesn't work.

Our system creates race, wealth and poverty, and simultaneously kills people for attempting to live in its juxtaposed structure that cannot work with parts broken, dislodged, or misplaced.

It is here that I say rest in power to **George Floyd** and **Breonna Taylor**, both murdered by and in consequence of said system. We say rest in power because we hope these terrible moments will create shifts in the tectonic plates of the earth and spark a joy that is lasting, and widely available.

——-

Not only do we need to witness and honor what we do that hurts others, we also need to be in alignment with what we do, ignore, say, and think that hurts ourselves.

When I pretend that I am not perplexed by the magic that is my life despite the circumstances, I am not honoring the weight of my reality. When I participate in transformational programming that chooses to wash over the historical disparities that persist due to slavery and colonization, I am telling the universe and the law of attraction that I am small and don't acknowledge my roots, my history, my story. I am saying that I would like to transcend my circumstances by discounting my truths yet they are innate and unwavering. And they are not mine alone. Which means I cannot heal and expect all to be healed. I have to know that the fabric is deep and respect the time it takes for us all to reach the middle.

But I am here, square in the center.

Waiting to expand.

33

How?

— I allow myself to be in awe of the magic it takes to persist and thrive

— I seek therapy

— I stopped doubting my truth

— I quit my job and began work for myself

— I received life coaching

— I spend my money on and consume what I believe in

— I acknowledge the symbology of familial cycles and remain in communication with my ancestors

— I am unapologetically authentic in my purpose and beliefs. Those who are meant for me understand that there is a spiritual and earthly reality — sometimes they coincide, sometimes they don't.

— I am BIG and I don't play small. I use all of my lessons and skill sets to propel forward and I don't hide to make others comfortable

— I don't stay places where I don't feel welcomed and celebrated

And when?

Now. I've changed my mind on respectability and I am on a mission to find myself. It's time. I've found that the sweetness within only gets sweeter when the fucks given are the fucks intended.

My reflections on Kyra's chapter

I was so drawn to Kyra - her power and warmth drew me in. There was a simultaneous softness and strength within her which I resonated with. We had had minimal interactions, a few messages here and there before I contacted her to invite her to be involved with the book. I followed my heart.

When I first read Kyra's chapter, I was riveted by every word - blown away by her writing. She enabled me to feel and to start to imagine the weight of racism on her and her loved ones. I have come to love Kyra - and so to read these words, and to be confronted with the reality of how racism has impacted her body, mind, emotions, and spirit so profoundly was sobering, shocking and devastating. The image of Kyra's body experiencing such a level of stress and anxiety, that would give cause to her experiencing chest pain and repeated episodes of vomiting, shook me to the core. Only once in my life has my body had such heightened anxiety that I vomited - the day after cremating my child. So, the thought that Kyra would be pushed to experience this level of emotional distress, again and again, because of, in her Grandmother's words, being unable to feel 'safe amongst all this Whiteness' was so eye opening for me.

It is easy to read statistics about racism and to feel detached but here Kyra was pulling me into her family life and emotional world - feeling the pain of knowing her Grandmothers' distress at being called the Egg Lady and Kyra herself questioning why she hadn't received a diagnosis and treatment sooner for her panic disorder: painful *and* - I cannot think of a better word - *wrong*.

When Kyra and I spoke, she talked to me about how hard it is to heal when you are ignored or denied. It made me think of the human body and how if one part is hurting or damaged it cannot heal without the rest of the body, working in harmony with it.

I hope this chapter enables you, the reader, to either feel seen and validated if you share these experiences or to start to comprehend, as I am doing, the extent to which racism and mental health are entwined. As Kyra says, racism represents *a mental health crisis* and should be responded to as such.

The main feeling I am left with upon reading Kyra's words is one of awe - just like what Kyra describes. Awe at how she triumphs in the face of such adversity. Awe at what an absolutely powerful woman she is, despite her anxieties. I feel joyful at how she has and continues to create bliss in her life as a creative, intelligent, and powerful AF Black woman.

It makes me really consider the amount of energy it must take to try and make sense of and live with racism as someone living in a Black body. Kyra's body was clearly in a state of fight or flight (I go on to discuss this further later in the book) - feeling unsafe and under attack - for a long period of time, as was her Grandmother's, and as were generations before her Grandmother. I wonder how Kyra, her Grandmother and all people directly impacted by racism would choose to spend this energy, if racism were not a barrier for them. Undoubtedly, these experiences powerfully impact both anxiety and joy, in countless ways.

Further resources

Resmaa Menakem – *My Grandmother's Hands*

Mary-Frances Winters – *Black Fatigue: How Racism Erodes the Mind, Body, and Spirit*

Tarana Burke and Brené Brown (Editors) – *You Are Your Best Thing: Vulnerability, Shame, Resilience, and the Black Experience*

PART TWO

My Anxiety

My anxiety and when it started

We can be born with a predisposition to anxiety and we can learn this way of being in the world. Often slowly and imperceptibly, the sum of our experiences. Retracing our steps through formative experiences can help us to understand our anxiety – and also to remember what brings us joy. I recognise that revisiting your past or your childhood might not be a positive proposal for you. Be gentle on yourself. Fast forward where you need to. But it might help you to join the dots. By learning more about when and where your anxiety first took root, you will be better able to see it for what it is, and to recognise and live with it as part of your story instead of your whole story. Throughout this book, I write notes to my younger self and to others. It might help you to do the same as you revisit your formative experiences. How can you lend some compassion to your younger self? What words do you now know that you wish you could have heard then? How might this new perspective or gentleness help you to change the texture of your memories?

Even writing the word 'anxiety' now creates resistance in my body; my inner guidance system is telling me not to focus on it (this is *key*, take note!). Given that I'm writing a book about anxiety, I'm getting used to it. Really, though, this book is about healing, loving, celebrating, and joy.

It's not an avoidance tactic. I don't avoid thinking about anxiety because it's too distressing. It's that, instead, I make a conscious decision to think about what I *do* want, not what I don't want.

I used to think about anxiety *all the flippin' time*. Every morning, as soon as I woke up. I thought about it for hours and hours a day. Any time I made plans or was invited somewhere, the *first* thing I would do was imagine myself in that situation blushing and shaking and humiliating myself. I would plan how I could hide my anxiety. I would assess if it would be 'manageable'. I would consider my escape plan. Sort of makes me laugh now! It seems wild. Thank goodness I transformed it.

Dear reader,

If this is you, if you are here where I was - you can completely overcome this. You can get to a place where the anxiety seems like a lifetime ago, where the fact you were ever so anxious seems wild and where you are at ease and present to life!

Trust me and have hope x

It reminds me of the saying 'worrying is like praying for something bad to happen'. I prayed for bad stuff day in and day out for decades.

As a young child I wasn't particularly anxious; perhaps a little preoccupied with approval from others. I loved playing with Sylvanian Families and making up dances. I loved my Grandma's dog, Chip. I loved penny sweets and remember throwing myself on the floor at nursery just to get a Smartie once or twice. You got a sweet every time you fell over, how cool is that? Bet that doesn't happen anymore.

I vividly remember sitting in the living room at Keswick Avenue, our first family home in Barrow-in-Furness, the town in the north of England where I grew up. I must have been less than 8. I would put Paul McCartney, The Hollies or Huey Lewis on the stereo, place the massive headphones over my little head, and get lost in a beautiful and fascinating world. I'd read the lyrics and feel fascinated! It was a wonderful escape. It's interesting I use the word escape, because life was great, but I guess at times the adults in my world were tense. Music enabled me to create my own wee haven. I loved reading the lyrics and thinking about what they meant. I adored the music and how it felt in my body.

I loved animals and became vegetarian at 7 when I realised a chicken on the plate was the same as the one in the field (whaaaaaat?). I carried on eating fish for a while until the day my goldfish Jason (I had two, Kylie and Jason...) stared me out whilst I was eating my fish fingers. I wish I had known then what happened in the dairy industry, but I didn't learn that until many years later. I absolutely detested racism and inequity, writing down my thoughts, loves and worries in the diaries I kept between the ages of nine and fourteen, trying to puzzle out why people behaved the way they did, what made the world go round. I don't suppose I've changed much.

I have some great memories of that first house. I remember the den I shared with my big brother Chris. The little patch of garden that mum gave just for me, and the amazing feeling of being given that responsibility. Choosing some flowers and watering it all by myself. I remember running round and round the house. A few times, Dad took us on torch-lit adventures under the floorboards, crawling around, creepy and exciting in equal measure. I remember amazing birthday cakes (a hot air balloon was my favourite). I remember being allowed to play out on the street but only past the second lamppost. I remember my mate Jenny next door and a girl Belinda from across the street who was older and cooler and once asked me if I knew what sex was. I had no idea. Like most kids born in the 80s, my brother Chris and I loved Bomberman, Street Fighter and Mario Kart on the Super Nintendo, and the inimitable sibling blend of fun with fighting.

Alongside the silliness, there was a good deal of stress around. Mum was always busy and found it hard to relax. She had and continues to have high expectations of herself and was juggling a stressful career as a doctor (both she and my dad were GPs) alongside motherhood. I watched her doing a lot for others and regularly aiming to please others (you could argue that she was co-dependent, more to follow on this). I watched and learned and grew up trying too hard to please others. I've worked really hard to lose this habit. Mum and I are very alike! Those things

40

that frustrate me about her are probably all the things that I see within myself (dominance, drive, a need to be in control) that I struggle with. Sometimes we clash, like many mothers and daughters. She is the most enthusiastic person you could meet; she is full of energy and she cares a great deal. She gives so much to her community and is loved by many in return. She was and is a great Mum. I wish she would give herself more credit for her awesomeness. She definitely worries about 'getting it wrong' as a parent, oftentimes saying that she did a terrible job when we were younger. This isn't true. She did her best and still does her best, just like all of us.

Dad is another kettle of fish; I'm smiling as I type this. He is quiet, funny and tells awful jokes. He, too, was juggling a stressful job, as a full time GP and parent. He hated being on call. So did Mum; that fear of being woken at any time of the night and not knowing what you would have to deal with must have been a nightmare. When we were growing up, Dad would withdraw physically and emotionally whenever stressed. He didn't know how to communicate his emotions and needs. In case this is you, I'm going to teach you how to do this in the best way ever in chapters on nonviolent communication, codependency and boundaries. A few times, I heard Dad lose it at people; he sometimes lost it at me. He was seldom physically violent. We were smacked the odd time, by both parents. Times were different back then, although I want to be crystal clear that I don't agree with any form of physical violence towards children whatsoever; again, though, they were doing the best they could with the knowledge they had.

Dad was definitely psychologically complex. He carried shame and that was directed at me and us a lot. I *was* a lot! I was loud, free, and uninhibited and I think this triggered him. When I use the term 'triggered' I am referring to a strong emotional reaction that arises in someone in relation to someone or something else. For example, in this case, I think my 'disinhibitions' triggered my Dad's feelings of shame. Dad carried sadness. He was and is a beautiful human. His calm and

41

quiet energy is gorgeous to be around. He is compassionate, gentle, and understanding.

Both my parents, with their love for me, the high expectations, their criticisms, their perfectly imperfect human-ness, made me who I am today. They prepared me in so many ways for life. My dad's difficulties with me led me on a beautiful path to accept myself more deeply. We have a wonderful adult relationship which I don't take for granted. My mum's high expectations have led me to achieve brilliant things. Her lack of compassion for herself led me to prioritise self-compassion and spread it in the world! They both did their absolute best to work ridiculously stressful jobs as doctors whilst getting to grips with parenting. All I have is gratitude for them exactly as they are. They were the most amazing support to my husband and I when Finn was diagnosed and when he died. We couldn't have done it without them.

If we cannot get things wrong, then what about other people? Can they get it wrong? This is an interesting one. If we are being so gentle and compassionate with ourselves then what about other people? What about our parents?

Coming from the world of psychology with a special interest in psychodynamic psychotherapy, where there is a real focus on the past, I spent years thinking deeply about which patterns I was recreating from childhood. I talked to friends about how and why we all were the way we were and who was to blame for the various pathologies!

I used to blame my parents for my anxiety. I used to carry anger regarding their high expectations and criticisms. Where did that lead me? Nowhere really. What did it do for me? Did it help me 'externalise' my anguish? I'm not saying that healing from past experiences isn't important; it is! However, there comes a point whereby letting go of the past serves you.

What if our parents were doing the best they could with the information they had available at that time? What if their parents were doing the same? I will dive deeper into these ideas in the later chapters on parenting, including some thoughts about those extreme circumstances when extending grace to your parents may not be appropriate and when acceptance is more complicated.

Back to life at Keswick Avenue. I remember clearly when I first found out about death. I just had this feeling that I wasn't going to die; that surely that would never happen to me. I was in the upstairs bathroom at the time, contemplating life and death as a 6 year old. It blew my mind, and it still does. I oftentimes thought about death, on and off as a child. I used to get a strange physical sensation in my body, associated with the thought of 'what would nothingness feel like forever and ever and ever'. It freaked me out big time.

I remember being bribed to be good in church (Catholic). If we sat still and kept quiet in church, we could go to the newsagents afterwards to get a reward. I remember the excitement of opening a chocolate bar, the shiny foil and the beautiful colour and smell of the chocolate. The level of joy from something so simple!

I loved going to Liverpool to see my grandparents. I was so lucky, they were beautiful. I felt so loved when I saw their excited faces. I loved how 'big' Grandma (because she lived in a house not a flat) let me put sugar on my cereal. She was called Maisie. She was and is my soulmate. My grandpa John (big Grandma's husband) once nailed lino to a piece of wood and polished it to make it slippy and then propped it up on a wall and voila! We had a slide! He died from mesothelioma, related to asbestosis, when I was 8 or 9. I remember him being poorly in bed and putting a pound coin in my palm and closing my hand lovingly and winking at me. *A whole pound* for sweets?! I bought a massive bag of Fox's Glacier Mints. It was amazing, I couldn't believe it, normally I only got 10p! When he died, I remember writing to my grandma Maisie on my new typewriter. I didn't know what to say. I remember writing, 'I hope you're OK'. Mum said, 'Of course she's not OK.' I felt embarrassed: I had definitely got it wrong! I've probably said such things to Isaac when stressed. Parenting is so challenging. I've dedicated a whole chapter to how it's impossible - and not even what our children need - to be perfect, to always get it 'right'.

I loved going to feed the squirrels in Formby with the other grandparents, Joan and Kev. I loved that they always had chocolate biscuits in the fridge. When we would go to bed in the living room - me on the sofa and Chris on a little camping bed on the floor - Grandma would *always* set the table for breakfast the next day and I vividly remember the place mats, how they looked and felt. There were always Kellogs variety packs. I loved the Coco Pops bowl that Grandma sent off for which I have downstairs in my house today. Grandpa Kev was the smiliest man and a really skilled carpenter. They all made me feel so loved. I am so lucky that I knew such love as a child. I know that is not everyone's experience. It's interesting how my childhood memories as so strong in terms of the texture of things. As though we notice the details more because we are more present to reality when we are little, as opposed to living in our conditioned minds or expectations.

Primary school was good overall. I remember playing 'kiss, cuddle or torture'. It was like chase: when caught you had to choose what you wanted to happen. I mostly chose 'cuddle' unless it was Jevon Turner (who loved whippets and was a drummer and I loved him with all my heart) or Andrew Clarke (loved him too, RIP Andy), in which case I'd have a sneaky kiss. I remember being made to stand against the wall for snogging. Mum asked me at home that night if I didn't think I was a bit young to be snogging. With a total attitude I said, 'Mum, I'm *eleven*', literally feeling about 25. I remember kissing with tongues and thinking it was the weirdest thing; the weird sensations, so non sexual for me. I was a late developer. We would clap and chant and count to see how long people could do

44

it for. Haha! I think 13 seconds was the longest I kissed. It was gross but fascinating.

Secondary school was different. I became painfully self-conscious. I hid it well, appearing outwardly confident, overcompensating a lot, but it was there. I felt scared of not fitting in and tried too hard to fit in which made me not fit in. I felt so uncomfortable in my my own skin. Too tall, too big, too uncool. I hated my hair and I felt embarrassed that we lived in a big house. I had some good mates and some mates who were probably going through their own troubles and sometimes said unkind things. I remember sitting down with them once and someone said, *'what are you doing?'* as in *why are you sitting with us?* I still remember that feeling of not knowing where to go or where to sit. I can't remember what I did. Mostly, though, I was OK. Sometimes, I was ashamed of how I was being treated and so, at times, I could be mean to others. This brought with it a shame I carried until very recently and there is still some residue. I was never intentionally horrible to anyone, I would have died at the thought of being considered a bully - but I wish I could have a word with my younger self about kindness and the impact of my words.

To anyone whose feelings I ever hurt, I am really, really sorry xx

After high school, I was a bit self-conscious about my looks, but I still wasn't particularly anxious. I was a people pleaser, but anxiety wasn't unmanageable. I loved how booze relaxed me but it wasn't bad. Sixth form was fun and I made some lovely new friends. I started going out with the boy next door who I had fancied *forever*. It was very exciting at the time.

I flunked my A-levels, by my standards, (due to discovering boys, pubs, nightclubs, and alcohol) and went through clearing to the University of Stirling. Uni was great, mainly because of Naomi, my pal who I spent every second with (you'll meet her later in the book). She introduced me to Japanese food. I felt like I was in heaven - adventuring to gigs, boozing on trains from Stirling to Glasgow to frequent The Barrowlands, a beautiful old ballroom and the best live music venue ever. Without a doubt, it was the most joy I'd felt so far in life. With Naomi, I felt a deep connection. Our lives revolved around talking about music, listening to it, writing out lyrics and travelling to gigs. She introduced me to Brighton which I fell in love with. It was so exciting for me. I adored this new brighter life that was unfolding in front of my eyes. I felt like I really belonged.

After uni, when I was around 21, something happened which I now believe was the main trigger of the terrible anxiety that followed for years. I met a guy in Romania, became pregnant and subsequently had an abortion. I thought he was dreamy, very good-looking, and exciting; I sensed danger, I think. I thought we'd used a condom but we hadn't, alcohol was always involved back then. I arrived back home to the UK thinking I was in love. One afternoon I fell asleep on my sister in law's couch. I told her I couldn't keep my eyes open and she asked me if I was pregnant. 'Nah, no way!' I went back to my parents' house. I'd finished uni and it was just before moving to London. I did a test with *zero* expectation it would be positive. It was positive. I phoned a friend who had been through a similar experience. I cried.

My mum came home, saw me, and told me I looked like I'd seen a ghost. I told her what had happened. Then dad appeared. Bless him - he obviously was trying to 'get it right' – '*is that a good thing, love?*'... whilst I was snot crying, devastated, and also without a boyfriend. 'No dad, it's not a good thing'.

I'd always told myself I would never have an abortion. I didn't judge others. I was pro-choice but I told a story that I could never go through with it myself. Then I got pregnant and I knew I needed to. My gut instinct was that it was *not* an option to have a baby with this guy. It's still hard to write that 20 years later. I remember my parents carting me off on a 45 minute drive out of town to see their lovely pal who was a doctor (RIP Jane). She

46

was kind. In retrospect, it seems ridiculous I didn't just see the doctor in my town. I can't remember whose decision that was. Might have been mine. I felt ashamed. I think it suited my parents at the time to go along with it. They didn't want people to know. Oh well, that's the cat out of the bag now I'm writing a book.

It was complicated. Mum burst out crying on me once, talking about her relationship with the baby and how she would have loved the baby. She is firm on her belief that abortion is wrong. She refused to refer her patients for abortions. My big Catholic family have had it drummed into them for generations. I felt shocked to see Mum so upset. I felt sad for her. Afterwards, when dad expressed that she should have kept it to herself, I felt conflicted; maybe it wasn't helpful for me to see that. But that was her truth, she felt sad about not getting to love this little grandchild. I understand. She was kind and tried to be supportive, despite her beliefs. Of course, though, she was not who I wanted to be supported by.

I remember going to see another doctor at the hospital. They examined me and I cried the whole time. They were telling me I didn't have to go through with it. But I didn't even consider the alternative. I knew it wasn't right for me. Now, nearly 20 years on, I feel compassion for my 21 year old self. I don't feel judgment. My body is tensing up a little as I write about it. But I've never written about it. This is new to me and there's no right way to do it.

I remember coming round from the general anaesthetic after the operation. I looked out the window; the sun was shining through the clouds, the colours beautiful. I felt a sadness so deep, deep down. I think I thought of all the missed beauty and small moments of joy I had deprived this child of, deprived both of us of. One tear came, I wiped it away then shoved that sadness down.

It was rough for a long time. I went on - many, many years later - to experience more child loss. I had failed PGD (a form of

47

IVF) and a miscarriage and, as I said, my first-born son Finlay died when he was 8 months old from Spinal Muscular Atrophy type 1. The thing with abortion, though, is that you don't receive the same love and support. At least, I didn't. I couldn't talk to my family members about it. Or, at the time, I felt I couldn't. I remember once, I was doing a dear family friend's hair, she was a mother figure to me, Colette. I SO wanted to talk to her and tell her. I wanted someone to understand me and hug me. But I couldn't find the words. I feared judgment. They were Catholic too.

I remember the first Christmas after the baby would have been born, I woke up crying. Then later in the day I remember feeling heartbroken with a lump in my throat, listening to Joni Mitchell in the kitchen, getting some space in the busy house. The same family friends were there. Dave, Colette's husband, came in to tell me how much he loved the song. I was holding back the tears. I distracted myself and made conversation.

I longed to talk openly about my grief. I held it inside. I wonder if my anxiety was just all that sadness shoved down time and time again; alongside the story that I had just done something *so completely wrong*. I missed that baby and I felt like a monster, for years. It was after the abortion that the anxiety spiraled completely out of control.

Dear previous 21 year old me. You did not get it wrong. You are not evil. You are sensitive and beautiful, and you are listening to your inner guidance system. Trust yourself. You cannot get this wrong. Other people's opinions do not define you. Trust yourself, don't give your power away. I love you x

Many people don't know about my abortion. Most of my close friends do, but it's just not something that I have ever found easy to bring up in conversation. A friend of mine and I were recently talking about my book and I said that I talk about abortion. She shared that she had also been through a similar experience. She shared that close loved ones felt critical and so she just didn't talk about it. I felt sad that she was unable to be free of judgment from others. I wonder how many other women I know have been through an abortion and have never talked about it. I am aware that people have strong feelings on abortion. Some people will judge me because of it. That's OK, though, you won't judge me half as strongly as I judged myself. Also, I don't need anyone else's approval. I have loved and healed myself through this experience and I hope by sharing this, that others may do the same. I have made peace with this decision and I know that for me, at that time in my life, it was the right thing. I couldn't get it wrong.

What debilitating looked like

What did my anxiety look like, when it was at its most debilitating? It looked like hiding in a bathroom full of utter self-loathing because I didn't know some piece of general knowledge in a conversation with someone I barely knew - that I told myself I should know. It looked like feeling like my skin was transparent and like everyone was staring at me seeing right through into the most shameful and repulsive soul. It looked like utter self-loathing. It looked like fearing leaving the house, hating public transport, worrying about the absolute most shameful thing happening, like defecating on the tube in London or something. It looked like worrying about shitting myself a lot - it makes me laugh to type that out - gallows laughter maybe.

It looked like taking 10 propranolol tablets at once even though I only was supposed to take one - feeling desperate for something to change. It was fearing everything and everyone. It was waking up in the morning and feeling the most heightened anxiety and adrenaline coursing through my veins. It was fearing and avoiding holding cups of drinks when in social situations, especially in formal work situations, out of fear that my hands would shake, and people would see me for the nervous wreck and the fraud that I was. It was having a panic attack if I had to introduce myself in a meeting – literally dreading this whenever I was in a group setting.

It looked like getting out of my mind on alcohol or drugs and regularly waking up not knowing where I was, having been intimate with someone I didn't know the name of and feeling scared and not knowing how to even get home - wandering the streets full of shame. It looked like - for twenty years - focusing only on my flaws, on what I perceived was wrong with me.

It looked like making myself wrong hundreds and hundreds of times, every single day.

The romance of this level of self-hatred

I miss the comfort in being sad
– Kurt Cobain

It was almost addictive, this level of self-hatred. I was (still am) obsessed with depressing music. When you make yourself a victim it can become addictive. You don't need to be an adult. You can be a child and fantasise about people rescuing you, doing things for you. Also, let's be honest, the getting drunk, partying and sleeping with lots of people in bands was absolutely not all bad. It was exciting and fun. Yes, it wasn't always healthy, but it was also fun.

I liked feeling sorry for myself. I liked other people feeling sorry for me. That's hard to admit but it's true. There is comfort in it.

I had no idea what I was capable of though, when I stopped avoiding life, the world, my fears. I had no idea how much more I would enjoy feeling proud rather than sorry for myself.

Previous me,

Although you sort of love feeling sorry for yourself and being self-destructive, wait till you see what is on the other side.

You have a belief that you won't be able to 'adult' - you are scared of your own power.

Wait till you see what it's like though.

You will be in a constant state of awe, in terms of what you are capable of - what is on the other side.

You are going to turn into one of the bravest people I know. You are going to start looking after yourself - in body, mind, emotions, and spirit. And guess what! It isn't going to feel boring like you feared.

In fact, it is going to be the biggest wildest ride ever.

You are going to blow your own mind, leading large groups of people to heal and learn to love themselves. Your social anxiety will be a thing of the past! Yes, you still get anxious, but you won't care! You won't even label it as anxiety anymore. It's just your body feeling excited, it's you putting yourself in situations that make you expand and grow. It's perfect.

You are going to fall in love with someone who loves you right back. On your second date you are going to fear that it's too safe to be exciting enough - but trust me - stick with it. He is amazing. You are going to have such an adventure together.

You are going to learn how to relate in the healthiest of ways - and it's the least boring thing ever, it's amazing. Learning to love and be loved in return!

You will stop putting everyone else on pedestals and telling a story that they are somehow getting life right and you are getting life wrong. Wait till you hear this! You are actually going to write a book about anxiety and how you overcame it - it is going to help others to do the same!

You are going to have some really hard times too. They are going to test you and stretch you beyond your limits. You are going to fear your ability to carry on in this life. But again - stick with it. What is on the other side will amaze you.

You feared being an 'adult'. You used to joke constantly about 'not being a real human'.

But you are a real human.

You are imperfect, you make mistakes, you feel anxiety, you feel joy, and you will learn not to live in a place of self-hatred, and it is going to be glorious.

Stick with it.

Sarah xxx

Panic attacks and my fear of blushing

My first panic attack happened when I was supposed to be presenting to a team I worked for, a charity for homeless Scots in London. It was a few months after the abortion. I started talking and felt my body and my central nervous system become totally overwhelmed. I was blushing and shaking, and my heart was pounding. I ran out of the room. I felt so shameful. It was awful (or so I told myself). I had to go back in the room and finish the presentation but it felt horrible. I told myself I was an absolute failure, that I had *totally* got it wrong and that everyone must have thought I was an absolute idiot. I phoned my Mum when I got home. 'Oh God, love,' she said. It didn't help. She was doing the best she could with the knowledge and information available to her but she really cares about what other people think. Her reaction confirmed my fear and shame that it was a terrible thing to have happened.

Dear previous me (or anyone else who has had a similar thing happen),

Do not worry about it. Don't worry about what other people think. You are entitled to experience fear. Their judgments are not important. They probably only felt compassion anyway.

What is going on for you? I wonder what the anxiety is about. Find someone to talk to about it; a friend, a therapist or a transformational coach. It is entirely appropriate that your body is freaking out at the moment, you have been through a lot.

I wonder what you can do to help yourself right now. Less boozing and more exercise would probably be a good start!

Don't torture yourself with the pressure to be 'together' *all the time. It's OK to lose your sh*t.*

You are beautiful,

I love you xxxxxxxxxxxxxxx

Around that time, I started blushing frequently - and fearing it *all* the time. I felt ashamed and uncomfortable in my skin. Thinking I was in love, I returned to Romania. It was a horror show. He called me fat and ugly for two weeks, stole my money, killed a family pig in front of me (as you know, I didn't eat meat). I came home covered in psoriasis and feeling even more disgusting. I already felt evil and now I felt fat and ugly, too.

The fear of blushing lasted for years. I would pile on makeup to hide, reapplying foundation again and again and probably keeping L'Oréal in business the amount I used. Every day, I prevented myself from realizing that I could cope without hiding. When that subsided, I began to use the drug propranolol to feel able to cope with life. I took it for pretty small things like one-to-one meetings at work. I just couldn't cope with anything - or that was what I told myself, anyway. I felt terrified of people seeing me as anxious. I felt deeply ashamed of my anxiety. This went on for years.

Dear reader,

If you are reading this and experiencing anxiety, please remember - you do not need to feel shame around it. You are beautiful, with anxiety or without. It is just a vicious cycle which has developed because of your fear of anxiety and your focus on anxiety. You can and will turn it around.

Ask yourself, are there any other emotions that you haven't processed? Like sadness or anger? It could be that when you process these or any traumatic memories, your anxiety will subside.

You do not need to beat yourself up about being anxious. You are just a human being in a weird fleshy body reacting to the events that happen in your life. Zoom out and see the bigger picture.

This will pass xxx

The propranolol made me feel sh*t. It also helped! But if I did something well, I told myself a story that the only reason it went well was because of the medication. So, I never allowed myself to celebrate myself (note, there is a full chapter on celebration later, and its pivotal role in creating joy). I trained as a clinical psychologist and worked in the NHS. A world where people did *not* routinely show vulnerability and were competitive high achievers. Brené Brown talks about how toxic these environments can be.

My years in clinical psychology were rich in learning and friendships. There were and are amazing clinicians in NHS clinical psychology doing brilliant jobs. It was just not the right place for me. I also feel strongly that NHS clinicians oftentimes fail to acknowledge their own emotional wounds. There were some exceptions, of course. It is, however, still not mandatory for clinical psychologists to undergo their own therapy. I met too many people who were dangerously unaware of their own issues and what they brought to the table. Sometimes, these clinicians viewed the people they worked with as different to them somehow; as 'ill' rather than simply as human beings just like them experiencing life and responding accordingly. Many healers are drawn to healing professions because of their own wounds (search 'the wounded healer'). That's normal and fine, as long as therapists have an awareness around it instead of being psychologically defended against it. By this I mean that people may unconsciously deny or distort reality in order to avoid unwanted feelings.

For years, I spoke to a therapist called Morag, who was trained in transactional analysis. She helped me process a great deal of the sadness and grief. Her consistent and loving presence soothed me and enabled me to relate to myself differently. When I think of this time the image of a fizzy bottle of drink comes to mind. It was like, on a weekly basis, having someone unscrew the lid and let the pressure out. It settled me immensely. Thank you, Morag.

During this time, I also drank a lot of alcohol. It calmed my nerves. I would sleep with people just to make up for my shame and for my low self-esteem; basically, anyone who gave me any attention. It felt validating. Then I'd feel more shame. All of this exacerbated the anxiety.

By now, I had a firm story: *I am an anxious person. I am a wreck.*

The words you attach to your experience become your experience
– Tony Robbins

This story led me to interpret any information as confirmation of this story. If I was excited and my heart was beating fast, could I lean into the joy of feeling alive and excited? No. It was proof of how anxious and weird I was. (I talk more about how you can break the vicious cycle of anxiety in the latter part of this book). Then I avoided situations that made me feel excited, preventing me from learning that I could cope. If we believe something, *anything*, we can find evidence to prove it. If we believe people are cruel, we can find *infinite amounts of* evidence to prove this. If we believe people are kind, we can find overwhelming evidence to prove this. If we believe we are strong, we find evidence to prove this. If we believe we are weak and anxious,

57

we find evidence to prove this. These are just *stories* that result in vicious cycles.

Past me: 'I'm weird' - normal bodily reaction to life - confirmation I'm weird - avoid situations- more confirmation that I can't cope and that I'm weird - take propranolol to slow my heart down- prevented from learning can cope further - only notice others coping well, compare self to others negatively - more proof.

Present me: 'there's nothing wrong with me!, everyone experiences aroused bodily systems' - embrace life, do scary things - feel amazing - still feel 'anxious' but tell a story that it's normal and everyone feels it doing new scary things - don't downplay other people's anxieties and overplay mine - don't compare - tell myself a story I cannot get it wrong - take pressure off - regularly challenge my fear of what people think - feel liberated and joyful - regularly do things that make me feel anxious - create a cycle of succeeding and winning!

The Danger Years

I talk openly on the online courses I provide about my anxiety –
it gives others permission to do the same and encourages them to
love themselves unconditionally too. When I spoke of these
years that involved lots of alcohol, drugs and sex, a client of mine
on a recent course (Eliott in fact! One of the guest authors)
referred to this time as 'The danger years'. It provided us all with
a good laugh. Anyway, I'm going to share with you some of the
music that I listened to during the danger years. Sometimes at
gigs, watching live music, drunk, with my best mates, it felt
perfect. The music I listened to made me feel less alone, less
wrong, less ashamed somehow. The power of music, for me, was
magical.

---

*"Now that I'm so sad and not quite right, I
could dance all night"*
– Clap Your Hands Say Yeah

*"And in our quiet hour I feel I see
everything, and am in love with the hook,
upon which everyone hangs"*
– Joanna Newsom

The Cure – Pictures Of You

The Twilight Sad – Cold Days in the Birdhouse

Frightened Rabbit – Modern Leper

Pixies – No. 13 Baby and Hey

P J Harvey – Rid Of Me

Jeff Buckley – Grace and Last Goodbye

Blur (everything by Blur)

Television – Marquee Moon

Clap Your Hands Say Yeah – In This Home on Ice

Joanna Newsom – Good Intentions Paving Company

The Beta Band – Dry The Rain

Laura Marling – Failure

Radiohead (everything by Radiohead)

Godspeed You! Black Emperor – Storm

John Grant – Marz

Bonnie Prince Billy – I See A Darkness

Nick Cave – Into My Arms

Sonic Youth – Teen Age Riot

Interpol – Leif Erikson

How Beautiful Could A Being Be

*How beautiful could
a being be*
– Caetano Veloso

In 2011, I was still sporadically struggling but mostly better. I was internet dating after feeling fed up of meeting the wrong kinds of people in bands! I met and fell in love with a beauty called Neil. I think the years of therapy really helped me to receive his love. We got married on the Isle of Mull. He was (is) hunky and we were silly as anything together, the emotional and physical connection amazing. We skinny dipped in lakes, we went on bike rides, we basically had (and continue to have) the *best* time. He is calm and strong, and he is my best mate.

We were *so* excited when we got a positive pregnancy test after 3 years together and three months of trying. We were so cute looking back. We wanted to do another test just to be sure. Neil drove to a 24hr Asda at 4am in the morning. We were delighted… beyond excited. I remember the first scan. Wow. I was smitten.

I adored being pregnant, the excitement of it. I *loved* my body, maybe for the first time. It was fascinating and amazing. I loved how my big pregnant belly looked. I had healed so much in terms of my body image. Neil was loving and accepting, and I had recovered from those dark days. I still feared how I would cope in pregnancy without propranolol but those feel-good hormones saw me through. It scared me, though.

Finn arrived and was very sick. He had to be resuscitated on birth. He then had to be taken by ambulance from Fife to

Glasgow for intensive care. It was terrifying. Meconium aspiration syndrome - and an undetected at that point genetic condition. We were told he was probably going to die within 24 hours.

He didn't die. He recovered and proved everyone wrong. We were discharged after 14 days and came home feeling so unbelievably relieved. We were told he could come out of it all 'unscathed'. We drank champagne. Mum, Dad, Neil and I stood in a circle and all toasted something. We all cried. We were so grateful for so much and we felt deeply connected.

His little body. When he was in intensive care, he had wires coming in and out of everywhere. He looked so poorly but all I saw was this amazing human that I couldn't believe I had birthed/created and who was perfect. I adored him. I felt a love I never knew existed.

Someone told us when we were at Yorkhill Hospital, the hospital for sick kids in Glasgow, that removing the wires is like unwrapping the most precious gift ever. It was kind of like that. It was amazing: the first hold at around 8 days old; the first time he opened his eyes.

It was excruciating, having to sleep away from him, not knowing if he would survive. But I also had this weird, deep sense of trust and peace. I knew he was strong. I knew he was a warrior and that he was going to be OK. When we were at Yorkhill, we stayed in this great accommodation provided by the Ronald McDonald House charity - across the road from where Finn slept and where I had previously worked years beforehand. My friend Claudia sent me a link to a song called 'How Beautiful Could A Being Be'. Aside from the fact we were terrified that he was going to die, we had also just become parents and this glorious uplifting song reverberated through our bodies as Neil and I danced together, in that room, amongst all the fear and terror cursing through our veins. It was a beautiful moment. Honestly, we couldn't believe how beautiful our baby was.

It was glorious, after those 14 unfathomable days, to come home, of course. To at least experience a tiny bit of normality. We were delighted, if not a bit shell shocked. Time passed, though, and Finn's body didn't look 'right' (though it was perfect). His little chest was tiny. Then his little wrists started to become floppy. His perfect little hands.

It was terrifying not knowing what was wrong.

We saw a lovely neurologist - I thought 'what's the point in this'. After the appointment, he called me late that evening. He asked me if we could travel to Edinburgh the next day for some results. He said it was important and wouldn't say anything else. I didn't push it. I f*cking knew it was bad. This doctor was so attuned and on it, I knew it was news he was unable to deliver over the telephone.

I remember once, even before this, walking on the beach and asking my dad, 'do you think his chest will grow?' Dad said, 'Of course it will, just like the rest of his body'. Sounds so weird now, but I knew it wouldn't.

That next day at the Sick Kids Hospital in Edinburgh, we were in an office. Me, Neil and beautiful Finny. Two doctors and a nurse. They seemed f*cking nervous. We knew it was bad. But not in a million years did we contemplate it could have been this bad.

'Finlay has got spinal muscular atrophy'. I must have asked him to repeat it ten times in the consultation. It felt so new to me then.

'He is unlikely to live past his 2nd birthday. The average life expectancy is 8 months.'

I had never ever ever loved anyone like I loved that little boy...

My world suddenly revolved around that little bundle of cells and glory. He was incredible. Now he was going to be torn away from me and it was agony. I felt like someone had shot me as those words reverberated through my body, mind, and spirit. My body probably didn't move but I felt like I'd been shot and my body had flown metres across the room and up against the wall.

I kept saying, 'fucking hell fucking hell fucking hell. '

I remember saying, 'oh my God we will have to have a funeral'. I couldn't believe it. Finny was smiling at me and then laughing. Looking like heaven. What the actual fuck.

Us poor little parents. And our poor little baby.

We went to see our friends. They were devastated too, of course. They were wonderful. Thanks Dan. Thanks Tops & Jonts. We then made our way back to Fife. I don't know how we walked. How we talked. How we ate. How we did dishes. But we did.

Another dear friend came over and delivered food. He had experienced ill health. He wasn't new to the darkness of life. It showed. He was comfortable to come and sit with us. It didn't matter what he said. It mattered that he just showed up. It mattered that we didn't feel alone. It mattered that we felt love. Thank you, Fenton. And thank you Aline for wandering the streets with your little baby, because he was snotty and we were being careful.

Dear friend of bereaved or traumatised friends. You cannot get this wrong. Just be there, don't worry about crying or saying something ridiculous. Just be there, say anything, show up. Xx

Finlay's life was beautiful, hard, terrifying, excruciating but mostly GLORIOUS. His smile and his noises and his ways. We

65

loved him as much as anyone has ever loved anyone. He had a great time. He was adored and held and loved and spent 99% of his life in physical contact with one of us, which must have been soothing. He looked so wise, like an old soul.

This experience showed me that love really is the most amazing thing. The love of our friends and family carried us through. Fenton told us it would and that we should let it and it did.

Dear friends and family, your love carried us through. Thank you for everything. If you showed up, thank you. If you said something ridiculous, thank you for trying. If you were too terrified to come near us or say anything, I understand and love you. Next time show up though. You cannot get it wrong xx

The love from Finny and between us and Finny carried us through. It was fucking hard though. There were moments we didn't think we could do it. We tube fed and gave medications every couple of hours day and night. It was exhausting. We used to say to each other, 'I don't know how much longer I can do this for', which is such an unbearable thing to think, let alone say out loud. Thank f*ck we had each other and were able to be open about all of this. It could have led us to feel like we were absolutely getting it wrong, as parents, but we didn't, because we had each other; and a beautiful team of nurses and doctors and parents and friends around us.

Neil, my absolute love. Thank you so much for hearing my pain, for accepting me, for walking this journey with me. Witnessing your love for Finlay is one of the greatest gifts I have ever been given, Sarah xxxxxxxxx

Finlay's nurses and doctors and all our family, thank you so much for your understanding and support and love. I carry it with me still, in my heart, 6 years on and it's so tender and beautiful and life-affirming. My heart could burst when I think of all the love that was expressed towards us in so many different ways; from comments on facebook posts, to his nurses turning up 20 minutes after texting them! So grateful xxx

David (Finn's community nurse) I still can't believe you turned up at the hospital at like 8am on that Monday before he died. You were amazing. We all knew what was happening, that the end was nearing, and it was bearable because of you and your love. When you offered to go and get me and Neil coffees from Costa and I asked for a decaf soya latte and you looked at me as if to say 'f*ck off' (I'm laughing). When you got back you slammed it down and said (in your strong, gorgeous Scottish accent), 'they didn't even hear me the first time so I had to say it again even louder in front of flippin' everyone' hahahahaha. It made me laugh so much, it makes me laugh and cry still and I will love you forever, Sarah xxxxxxx

Phyllis (Finn's other community nurse) and Jamie Cruden (Finn's pediatrician) thank you for, on your days off, coming to see us at the hospice. Wow. We were so comforted by your love and your sadness and it meant the world to us xxxxx

In the middle of the night when Finny was asleep and I wasn't trying to hold it completely together, I would cry in Neil's arms. The warmth of Finn's soft head on my inner forearm was so beautiful and I didn't want to live without that warmth. I didn't think I would survive his death. I thought my heart would stop beating when his heart did. I really thought this. Neil and I used to say to each other 'shall we just kill ourselves'. We discussed how we honestly would if it wasn't for the people in our lives that we didn't want to hurt. Then we would joke and crack up laughing. Neil suggested we have a massive party and invite everyone we know and just get the place bombed, take everyone out. Then no one would miss us. But what about the people of the other people? We could invite them too! But what about their people? It gave us light relief. We would never have done it (obviously!) but we longed. We longed to think of a way of avoiding the inevitable pain that was coming our way. That had already come our way. It was unthinkable.

The worst thing for me was not knowing what his death would be like. I was so scared Finny would feel scared or in pain. I was so scared of him looking at me with those beautiful eyes willing me to help. And me being unable to do a f*cking thing.

His death was incredibly peaceful, though. It was intimate and beautiful. I sang and Neil held him, we both kind of held him but it was painful for him to be passed at the end. We loved him and made promises to him. The morphine helped him relax. I sang 'Farewell and Goodnight' by The Smashing Pumpkins, one of my favourite songs.
The poor grandparents were in the other room. Little loves.

Obviously, I could write a whole other book about this experience, but I want to talk about this in relation to anxiety.

The events that followed this experience gifted me with a new environment and with people and new activities that totally transformed my anxiety. Without this experience, I believe I may well still be working within the NHS in the wrong environment, feeling anxiety throughout my body, trying to be something I am not, feeling like I was getting it all wrong.

Finny, thank you for leading me on this mysterious and astounding path and for teaching me so much. Thank you for the beautiful and amazing ripple effect of all the love and joy you were and are. I love you forever, Mummy xx

The anxiety the day after the funeral was probably the worst I've ever felt. It was on a whole other level. I feel for people who experience that level of physiological feelings. We went for a walk in a forest and I vomited. I had been holding everything in, being strong for Finn, for months, then the funeral to focus on. Then suddenly there was just emptiness. No Finn, nothing to do, nothing to plan, no medications to give Finny, no secretions to suck up with that weird machine. Silence.

We came to bed and gave each other massages just to try to deal with that unbelievably heightened anxiety.

It felt brutal.

We just didn't know what to do.

The mystery

Although I have just talked about the anxiety and the bleakness, there was also absolutely unbelievable magic unfolding in front of our eyes over this period. It was hard to fathom or believe.

Although our baby had just died, that period of time after he died until the funeral was magical. It was the time in my life when I have felt the most connected to love, warmth, 'the universe', trust and the 'mystery' (some people might call it God or Source). Look what happened in the sky whilst Finn died (for the full impact and the beautiful colours, please see the E-book):

SEPTEMBER 28TH 2015.

70

The morning after he died, Neil was having a moment in the garden on his own. One of Neil's main interests in life is butterflies. He used to work for the Butterfly Conservation Society (*where he met David Attenborough! Twice!*). This day, Neil was in the garden alone escaping the busy house (full of grandparents and our community nurses) and he said out loud, 'where are you Finn?' As he said this, a butterfly landed right in front of him and started opening and closing its wings. It felt comforting to Neil.

Then I had a moment of fiercely heightened anxiety. I needed to ground myself and get away from everyone. I asked Neil to come to the beach with me. We walked down there, and I lay on the sand, eyes closed. It was the weirdest feeling but I felt sure that someone was standing next to me, standing over me. I knew it. I thought Neil must have just come to be with me. After I opened my eyes and Neil was still far away, I wondered what had happened. On our walk home, Neil said to me, 'that was really weird but when you were lying on the beach a butterfly flew down and hovered above you for ages. Wow. That was strange. Butterflies don't often come to the beach with little vegetation there...' It felt very comforting. It felt like it was Finn's spirit.

Anyway, at this point it *felt* magical and mysterious in my body but could still be explained away by some sort of coincidence. We then drove up to the children's hospice in Kinross where we would all stay until the funeral 9 days later. There was a beautiful room - the 'rainbow room', which had a wee sign on the door that someone had made that said 'Finn'. How gorgeous that someone had taken the time to do that. Finn's body had a lovely little bedroom waiting for him. He had a crib. We could sit in there with him when we wanted. We could 'wean' ourselves off his physical body gradually and gently. There was a little room next to the rainbow room with comfortable chairs and daily homemade traybakes. These small touches, what a difference they made.

71

To the person who made those traybakes, probably a lovely volunteer, THANK YOU.

Those cakes reminded us that the world was a loving place when it felt like a dark cold place and they made us feel so cared for and loved.

I love you xx

The staff were out of this world; giving us space *and* being there when we needed them. The parents of the child in the rainbow room get a whole beautiful garden all to themselves. We couldn't believe the love that was being extended to us.

Our community nurse Phyllis came to visit us one morning. She sat with us in the garden. We told her about the butterflies. We said how nice it was. She said that she believed in that kind of thing, even if some people didn't. Then the most magical thing happened. A red admiral flew and landed on Neil's shoulder. It stayed there for about 20 minutes:

OUTSIDE RACHEL HOUSE HOSPICE IN KINROSS, FIFE.

It was so moving. Absolutely amazing. Never in Neil's life had this happened. On his shoulder, too, as though someone was putting a comforting arm around him.

I was scared of missing Finn's warmth - the warmth of joy and love in my body, the absence of the warmth from his body against my body at night, his cuddles. I was terrified of the cold. I was terrified of his absence. And for that whole nine days, the sun shone. It was amazing and it felt like Finn was keeping me warm.

The funeral was a small gathering. Immediate family. David and Phyllis, our amazing community nurses who were like family. Naomi and Sam, one friend each for Neil and I. After the funeral, we sat in a circle in the sunshine in our garden. There were a bunch of red admiral butterflies on the buddleia and they came and flew around us in a circle for 5 minutes. Then they went back to the plant. Then they flew around us again. It happened again and again. It was astounding. This had never happened in my life and has never happened since. It felt like they were performing a sacred dance for us.

There are other stories, too. Neil and I would hike up a hill and find a red admiral at the top:

**RED ADMIRAL ATOP A HILL ON WEST
COAST OF SCOTLAND SOMEWHERE.**

After IVF/PGD implantation (with a baby I went on to miscarry) I was sitting in the garden one day with my bare belly out so I could feel the sun on it. I was feeling sore (physically and emotionally), and a butterfly came and landed on my bare tummy.

The mystery and beauty of all of this was immense. We decided not to try to explain or use logic to understand it. We wanted just to experience the beautiful feelings it conjured up for us. There was a wonderful man who worked at the hospice. When we told him about these experiences, he said that this kind of thing happened all the time. He said there were numerous examples of these kinds of things that people wouldn't believe.

I know so many friends who have also said the same thing about butterflies and feathers and robins. It feels magical and mysterious. (I'm laughing with delight, I just finished writing this chapter and went downstairs to grab a bowl of cereal and there was a red admiral just hovering at the window saying hello to me! Ha ha!).

(Also! The next day after writing this chapter my friend was on a boat and we texted him saying 'let's have a day out all of us together on the boat' and when Jonty told his brother that Neil and I wanted to come on the boat and Paddy agreed, a red admiral landed on the boat!). Since these experiences, another friend has sent me two antique badges of butterflies and my mother-in-law sent us a beautiful piece of wood with a painted red admiral on. How lucky are we that all our dear friends text us photos of red admirals and tell us their red admiral stories. I have one tattooed on my arm and I just feel so warm inside at the mystery and the magic.

This period of my life was the point at which I began to heal. I already understood the mechanics of anxiety from my work and research as a clinical psychologist. But this was when I began to rewrite my story. Where I began to move into my body and step into joy. This was my turning point, towards transformation.

MY FAVOURITE PHOTO OF FINN

The songs that soothed me so during this time of grief

Sufjan Stevens – Death with Dignity

Fionn Regan – Dogwood Blossom

The Source & Candi Staton - You Got The Love (I would listen whilst running and think of how our love got each other through)

Bob Dylan – Boots of Spanish Leather

The Gloaming – The Sailer's Bonnet & The Weight of Things

The following 3 songs are the songs we played at the funeral

Coldplay – O (this was Grandma Barbara's 'Finn song' and we grew to associate it with Finn and to love it)

The Beatles – Blackbird

Ludovico Einaudi – Berlin Song (listening to this just now and having a little cry. Once this song came on whilst I was at lunch with two dear friends not long after he died and they just held my hands – so grateful for their love and everyone's love.)

PART THREE

Transformations

Dance

Strangely enough, dance had never been a big part of my life. But when Finn was poorly, I once dreamt that he was dancing. It was before the diagnosis when I was desperately willing his body to heal and his movements to strengthen. I woke up and cried. I just wanted to dance with him. Little did I know at that point how absolutely central dance would become to my healing and joy.

I woke up one morning a few months after Finlay died and I felt like my body wasn't attached to my head. I needed to stop my brain. It was racing and racing - there was no peace. I *knew* I needed to move my body to do this. I knew I needed to move my body to survive the grief I was feeling. It was a physical feeling and knowing that just hit me one morning. I didn't love yoga, though; I'd tried it many times over the years but never found the right teacher. But I knew I needed yoga to survive this - or at least I thought. Until this point in my life, I was almost constantly living in my head. I have observed that this is not an uncommon thing for humans in these modern times. It took losing my child to force me into my body.

I was seeing a beautiful therapist in Burntisland, to manage my grief. She was gentle, understanding and helped me to connect to my trust. I told her I needed to move my body to survive the grief. I said the words, 'I need to move my body to heal.' She looked at me. 'Sarah, this is wild, but I need to tell you about Nia. It's a dance form that I love and there is a guest teacher from America here *tomorrow* who is teaching a class called Moving to Heal.' She paused. 'If you start coming to Nia regularly maybe I can't be your therapist but we can become friends instead.' Another magical moment to lean into. We celebrated.

If that wasn't the universe guiding me, I don't know what was. I went along to that first class shaking and terrified of 'free dance'. Any readers familiar with the British TV comedy *Peep*

Show might remember the episode where Mark attends Rainbow Rhythms. I expected a version of that - and feared being just as excruciatingly uncomfortable and self-conscious as Mark! In reality, my experience couldn't have been more positive. My pal Aline came along to the class with me. We were met at the door and warmly welcomed by the lovely Karen, who taught a regular Nia class a few minutes from my home here in Burntisland. Then Siere Munro, who was leading the class, came to meet me. She asked why we were there. I told her about Finn. She was beautiful. I feel deeply that she was an angel who flew into my life exactly when I needed her somehow. It changed everything.

I hid at the back of class like many newbies do. Then the music started. Isn't music the best? It was beautiful. The combination of the music and the gentle moves made me cry straight away. I cried with *relief*. I instantly knew I had found what I needed. After a few slow songs, the music became more upbeat, the movements faster. The tears stopped and I started to smile. I was feeling a *joy* I never *ever* thought I would feel again following Finn's death. It felt absolutely amazing.

Apart from when I was drunk in a nightclub or forced to attend ballet as a kid, which I hated, I had never danced! Oh my goodness. I felt free! It was glorious. *I was hooked.*

I have since gone on to train in Nia and I now teach. It's one of my biggest joys. It enables me to help people not only challenge the stories in their minds but to shift patterns and stories in their bodies. I will tell you more about this imperative combination of mind body healing methods in the chapter on 'reclaiming joy' and brain development.

Thank you, Karen, Jinti and Britta and Leticia. Siere. And Debbie and Carlos. And my freerwithnia copilot Bronwyn.

One of the *main* things in Nia is that '*you cannot get it wrong*'. It's so funny. I have been writing this book without making that connection. Only yesterday, my pal Fenton pointed this out to m*e*. Nia is about feeling the *joy* of moving your body. For me, it is about reclaiming my right to dance. I used to tell a story that I couldn't dance. Only professional dancers had the right to call themselves dancers or dance teachers. Now *I am a dance teacher* - and I adore it. I adore watching the joy and fun and healing in my class members. It's incredible. People laugh in class, cry, have *fun*, are silly. I have the added joy of witnessing that transformation in others. It makes me feel more alive than ever.

Nia released trauma from my body. It released what wasn't supposed to be kept there. It fed my spirit. It made me feel happier than I ever thought I would feel again. It released trauma that predated Finn. It made me question the story I'd been telling myself about my body and its place in the world. I began to realise the power in this thought: *What if we are supposed to feel great, in body, mind, emotions, and spirit?* It felt, for the first time, possible.

I remember one of Karen's classes. The sun was shining through the window. Gabriel, my Nia friend who is around seventy, was dancing. We were all smiling at each other as usual. I thought, 'I need to write a book about joy after loss. It c*an* happen. My life is more beautiful now than ever.' I cried tears of joy.

Dear reader,

If you tell yourself you can't dance, that you are not a dancer, or you are not coordinated enough… it's not true! Dancing is your birthright. Joy is your birthright. Every toddler in the world dances. Put on some music and let your body move. Free your body. Find a dance class (there are Nia classes worldwide!) It

81

will transform your life. I had to go so low to listen to my body and find dance to heal but you don't have to.

Dance dance dance!

Further resources

The Nia Technique – Debbie Rosas & Carlos Rosas

I also recommend 'Nia TV' which you can use from home:

www.niatv.fit

I provide online Nia classes – email for more info drsarahmadigan@gmail.com

*Some of my favourite songs to dance to
(some I discovered through Nia and
others not)*

Lizzo - Juice

Da Cruz – Boom Boom Boom

Cosmic Vibration – Show Me Your Love

The Babysitters Circus - Everything's gonna be alright

Todd Terry – Something's Going On

Dua Lipa – Don't Start Now

Kaya Project - Saranghi Breaks

Mystic Rhythms Band - Victory Dance

Hilight Tribe - Indian Trance

Strobe's Nanafushi – Satori Mix

Charli XCX, Lizzo – Blame It On Your Love (feat. Lizzo)

Lizzo – Ok anything by Lizzo, Tempo, Boys, Good as Hell

Transformation and the power of community

I could never have foreseen the ways in which moving my body and embracing Nia opened up space in my life for other shifts to occur. I ended up leaving my well-paid job as a clinical psychologist in the NHS workplace. While on maternity leave with our second son Isaac, I had to be interviewed for my job and I didn't get it. I felt so shameful but oh my goodness, Universe. Not getting that job was the best thing that ever happened to me. I was offered other roles in the department, but I didn't want them. I decided to retrain as a transformational coach.

After leaving my job, I combined private clinical psychology work with teaching Nia. It was OK. Then I met an angel called Jane Mann. She was a yoga teacher in the same studio where I taught Nia. She was training as a transformational coach with a company called The Little Volcano, who are based in San Diego. I completed their Get Yourself Together challenge, a week-long extravaganza. It blew my mind. They were *big, loud, fun, colourful, wild, really vulnerable, authentic, and they swore*! They call themselves 'the tribe of too much' but they were exactly the right amount of much for me. They were what I had been looking for and exactly what had been missing for me in the world of clinical psychology. I said out loud on their first webinar, 'at *last*'. They gave me permission to be myself: to be 'too much'; to bring myself into my work; to be 100% authentic; to be vulnerable; to forget being 'professional'; to forget fitting into a box; to wear what I wanted and to swear the odd time (I've tried to reign in the swearing for the purposes of writing a book...).

I'm now a transformational coach. I'm absolutely 'too much' and I'm perfect for my clients. I am finally *free* and totally myself and the people who are meant for me can actually find me now because I'm not hiding! I'm not pretending to be something I'm not. Finding this community who lift me up and believe in me and encourage me has been *the biggest* game changer.

84

Dear reader,

If you are not surrounded by joy seekers or people who support you - find some new people. I'm not saying get rid of those people who are sad (although there might be some people it's healthier to distance yourself from) but I'm saying the power of a big community of loving people is life changing and it will massively impact on you attracting new positive emotions. Join a dance class, change jobs, find a Dungeons & Dragons gang if that's your thing. Find what makes your soul light up and find others who light up about the same things. There are heaps of online communities, Facebook groups and in-person groups.

If you are telling a story that you wish you could leave your well-paid job for a job you love but that you are just not that kind of person...

If you are telling yourself that you need that pension or the security...

...just think for a minute. What are you trading for that security? Imagine if you could find a job that you adore. What would be the ripple effect on your body, mind, emotions, and spirit? What would be the ripple effect on all the people that you love the most? What would you be modelling to your children?

Maybe you could find a job that pays even better. Something you adore, like I have. When you are lit up and doing what you are supposed to be doing, imagine the bigger impact you could have in your lifetime! The timing will never be perfect. What small steps or leaps would you make if you trusted that you couldn't get it wrong.

Xxx

I found my community in both Nia and coaching. I found people who prioritise joy through dance.

I discovered a glorious coaching community based all over the world who are committed to positive transformation.

I left a workplace of stressed-out people. I surround myself with people who focus on what they *do* want in life; who want joy, fun, freedom, ease. It has changed everything.

I have now created the most beautiful and supportive high-vibe community of my own too, and I get to witness how this inspires, supports, and empowers people every day. It is one of my greatest achievements and deepest joys.

Further resources

You are welcome to join my private Facebook Group – 'Bliss Seekers' for weekly inspiration and guidance – you can search for it and request to join

I run four day intensives called 'BS to Bliss' three times a year too. 8 week 'Relationship Magic' courses and a 'Spectacular School'. For more information follow me on Facebook, Instagram or visit my website:

www.drsarahmadigan.com

Also feel free to email me at drsarahmadigan@gmail.com with any queries

Facing My Fears

Taking such a leap of faith and landing within supportive communities helped me to face other fears and to finally stop caring about how I am perceived by other people.

I used to play in bands. That love of music had carried through from childhood to become a central part of my early adulthood. Yet the sheer joy - of being that kid with the headphones on in my childhood home - had been tainted by my anxiety.

To cope with the fear of performing onstage, I would get drunk or take propranolol. I didn't think about any of the positive aspects of performing - I didn't think of the fun, the joy, the music. I just focused on my anxiety. On how humiliating it would be if people saw me shaking or blushing or if my hands shook too much to play piano or if I couldn't sing in key. I robbed myself of so much enjoyment because of where my attention was focused. In the end, I focused so much on the anxiety that any joy was lost entirely. I stopped performing.

In early 2020, pre-Covid, I was being group coached in front of about 25 people by my dearest Little Volcano mentors Kit and Rosie. It had taken me months to build up to stepping forward on the group coaching. Now, I was finally talking in public about my anxiety. I didn't know how life-changing it would be to make myself vulnerable in that space.

I spoke about how I wanted to sing again but had a story about getting too anxious. Their first reaction was pure support. They told me that all they saw was my power and amazingness. It was the first rebuttal against a lifetime of anxiety. I'm deeply grateful in my heart that they saw and continue to see this in me. Kit said he didn't think I needed coaching on this. His belief in me *still helps me to this day.*

Then they asked me why the anxiety was perfect. I was confused. They wanted ten reasons. I couldn't think of *one*. I had such a negative relationship with what I called anxiety. With my body just doing its thing, responding to its environment. Here's what I can remember saying:

1. I suppose it's perfect because it shows I'm doing something I care about
2. It can make you perform better and focus better

I stopped.

'There are no more positive things about anxiety, it's awful.'

'Carry on, Sarah,' Kit said, *'you've got this.'*

3. Maybe it actually makes you more relatable
4. It shows I'm expanding
5. I'll feel great afterwards if I do something that makes me anxious
6. It will motivate me to practice and make the performance decent
7. I actually find anxiety and vulnerability in other people beautiful - I don't judge others negatively for getting anxious
8. It means I have a human body and that's pretty cool
9. It's an opportunity for me to practice not caring about people seeing me as anxious
10. It's an opportunity for me to break free

… (something like that anyway, I can't remember word for word).

I had *never* thought about how anxiety was perfect. It was just an enemy of mine. I hated it. I felt like I had no power or control over it. It ruined my life. I resisted it. I avoided it. I had nothing positive to say about it!

I was pretty stoked with how the coaching session was going. It already felt like a breakthrough. Then, Kit asked me, 'How much do you want this? How much do you want to transform this and be free from this?'

Without hesitation. 'So much.'

Then the penny dropped. He was about to ask me to sing in front of everyone. *I knew it.*

'Sing for us.'

Face in hands. 'Are you f*cking kidding?' (I'd been avoiding performing for years, passing by any opportunity that presented itself, deflecting to my story that my anxiety would ruin everything.) I knew there was no way out of this one, no real reason to say no. 'Are you f*cking serious?'

Kit paused. 'Are you f*cking serious about your life?'

Oh my God. I couldn't argue with that. I took my laptop to the piano, I took some deep breaths and I made my way through part of a song I'd written years before. I messed up a little but I managed something fairly decent. The 25 people in the group session were like absolute angels. They supported me, encouraged me, celebrated me!

Dear reader, this community I am talking about… find it! Find people who will support, encourage and celebrate you. Join my Bliss Seekers group on Facebook, there's a place with your name on it.

If you are telling a story that you don't belong or that you won't be able to find your community, this is just a story. It is not reality. You create your reality and you can create or find a loving amazing community of people x

Then (as if that wasn't enough), Kit told me to sing *every* day for weeks *live* on my Facebook page.

Oh.

My.

God.

Dear reader,

Think about how fears of what other people think of you impact your life. How do you torture yourself with fearing the thoughts of others? How do you keep yourself in a box? How do you steal joy from yourself with these stories? How do you put yourself in prison?

I did it. I found a venue for an acoustic night and for every night until the performance I sang online on my page. It was awful at first. Some days, my horror stories about being judged felt unbearable... but you know what?

It was so free-ing!

I faced my worst fears. People could see I was anxious (although I didn't look as anxious as I felt!). I knew that some people would judge me. I knew that I might also trigger *their* shit about taking up space or whatever. I did it anyway. I learned to stop giving a f*ck.

My vision for what I wanted in life was bigger than my fears.

My focus on joy was starting to become bigger than my focus on anxiety.

Dear reader,

Think about what you really want in life.

What emotions do you want to feel?! Think think think about them, focus on them, talk about them.

Make your vision bigger than your fears.

(Also, check out Abraham Hicks).

It's around this time that I was introduced to the central premise of this book. I had a coaching session with an absolute beauty called Corey Thomas. We talked about my anxiety. She said to me, 'What if you couldn't get it wrong'.

I cried.

Oh. My. God.

What if I told myself that I couldn't get it wrong. What if I decided from that day forward that I didn't care what others thought. That I only cared about how I felt about myself. That I could choose to think *'I cannot get this wrong'* (Hello book title!). That if I chose to love myself no matter what, even if I blushed, even if I showed physiological symptoms of fight or flight… so what.

I could choose that I was always doing things perfectly. I could choose that I couldn't get things wrong. I could start saying *yes* to those amazing opportunities I turned down regularly. I could change my relationship with my anxiety. I could stop avoiding.

It was actually that simple. I tell myself 'I cannot get this wrong' Every. God. Damn. Day.

Thank you, Corey.

I began to reveal the parts of myself that had been so central to my identity before anxiety took hold. Music. Performance. Fun. This lightness had always been there. The gallows humour that saw me and Neil joking together through our darkest moments. Our capacity for laughter. Our openness to the inexplicable magic of life following Finn's death. It got me thinking about the transformative role that performance can play within community. How standing up and telling our deeply personal truths onstage can bridge gaps between individual experiences and open up space for our collective healing. The more authentic and unglossed the story, the more powerful its impact. I thought of my friend Eliott, standing on a stage and using comedy to disarm his audience and tell his story. Here it is.

Sex, Love, and lack thereof
By Eliott Simpson

Hello reader! My name is Eliott, spelt with one 'L' and two 'T's'. It makes an anagram for Toilet if that helps you remember. That alone might give you a slight indication of the type of person I am. It's never been a secret to anyone, let alone myself, that I use humour to both defuse tension and deflect hard questions - but I also use it because I genuinely enjoy spreading joy to others, even when I lack it myself. The fact that I'm able to admit that and display vulnerability is a true testament to how far I've come on my journey of self-development.

I may only be 24, but my journey of self-compassion, self-acceptance and self-love has been a strenuous and complex one, and one which still has many more stages to come.

I'm writing this chapter to provide a unique perspective to vulnerability that I think is not often touched upon (a phrase that you may find ironic by the end of this piece). I'm a gender fluid autistic asexual comedian and filmmaker and, until very recently, I had never once said a kind word to myself. Even now it's still something I'm working towards but, much like anything involving self-development, it's an ongoing process that requires constant learning and attention.

To say I spent childhood as an outcast would be an understatement. I was diagnosed with Asperger's Syndrome at a very young age and so was already aware of the way in which I saw the world and how I struggled to understand others. However, my journey through puberty ended up being far more complicated than I could ever have anticipated.

I was naturally outcast at school, perceived as weird, strange, and not as socially competent as others. This was probably most prominently pronounced by my inability to detect sarcasm or tone, where any slight tease or joke at my expense sent me into a wild state of anxiety. The fact that I've now weaponised that anxiety - as a means to now have a career of making jokes at others - could be seen as concerning. I've chosen to see it as catharsis. But while the feeling of being outcast is familiar to me, it's certainly never helped me to escape my cage of self-betrayal. Being surrounded by people who judge you for your differences inflicts a constant state of paranoia and self-criticism. Despite being aware that I was peerless, it was my own self-criticism that prevented me from truly embracing my good qualities. I allowed my fear of judgement from others to inhibit my own self-worth; forcing myself to become things I wasn't or to appease people who didn't care for my existence. I fell into a cycle of self-destructive behaviour, convincing myself that I needed others' approval to feel happy. I felt that my authentic self was responsible for my ridicule, and so it was my authentic self that I began to despise.

People were hard to understand, in fact they very much still are, but that lack of understanding should never have impeded my love for myself, nor should it have prevented me from accepting love from those who truly did care for me.

Matters of acceptance were drastically complicated by the dawn of my sexual awakening, or rather, my lack thereof. Although I wouldn't know this until many years later, I identify as a panromantic asexual; 'asexual' meaning 'a lack of sexual attraction'. Unlike my peers, I never felt an urge or desire to pursue sexual relations, I never had an interest in pornography or masturbation and although I never cared for ironing, I still wasn't into kinks, either on or under the sheets. You'd be forgiven for being unfamiliar with the term 'asexual', as it's still a 'relatively uncharted area of sexual variability', which as you can imagine didn't make feeling validated an easy task.

Having any identity outside of the 'hierarchized binary' of heteronormativity presents challenges of feeling outcast and ridiculed by wider society. Due to our culture's general lack of asexual awareness or representation, I spent almost my entire early adulthood feeling broken, wrong, and incomplete. Although I no longer feel that way, those emotions of fear and anxiety did nevertheless impact my 'coming out' process; a process hindered even further by complications concerning my gender.

Although I now identify as gender fluid, this was, very much like my sexuality, a revelation that took several years to fully accept. When I was coming out as asexual, I still thought I was just a man because that's what I had been assigned at birth. It was simply what I thought society expected of me from the way I appeared and presented. Thankfully, I am now much happier in the knowledge that gender is simply a societal construct and that our biology holds no bearing on how we choose to identify ourselves. Now I am happy to flow freely across the spectrum, not feeling permanently attached to any one specific gender. But for someone who had grown up being perceived by everyone as male, facing pre-conceived notions of 'manliness' and 'manhood' were difficult to say the least. For a vast majority of my academic life, pervasive ideas of male to female interactions being seen as competition not only forcibly pushed standards of straightness, but also the expectations for sexual accomplishment. In both school and social events, sexual activity was constantly framed as a firm desire that all men should aspire to. Moreover, we were encouraged to use any means necessary to obtain it. I existed in an environment where socially constructed attitudes describe men as aggressive, strong and unemotional. With no knowledge of the existence of alternative communities, I was instead left to feel alienated and broken for not being as openly engaged with the pursuit for sex as my peers seemingly were.

Even after finally becoming aware of the asexual spectrum through independent research, perpetuated sexual expectations still slowed my journey towards self-acceptance. The constant underpinning theme of sexual attraction as a necessity of adulthood only cemented the notion that I was unwelcome within any community.

Although my rejection of stereotypically masculine activities did aid the eventual revelation of my sexuality and gender, our society's obsession with withholding standards of heteronormativity may very well be preventing others from feeling safe to do the same. My own lived experience taught me just how much *awareness* could help those struggling with self-identity and self-acceptance. This experience allowed me to find my voice through comedy.

Being on the autistic spectrum, my biggest difficulty comes with reading emotions and tone. You can say nothing but compliments to my face, yet it's still highly probable that I'll assume you were being sarcastic. Because of this, I struggle to receive clear, sure-fire messages that tell me someone's emotional state. This is why comedy has always appealed to me, both to watch and to perform. Comedy can provide and discuss a multitude of things. Primarily, though, its goal is always to elicit laughter from others. Laughter is one of the clearest, most defined reactions that we possess. Unless you're theatrically trained, faking authentic laughter is no mean feat. To my autistic brain, hearing laughter is one of the few definitive signalers that someone is expressing joy as a result of something I've done.

Coming out as asexual was one of the most liberating experiences of my life, so much so that I've dedicated my career to spreading awareness about the orientation in order to help others like myself. However, although my campaigns were well received by those in my social circle, any attempt I made to explain asexuality fell on deaf ears outside of that confined bubble. This is how I discovered the remarkable transformative nature of comedy. Once I started using jokes to explain my orientation, not only did people laugh, but they understood; furthermore, they were intrigued and wished to learn more even after I'd left the stage. In some respect, comedy is almost like a magic trick; audiences don't go to watch comedy with the intent to learn or to hear about a specific topic. The only prerequisite is that whatever is said elicits laughter, and with that you possess the power to educate audiences through subtlety and humour.

Growing up in the 2000s, it was not uncommon to see comedy used as a means to perpetuate stereotypes of autistic people being selfish and unfeeling with 'atypical ways of forming relationships'. Nor was it uncommon to witness 'ridiculing of effeminate queerness' at the expense of LGBTQ+ people. Through comedy, you possess the ability to influence people by making an audience feel that they're supporting the 'preservation of the status quo'. For centuries, this status quo has been heteronormativity which 'presumes heterosexuality to be natural' and thus asexuality to be an unnatural 'disorder of sexual desire'.

Therefore, the ability to bring joy and laughter to others is more than just a privilege, but a moral responsibility. In a world where division is one of the greatest enablers of corruption and injustice, the question we must ask ourselves is not why we laugh, but who we are laughing at and who we are laughing with. Being aware of the power granted by a literal platform and microphone, I've dedicated my life to shifting the status quo to not mock those who are different but to instead mock the culture which makes us afraid of what's different.

Ironically, being silly was the only way to be taken seriously. I used to believe that the harsh reality was that being an outcast is forgiven provided you are of value to society (at least that's the message I always got from watching *Rudolph*). If you were a freak and you were funny then that was fine, but if you weren't funny, then you were just a freak in the eyes of the public. Thankfully, through practicing self-gratitude, I've learnt to adopt a healthier mindset; to instead be proud of my differences and the work I do in helping and educating others through comedy.

Sadly, I would be lying if I said I hadn't experienced trauma on account of my sexuality. When you're different, or when people don't understand you, they try to correct you, which is rather uncomfortable if you don't feel like you need correcting. Previous partners made numerous attempts to fix part of me that wasn't broken or berate me for resisting their attempts to change me. As bizarre as it sounds, being silly and wacky on a stage with prop bananas and googly eyes is the only way I know how to fully talk about those experiences. So as much as I'm aware that I use humour to disguise and overcome the pain of my past, I'm no longer ashamed of it. My trauma is still important, because without it I very well wouldn't be as confident in myself as I am now, I wouldn't be able to use that pain to bring enjoyment and awareness to others, and I certainly wouldn't have been able to truly embrace and love a partner who in turn accepts and loves me for who I am. I am incredibly fortunate to now have such a partner, to have someone who demands nothing but my authentic true self, and not a day goes by where I am not grateful for that bliss of being unashamedly myself and loved for it.

I am not broken, damaged, incomplete or something in need of a cure. I like myself just the way I am. While I still have a long way to go in regard to loving and embracing every aspect of myself, it has been an abundance of honesty, vulnerability, gratitude, and acceptance of love from myself and others that has allowed me to overcome my anxiety and my trauma.

Before learning about the practices and methods of self-compassion, I had never once shown gratitude or any kind of positive thinking towards myself. Everything around me, from my peers to the media, told me that who and what I was - was wrong. I didn't fit, I didn't feel the feelings I was supposed to, and I didn't interact like I was expected to. The anxiety I felt during childhood and early adulthood still resonates with me today. I came to realise, though, that while society had placed barriers in my way to make me doubt myself and my existence, the greatest barriers I had were those I had made for myself. People saw me as something that didn't fit, so I hid away to make sure that I couldn't even try to fit. I allowed fear of people's judgements to stop me from doing what I loved. I couldn't even accept and believe genuine compliments from others, because I no longer believed that good things about myself were true.

Fear makes companions of us all but when we are afraid, we are irrational, paranoid, desperate, uncertain, or quick to anger. The weakness of fear lies within the uncertainty, and thus I discovered that honesty was the path to strength and confidence. In vulnerability lies strength. By being honest with yourself, you understand and appreciate your needs, wants, fears, aspirations, accomplishments, and desires. It takes courage and strength to show vulnerability but doing so makes you more confident than anything in the world; and I can personally attest to how wonderful creativity is as a means for loving yourself for your quirks. Before, nervous twitches and responses made me feel embarrassed and ashamed. Now, they act as punctuations that emphasise my comedy and bring joy to thousands of people. I love myself for being excitable and nervous. It's what makes me who I am, it's what makes me an unpredictable, funny stage presence, and it proves to myself and others how much I care. While I still struggle at times, I'm now learning to fully embrace compliments from others because I can now begin to earnestly concur with them.

Now, whenever I'm confronted with any challenge, I ask myself, 'How can I get this wrong?' Whether I was bullied or outcast or misunderstood, I was always myself. I was always doing what I could to make others laugh, in spite of anxiety or trauma. I'm proud to be where I am now. I'm proud to be here, I'm proud to be queer, and I'm proud to have no fear (okay there is still a bit of fear but, like I say, work in progress).

Instead of dwelling on how I was feeling, I started to focus on how I wanted to feel, and on the steps I had to take to get to there. I asked myself, 'What if you don't think you're wrong?' Asexuality is not wrong. Autism is not wrong. They are not a disease, or a condition, or a defect. They are natural, they are valid, they are me, and they're beautiful, and I'm tired of pretending that they're anything else. I worked towards challenging those beliefs about myself. I began to consider that perhaps people truly did love me. Perhaps the person who was really the most doubtful of my validity was myself. Now I am proud to sustain my joy in the face of discrimination, in the face of ignorance, or misunderstanding, or stubbornness. Discrimination will still be there, and it will still confront me, but allowing it to force self-loathing upon myself is not a choice I allow to happen anymore.

Society didn't accept me, so I didn't accept myself either. Having autism made communication hard, being asexual made communication harder, and having self-loathing made self-communication the hardest of all (again, an ironic use of phrase). I didn't have clarity then, but I do have clarity now because now I have vulnerability, now I have love, and now I have pride. Now I strive to create joy, to heal collectively with my friends and family, and it has completely changed the way I think about anxiety. I may still have barriers to self-confidence, but I guess that's unsurprising when your job involves telling jokes in order to gain validation from drunken strangers in dark rooms. But while I know I still have barriers to overcome, I will always be grateful for where I am now compared to where I was, and even more grateful to know where I'll soon be. The things I hated about myself are now the things that make me feel empowered. I'm empowered to be autistic; I'm empowered to be asexual; I'm empowered to be myself.

People still tell me that I'm missing out by not having sex, and while it has never been an interest or concern of mine (and I would still take hummus over sex any day), I now simply ask: why would I ever even need sex, when I already have love.

My reflections on Eliott's chapter

Eliott is such an absolute treat of a person. He is one of the funniest people I have ever met. I met him as the partner of a friend of mine and we have since become friends. He has taken part in two of the self-development courses that I run, so I have had the privilege of getting to know him deeply, witnessing his beautiful vulnerability, joy, and humour - such gifts that he has shared with me and the community I have built.

Eliott refers to the expectations of society in terms of gender, sexual orientation, and neurotypical/divergence. He talks of his perception that society rejected him, and in turn how he rejected himself. His awareness of this process has given him power - and him taking control of his relationship with himself has enabled him to turn this round - and to turn around his relationship with society. I adore that one of the ways he has taken control and empowered himself is to use his comedy to shift the status quo, like he said, to mock not those who are different, but the culture which makes us afraid of what's different.

It is poignant when Eliott acknowledges that when you are a 'funny freak', you are accepted in your 'weirdness', but when you are not funny you are just a freak - this made me consider the people living in our society who may belong to LGBTQ+ communities or be neuro-divergent with perhaps less 'protective factors' in their favour - it made me consider the potential societal barriers they face to creating a life of joy.

My own journey with anxiety, and my putting an end to resisting anxiety and shaming myself for experiencing it, is mirrored in Eliott's journey. He talks of transforming his feelings of shame around how his anxiety manifested physically (nervous twitches for him, blushing for me), into celebration. He shifted his mindset about anxiety, viewing the ways in which it was perfect, in a similar way that I did in the group coaching session I wrote about. He claimed these previously shameful parts of

102

himself and actually attributed his success in comedy, in part, to them. Recognising that they help him spread joy, to bring himself joy. He celebrates anxiety, loves himself, not despite it, but because of it. It is part of him, it makes him who he is, and he has started to love the *whole* of him, not just parts of him. It proves to his audience members that he cares; it makes him funny and unpredictable. In so many ways his anxiety is perfect. His mindset shift around his anxiety utterly transforms his experience of it.

What also interests me is again, the form that celebration takes for Eliott. Not only is he learning to love and celebrate his anxiety, he is loving and celebrating all of his identities - asexuality, autism. Not only this - he is celebrating the very fact that he is celebrating. He is recognising his strength at sustaining joy in the face of discrimination, in the same way Kyra did when she used the word 'triumph'. Eliott acknowledges that discrimination will still confront him, but the key is, it will not impact on his love for himself - he will not let that happen.

My identity as a woman

Eliott touches upon the power of an externally defined identity to brand us from birth or from childhood, and on how difficult and powerful it can be to rewrite those rule books. In many ways, my anxiety was tangled up in my identity as a woman and my relationship with my female body, with everything I had imbibed about what it meant to be a girl and then a woman. Why, when I was a little girl with two doctors as parents, did I think that nurses were female and doctors were male? How deeply the social conditioning embeds itself. Why, when I was only maybe nine or ten, was I *devastated* about being taller than all the boys?

Why did I think I needed to be small?

I wished I was shorter. I always weighed about two stone more than my friends as I grew up. I was a *lot* taller than most of them and I felt like the Big Friendly Giant. I was really slim, and I thought I was *massive*. I received praise within my family for being slim. I watched women within my family talk negatively about their bodies. I watched men in my family speak negatively about women's bodies at times. I seldom met women who *loved* their bodies. I watched my Mum hate on her perfectly beautiful body. She commented a lot on my body.

I fantasised about being smaller, shorter, quieter, demure, and shy; I thought I would be loved more if I was like that. But I was a *loud, wild, tall, big* person.

I took up space.

I felt like I was *getting it wrong* as a girl and then as a woman.

Having an abortion exacerbated this; made me feel like I had *really* got being a woman wrong. After Finn died, we were left in a distressing and complicated situation in terms of two humans who really, really wanted to have another baby together. We both

104

carried a genetic disorder. It was an autosomal recessive disease. It meant that each time we got pregnant there was a 1 in 4 chance that the baby would have a terminal illness.

Sex become something associated with deep sadness: potential trauma; confusion; distress. I wanted sex to feel light, fun, and intimate again, but it didn't; it felt like something which could lead us to horror, to inflicting something so awful on the baby and on each other and our loved ones.

I missed the way things used to be and I missed Finn. My heart ached. You know when you leave your baby for a period of time and then you feel so excited to see them again? And the reunion is absolutely perfect? Or when you've been apart and you just feel like it's been too long? The freedom you yearned for was good but now all you want and need in every cell of your body and heart and soul is to hold that baby close again and smell them and sense them? Well imagine that feeling constantly... that feeling of, 'OK, it's just been long enough now, I can't cope any longer without them, I need to see them.' Except you don't. You don't ever get to see them again.

I missed sex being straightforward and I missed life feeling easy. I started to feel incredibly jealous of people who found it easy to become pregnant.

We decided to start PGD (preimplantation genetic diagnosis). This would avoid the distress of having to terminate a pregnancy of an affected baby. There was no way we would inflict such an uncomfortable and distressing disease on another little human; there was no way we would survive it again.

We started the process, which is similar to IVF except they test the embryo for the disease prior to implantation. It took months to be given the first appointment and then months to start the injections. My memory is actually hazy of this time. I had to inject various things into my body. Then we had to attend scans to see how the eggs were doing and to guess the prime time for extracting the eggs. I was told various things about my body; it was very invasive and although we felt incredibly grateful for the medical science and input, it felt so disempowering.

At our first appointment, we were excited about the sense of possibility yet at the same time the whole clinical atmosphere was just weird. We were given an *infertility number*! What. The. Actual. F. I wanted to scream and say to everyone, 'We are not even infertile, we got pregnant easily, there's nothing wrong with us, nothing wrong with our bodies, we are not infertile.' Where does all that language come from? Imagine if you did actually believe that you were 'infertile' and unable to have a baby and then you were given an infertility number, thereby

1) making you feel like a number in a system and

2) confirming your belief that you were not going to be successful in having a baby.

Don't these people know about the power of mindset? I might provide some feedback: is four years too late to do that?

The first time Neil had to do a sperm sample, we were waiting for the (let's be honest) Wanking Room to become available. The universe just started to have a laugh with us. 'Beat It' by Michael Jackson came on the radio. *No joke!* There was another dude in the waiting area and we all burst out laughing. It was fun and funny, and we felt so connected in that moment.

I did not feel like I was getting it right as a woman, being unable to have a baby. We couldn't easily get pregnant anymore and during that time after Finn died, after failed IVF, etc., I began to feel so envious of other women. It was a lonely, horrific place to be. Everyone else seemed to get pregnant without even trying (obviously this wasn't always the case) but it was so hard. I remember even feeling envious of my mother's journey to becoming a mother. She didn't experience any loss or difficulty and I remember thinking, 'you don't understand me'. I hated myself for feeling this way towards people. I met a friend for dinner around this time and she showed me the photos of her 20-

106

week scan, glowing with happiness. It was awful. I couldn't feel happy for her and I didn't have the insight or skills at the time to communicate that I wasn't in the kind of place to cope with that. I felt consumed with jealousy and was shocked that she was so out of tune with how I was feeling. It was my responsibility to communicate this, though, and at the time I didn't feel able to.

I felt that my body wouldn't work properly and that I was 100% *getting it wrong*. The expectations we have of our bodies as women can be so high, can't they? Not just in terms of making babies but also in terms of how our bodies appear to others, how fat or thin they are.

Have you read *Untamed* by Glennon Doyle? It's a masterpiece. I had an epiphany when I read it. I am a feminist *and* I realised that I *still* hold shame around how much I weigh. My body looks great, I am fit and strong *and* there is still the voice telling me I should be smaller.

Glennon talks about her children having a sleepover and her popping in to offer the kids food. All the boys didn't even look up and said yes they wanted food and all the girls looked to each other for approval.

Weirdly, I realised that I *still feel this sh*t*. I didn't want my husband to see how much I weighed for the first few years of our marriage. I was very comfortable being naked in front of him, but I still felt like I was getting something wrong because I weighed more than some of my smaller mates. WTAF?!

Last week, three beautiful friends and I were standing in a circle, being the gorgeous hippy witches that we are, setting intentions and manifesting. I was hungry and opened a massive bag of crisps. I said I was relieved that the others had joined in to eat, too, otherwise I would have felt like a fat bastard; self-conscious of eating junk food in front of others when they weren't eating - just like those kids at Glennon's sleepover!

Do you think that Neil has ever felt self-conscious of eating crisps in front of his friends? I am not saying that eating issues affect women exclusively, but blimey, I really couldn't believe that as a woman of 40 who is mostly super comfortable in her body, that *I was still like those kids* looking to others to see if it was OK for me to eat the damn crisps.

Dear younger me, and current me,

You are loud, you take up space, you are tall. Sometimes you weigh 11 ½ stone sometimes 12 ½ stone. This is perfect. To all of the extra cells from corona time lockdown - welcome to the f*cking party, I love you. Join in. Body, you are amazing. You do so, so much for me. You dance for me, you are loved, you nurtured and birthed two amazing babies.

Sarah, you do not need to be quiet, or small or lighter. Eat the crisps. Shove them in your gob, Tell the world that you weigh 12 ½ stone with zero shame. Don't waste any more energy worrying about your size.

Be big, be bold and wonderful.

Be bigger!

You cannot get this (or being a woman) wrong!

Sarah xxxxxxxxx

To the people who want but are unable to get pregnant,

Do not feel bad about experiencing envy towards other people. It is normal.

Set boundaries if friends talk about their pregnancies; communicate to them what you can and can't hear. Allow yourself to avoid situations or people if you want to. Celebrate yourself if you are able to manage these situations and feel joy for others. Also celebrate yourself if you want to scream at every pregnant person you see. Both are OK.

Grieve, love yourself, know you are not alone.

Whether or not you can get pregnant does absolutely NOT mean you are getting 'being a woman' right or wrong.

There is no such thing as getting it right. You are no more or less a woman with or without a pregnancy or baby.

I know how all-consuming this can feel.

I love you xxx

Sexual assault, abuses of power and the impact this had on my spirit

It is impossible to talk about being a woman in a patriarchal society without discussing the sexual assaults that my body has experienced. There are many times, mainly as a young woman between the ages of 16-25, that men abused their power and sexually assaulted me. The number of women I know who have multiple, similar stories to tell is astounding and grim.

The first time, I was 16. The same age that my niece is now, which makes me connect to just how young I was. I was with my boyfriend in a nightclub and we were talking to a man he knew, a huge bodybuilder perhaps 6 foot 6 or so. When my boyfriend looked away, the stranger placed his whole hand on my vagina, rubbing and grabbing me there. I remember what I was wearing (tight black velvet trousers) and how time slowed down. I decided not to say anything because I didn't want him and my boyfriend to fight; out of fear that it would harm my boyfriend. I couldn't speak to the bouncers because they were friends with him or I presumed so, I can't remember. I felt powerless and silenced.

Another time in the same place, a man grabbed my breasts and started commenting on them. I was only 17. I remember being disgusted but also confused. I kissed him. I didn't realise how wrong it was that he did that. I was drunk. I wish I could return to that time and respond very, very differently. I felt powerless and silenced.

Still 17, I got a job in the bar of a working men's club. My boss touched my bum, with both hands, to 'move me out of the way'. He continuously made sexual comments, too. I left the job and put in a complaint and had to go to a 'board meeting'. Ten men asked me about what had happened. My Dad came with me and they addressed him and not me. One of the men was a patient of my dad's.

'Dr. Nugent, this must have been upsetting for you.'

Dad: 'I think you should reword that question and ask it again to my f*cking daughter.'

My friend who had witnessed the event wrote a letter of support. They argued that our letters contradicted each other because I said he placed both hands and she didn't specify this. What a crock of sh*t.

I'll never forget a beautiful handwritten letter from one of the old men at the bar, though, telling me that all the regulars hated this guy and that they all believed me and missed me. Heartmelt.

I was learning to be less silent, but it was stressful. I overheard a group of women in the pub one day say, 'she asked for it'.

Another time, I was in the family home of a friend. A man my father's age came over and touched my bum. 'You've got a hair on there,' he said, handing me a hair he picked up whilst touching me. I looked right at him and dropped the hair on the ground, I was furious. I had to stay in his home with my friend. I didn't want to upset my friend or the man's partner and child, so I didn't say anything. I just felt so uncomfortable for the rest of the visit, of course. I don't know why I wanted so badly to protect everyone else; I perhaps questioned whether they would believe me. Again, I felt powerless and silenced.

Another time, I feared I was going to be raped. I had been joking with a man at a house party but now he was forcing my hand to his penis. I was resisting again and again. I was telling him No but being ignored. I got up to leave the room. He shut the door and blocked it with his foot and wouldn't let me leave. I can't remember how but I got out and ran to find my friend. I was so scared.

111

Another time, I was walking home in Edinburgh to a flat where I lived alone. A group of men had pulled up in a car, the passenger door open and blocking my route past. They started making sexual comments about me. My body sensed real danger. They let me past in the end but I was terrified walking home in the dark, scared they were following me. It was right after a music festival I had attended where a 17 year old girl had been gang raped. I had just moved into a flat on my own and it significantly impacted on my sense of safety.

I am grateful for how, viewed retrospectively, having transformed any shame around these experiences, they now embolden me to stand more fully in my power as a woman.

I love being a woman. I inhabit my body fully. I love my body. It's mine and mine alone. I suppose it homed my babes for a while so it was kind of theirs too. I gladly shared it; what a gift. But it's my body.

I've lost count of the times when men have assumed power or superiority or made sexist comments about how women should appear or behave. I once went to a senior clinical psychologist for advice on how to succeed at my interview for the doctoral level training course. I wanted advice on how to prepare and structure my knowledge. He told me not to wear too much makeup and how to dress.

I have had boyfriends who told me what to wear, how to cut my hair, to lose weight or how to act.

I won't heed advice from culture or men on how it should appear, on how I should behave or what I should wear.

I love that I now work for *myself*. That I wear what I want (low cut sequined onesies at times). That I earn more money than I've ever earned. That I built this and created this as a woman and that I provide fun work for other coaches. That I help people more powerfully than I've ever helped them and that I often do

112

it in bright red lipstick (the specific shade he advised me to avoid).

And if joy and confidence make people trust me less? (Research shows that people trust and like confident and joyful men *more* and joyful and confident women *less)*. Then you better believe I'll work tirelessly on my joy and continue to grow in power until I take my last breath (wearing that bright red lipstick probably).

This is your invitation as a woman, as an act of rebellion, to fully inhabit, celebrate, love, and own your body. If people trust confident and joyful women less, then let's become as untrustworthy as possible.

Shame and guilt

Shame is central to many of the experiences I share within this book. When editing, I realised that the word 'shame' appears 90 times in the pages of this book. It is something I encounter and work on day in and day out with clients.

'I am not enough.'
'I get things wrong.'

Such shaming stories, deep within so many of us.

My shame looked like shame at being too big, *'too much'*, shame at my curly frizzy hair, shame about my looks. Throughout primary school, I constantly received praise for 'getting it right.' I was clever, I was moved up a year with some other kids, I felt proud of how quickly I completed my work and of my achievements. I received praise from teachers and family members (although oh how this changed when I discovered boys and rebelled and stopped studying and flunked my exams!). Achievement was emphasised and rewarded.

In retrospect, I wonder how it felt for the kids who were too bored or traumatised to concentrate, or who didn't find the work easy for whatever reason. If I felt proud, they perhaps felt shame (the same deep shame I felt on A-Level results day, I guess).

Wow. Shame shame shame.

Looking back, I recognise that my body was full of shame. The abortion was the big trigger. That, coupled with the arsehole who called me fat during that vulnerable time, triggered *all* the shame. Now, I actually take full responsibility for attracting him into my life; I was vibing at such a level that he was who I attracted. He confirmed all my worst fears about myself.

The shame lifted when I had therapy and began to open up with friends about those experiences that had made me feel shameful. I remember being in a pub with my dear friends Naomi and Mark. I wanted to tell them what had happened in Romania with the fat shamer but I seriously thought they would agree with the things he'd said. Looking back, it's unbelievable that I felt that fear. I told them anyway. They were furious. They wanted to send him hate mail. They made me laugh. I felt such *relief.*

Maybe there wasn't something wrong with me.

Naomi and Mark,

Thank you for your love during that time. Mark, thank you for driving me to my appointment about the abortion and for making me feel everything was going to be OK.

Thank you for both being so loving and helping me see things clearly again,

Love you both xxx

The work is always ongoing, isn't it. We reveal and hide parts of ourselves depending on how we're feeling at a given time. Yesterday, I was talking to a friend about IVF and PGD (pre-implantation genetic diagnosis). I mentioned abortion. It struck me how I would never have usually brought that into the conversation; my shame would have kept it hidden. Even now, after all these years. But it was relevant. It opened up the conversation to another level of honesty. I've had enough of hiding beneath shame that no longer serves me.

The shame was always about looking wrong (too tall, too heavy, too curly), speaking wrong (too loud, too un-cool, too laughable), getting things wrong (A Level results, acting or

115

saying something wrong, having an abortion, blushing, appearing anxious)…

When my moto became

I cannot get this wrong…

it changed everything.

Dear reader,

Spend some time tuning into where you feel shame. Do memories of things you have previously done in life still haunt you or make you cringe of feel ashamed?

How can you bring love to these areas?

How can you allow yourself just to know what you know, then do things differently and better when you know better?

Like me and this book; not even initially considering inclusivity or discrimination. I felt deep shame at first. But that's OK. I could feel it, allow it then celebrate that I now knew better, knew more, and could do better.

Where can you allow yourself more?

Speak aloud the things you hide from people. Tell your partner or trusted ones about things you have never told anyone before out of fear of judgment (choose your person wisely, of course!).

By speaking out loud the things we are ashamed of, we allow ourselves more fully!

Sarah xx

And while we're diving into shame, let's drop in on its morose sibling, Guilt. Guilt is an interesting one. Slightly different to shame and involving a feeling of remorse or responsibility for having done something wrong. For those who are, like me, familiar with Catholicism, guilt is probably not an unfamiliar emotion or concept to you.

The things I have felt guilty for in my life?

- Being mean to people
- Being irritable with my mum
- Not being a good enough parent
- Being snappy with Neil
- Having an abortion
- Wanting to be successful and have money
- Being happy

Wow. At times, it's felt like we as a society are addicted to guilt. How does guilt show up for you?

The 'I'm not enough' or 'I'm too much'? Or 'I've done something bad'. 'I'm bad'?

Write a list of the things you feel guilty for. How can you give yourself grace?

Later in the book, I will explore what to do when you *do* feel you have done something wrong. It involves taking full responsibility and deciding to commit to doing something different next time, but without the guilt and shame!

Pattern interrupt

One of the things I love about transformational coaching as opposed to traditional therapy is the focus on the FUTURE and not on the past.

We are conditioned to respond in various ways in life. Maybe the only time you received attention was when you were upset so you associate pain with love.

Whatever your patterns, you can learn to reprogram yourself.

Instead of feeling like crap every time you tell yourself that you are never going to succeed in life, you can reprogram yourself to feel differently.

Try this (an exercise inspired by Tony Robbins).

Think of your one biggest limiting belief. It could be 'I can't cope'. It could be, 'I don't want to humiliate myself.'

Or it could be, 'I'll never succeed '

Whatever it is, it probably makes you feel rubbish.

Guess what.

It's NOT REAL. You are just conditioned to think and feel it because of your previous experiences.

Now.

Jump around the room pretending to be a kangaroo whilst shouting out your limiting belief in an Irish accent. (If you are Irish, pick a different accent!)

Seriously! Do it!

Does it suddenly feel different?

Do it LOADS of times! Start to interrupt that old pattern!

YES! Are you smiling and laughing?

Take the power away from those words and start associating new physiological and emotional feelings with those words. A pattern interrupt is so powerful.

Also, right now, choose something new to do with your body and your voice every time your anxiety creeps in.

Want to know what I do? When I'm annoyed at my husband or feeling angry or sad or worried?

I yodel! Yodle ey hi yodle ey hi yodle ey hi hooooooo! And I do star jumps.

Maybe now I've disclosed my techniques in a book, I'll need to do teeny tiny star jumps so my husband doesn't notice.

Do something to interrupt the pattern that has been conditioned in your body. You can do it! You are not too much or too lacking in anything. You deserve to be happy. You cannot get this wrong.

How do you get grieving for your child right?

My grief since Finny died is nothing - and I mean *nothing* - like what I expected it to be. I didn't think my body, mind or soul would survive his death. The thought of it was unbearable. It was wretched. It was terrifying, knowing that he was going to slowly deteriorate, knowing his little body would stop working one day. His beautiful little heart. My favourite organ in the whole world. His beautiful, beautiful body. His soft body, which had been attached to my body for so long. His little creases, his little noises, his little ways. The reindeer vein on his eyelid. Where would they go? How could they be here now? Then stop being here?

When I look back at Finny's life, I do feel that we '*got it right*'; I feel a strong sense of pride in how we managed to get through it and stay in the moment. We dug deep and showed Finn what love was; how utterly blissful love can be. We showed him what joy was. We shared something which was glorious and amazing. When he was alive, I did fear that I would feel regretful. I once wrote 'future me' a message, to open after he died. It said something along the lines of:

'*You were a great Mum. You didn't play Candy Crush too much. You only did it every so often whilst he was breastfeeding and you needed the distraction. Don't worry about it. I love you x*'

Hahahaha!

Then he died. And I didn't know what to do. I didn't know how to deal with it all; my feelings, other people's reactions, other people's feelings, other people acting like nothing had happened, going back to work, the grandparents, my husband, my friends.

Am I talking about Finny too much? Am I making people feel uncomfortable? Am I sharing too many old photos of him on

120

social media? Focusing too much on the past? Am I over-sharing? Am I sharing enough? Am I a bad person for feeling so unbelievably jealous of my friends who have children the same age as Finn, except their children are alive? Am I wrong for not wanting to see those people? Am I wrong for sometimes not wanting to talk about Finn when Neil wants to? Am I sad enough? Why am I feeling OK some of the time? How the f*ck can I be so excited about Christmas when my child died only two years ago? I'm a monster... Am I the worst mother in the world? Why is my heart still beating? Why am I still hungry and still eating food? How can I still laugh? Oh my God, I think I just went a full day without thinking about Finny, I feel awful. Is my identity too wrapped up in being a bereaved Mum? When people ask me if Isaac is my first child should I just say yes? It doesn't feel right, is it too soon to have another child? Someone just basically told me they thought it was too soon *whilst I was pregnant!* Why am I so furious at that person? I can't remember all the small details about Finn anymore... this is awful, this person seems so uncomfortable with me, they can't handle my words or my emotions, I'll just keep quiet.

Even writing this book brings up similar feelings for me; am I sharing too much sacred information with the world? Then I remember '*I cannot get this wrong*'. I trust myself. I trust that this is flowing out of me like a river for some reason. Perhaps someone will read this and resonate with it and feel less alone. I hope so.

I have found such peace and harmony with how I grieve for Finn. It's nearly five years since he died. His little mates are starting school tomorrow. Tomorrow. Previous me would have questioned my feelings around this and whether or not they were OK. Now I flow more. It's painful to be reminded of what he would have been doing. It hurts. I tend not to focus on what we have lost, on what he would have been doing, and times like this that's tough.

121

Right from the beginning of our grieving journey, Neil and I decided to always check in with each other if we wanted to talk about Finn. What we went through, and some of the things we saw, was so traumatic. We agreed that, if one of us was having a good day, we might not necessarily want to be triggered. It was helpful for us to have realistic expectations of each other (more about this in the Boundaries chapter). As a self-confessed *co-dependent in recovery*, I still at times feel responsible for other people's emotions. Previous me would have told a story that, to '*get it right*' as a wife and partner, I should be there 100% to support my grieving husband. I don't know how we landed upon it but somehow, thankfully, we both decided that we just could not be responsible for each other's emotions whilst our own were so big. We both found counsellors and we talked to them about the difficult stuff. Overall, this has worked well for us.

I will speak in further detail in Part Four about how receiving EMDR (Eye Movement Desensitisation and Reprocessing) therapy helped me to process traumatic memories and alleviated some deep fears around Isaac's physical health. During those EMDR sessions, the psychologist made the interesting point that although mine and Neil's method of not putting our emotions onto the other person worked for a while, at times it may also have prevented both of us from processing some of the trauma. Perhaps, because of our agreement, we sometimes felt too responsible for the other person. Sometimes we may have stayed quiet when in fact the other person wouldn't have minded talking about Finn or would perhaps even have liked to. The psychologist asked if I spoke to anyone else, friends or family, about the difficult memories. 'Absolutely not,' I answered. Again, a co-dependent response, perhaps. It's not exactly something that you can bring up over the dinner table, talking about the death of your child. That being said, I began to realise that maybe with my closest friends, *maybe* they could handle more than I gave them credit for. I wasn't about to start going into detail but perhaps I could start to be a bit more open with them about when I felt traumatised or when I felt rubbish; or even about the vague themes of what continued to disturb me.

122

I did begin to open up more with them and it brings me to tears to think of the love and support I received. *Thank you, Naomi and Tara xx*

Previous me,

You have been through so much. I am so proud of you. You have done such a good job of loving that baby. I'm gonna tell you this right now; you cannot get grieving wrong. There will be times when you feel that you have shared too much with a random stranger on the train, but you know what? Trust yourself; maybe that share was a real gift to that stranger that day. It is OK to feel totally, totally full of anger and rage. It is OK to feel jealous of others. It is OK to avoid people. It is OK to hate the world. It is OK to write God a letter that starts with 'F*ck you'. You are hurting so much and you do not understand why this has happened and why if there is a god he took your baby's life away from him. You will find peace with God/ Universe/ Source/ Whatever you want to call it. I promise.

The hardest bit in some ways is going to be when you start to feel better. It's OK to start to feel better. Allow your tender heart the healing and the peace. You deserve to experience the beauty and joy in this precious life. You deserve to feel love and happiness. You deserve to feel excited about life. Finlay is part of you now and forever and he would want all of the beauty for you. Imagine him looking down celebrating all that you are. He is everywhere; he is the butterfly, the feather, the sparkle of the ocean, the bud on the tree, the stars in the sky, the rain falling, the storm, the thunder, the sunrise, the sunset, he IS the beauty, he is the love. Feel it all.

There is no right or wrong way to grieve. You get up every day and get out of bed. This is a beautiful miracle, and anything else is a bonus.

I love you,

Sarah xx

I thought grief would be completely relentless. I thought it would be unforgiving, brutal and unbearable 100% of the time. I wanted to escape this, of course, that's why we joked about killing ourselves off in that massive party. But it's not like that.

Since Finlay's birth and death, I have known a new level of love and a new level of gratitude. I was so relieved that his death had been peaceful and felt so grateful that he had come to us to be with us for those 8 months (17 months including the pregnancy). He gifted us so much.

And since then, grief comes and goes. I still function throughout it all. There were and are times when I didn't even feel at all distressed; I couldn't believe this. Then, as time progressed and over the last five years, it gradually started to feel easier. The awful days became fewer and farther in between. And the good days are better than any days I had before Finlay came into my life. As I type this, editing, it is February 5th 2021. He would have been 6 tomorrow. We are going to collect our *first ever campervan!* on his birthday! What an absolutely amazing gift; and such synchronicity that it happens to be ready on his birthday! We are going to play 'bug bingo 'in the camper with Isaac tomorrow, and eat cake and drink champagne and celebrate the incredibly significant date of February 6th. The day our lives and worlds changed forever.

What I have also come to realise is that when I block the grief out too much - when I disconnect form the pain - I also disconnect from the joy. When I resist watching videos of Finlay because seeing his poorly body pains me, I also avoid the joy of seeing the sparkle in his eyes, how they danced. I have developed rituals which help me connect and honour my continued relationship with Finn. We still have a relationship, which

124

changes over time like all relationships. We have a beautiful blossom tree in the garden - each year when it blossoms, it helps me feel connect to him. We light candles for him regularly, we talk to him. I dance with him and for him sometimes, I dance my love for him. I am learning to let it all be there at once - the pain, the joy, the grief, the love, the anger, the peace. But just like the blossom tree, the peace seems to be blooming more and more.

PART FOUR

Anxiety Explained
And The Actions That are
Always Within
Your Control

The origins of anxiety, what even is anxiety?
(with no annoying jargon)

So far, I have shared my story. I have spoken about how anxiety can be tied to our identities. I have explored the role that discrimination can play in how we experience the world and how the world interacts with us. I have spoken about how shared experiences of community and authenticity can create opportunities for supported healing. But, before I dive into the methods and practices that can help us all to cope and thrive, I want to think more deeply about what anxiety is.

Anxiety happens when our bodies go into 'fight, flight or freeze' mode and prepare to either fight, run away or freeze. When we perceive danger, anxiety is our body's way of preparing us to ensure survival. This was super helpful in the old days when we were faced with a wild animal. Perhaps less so when you are, say, in a meeting at work. But why are some of us more anxious than others? What makes one person more likely to develop anxiety?

For years, these scientific enquiries centred around 'nature or nurture' debates. Are psychological dispositions inherited (nature - passed down to us from our parents) or learned (caused by the manner in which we are nurtured, our environment)? This approach is now considered outdated because it is widely accepted that a mixture of the two are absolutely at play. It is not 'either/ or'. It is both nature *and* nurture (more on this in the chapter on Brain Development).

Some people are born with more of a genetic predisposition to anxiety, but our worlds are a huge part of how we respond to emotions. I love the work of Suzanne Zeedyk who I have had the pleasure of working with a couple of times. She talks about 'attachment' in a beautiful way which is easy to understand and doesn't focus on all the annoying categorisations of attachment which people can sometimes get lost in. I thoroughly recommend her book, *Sabre Toothed Tigers and Teddy Bears*.

The basic premise is that parents respond to their babies when they are distressed. When a baby is hungry or scared, they cry. Their parent picks them up and comforts them and this teaches the baby that their emotions are manageable. They learn that sadness or anxiety are manageable, that distress is temporary and that humans can be trusted. This process is referred to as 'containment', a concept developed by psychoanalyst Wilfred Bion in 1962. Some of Bion's wisdom developed from his wartime experiences.

This process of containment is important throughout life, not just for babies. You will be able to call to mind, I'm sure, a time when you were feeling overwhelmed or anxious about something. You told a family member or a friend and they listened carefully, remained calm and this in turn restored your capacity to stay calm and think straight. This is containment. Your feelings did not overwhelm your friend and their lack of overwhelm impacted positively on your emotions, too. It's a glorious process.

My husband is *a very containing* person to be around. He is so calm. His mum, my wonderful mother-in-law Barbara, says that he is so laid back that he is horizontal! When I have been overwhelmed (*many* times over the past 9 years of our relationship) he remains so calm that it helps me to restore this calm too. It's fabulous.

Conversely, I bet you can call to mind a time when you have felt worried about something. You have told someone, they have panicked and you have left feeling even worse about your worry! I remember one such occasion. I was conducting university research that required consent forms. I forgot to send out the forms to participants and unknowingly went ahead with the research. It wasn't until I was writing up the project that I realised. I was *so anxious* about my mistake and about getting into trouble. I called my mum. What follows is an example of the *opposite of containment.*

Me: 'Sh*t, Mum I have forgotten to get consent forms for this research project I'm doing! I'm shitting myself, what if I get sacked?!'

Mum: '*Oh my God, Sarah, how could you do that? What were you thinking? How did you just forget?*'

Me: 'Nice one Mum, that's not helping! I've got to go now, bye.' (hangs up)

Hahahaha!

Mum, if you are reading, I'm just sharing this to have a laugh; I'm sure one day Isaac will write a book about my parenting highlights!

(To be clear, everyone gave verbal consent and I collected all the forms retrospectively and I didn't get sacked!)

Depending on how the adults in our lives respond to our emotions when we are little, we either learn that emotions are manageable, or that emotions are really scary. This can significantly impact our susceptibility to anxiety in later life.

We also learn how to manage (or *not*) anxiety by watching the people around us and how they manage it. This is called modelling. We learn plenty without realising, simply by watching other people do something first then having a go ourselves. Some people may watch their parents remaining calm and being able to take a few deep breaths when feeling overwhelmed. They may observe them partaking in helpful activities for anxiety, such as exercise, healthy eating, moderating the intake of caffeine or alcohol, meditation, dance, and therapy/coaching. These activities will vary across cultures. They may also learn how to relate to anxiety in a healthy way, i.e., by 'feeling the fear and doing it anyway', (a great book by Susan Jeffers, check it out!) and by not overthinking anxiety or feeling shameful about it.

On the other hand, some people may watch the people around them coping less well with anxiety and partaking in coping strategies that worsen it. They may observe them drinking alcohol, avoidance, over or under eating, focusing on the anxiety (Previous me!) or carrying a story that anxiety is shameful and must be hidden.

Dear reader,

Make sure you have people in your life who you can go to for containment. Some people are amazing, and others less so. Work out who is best able to be calm and not overwhelmed by your distress. Go to them.

We all need help and containment at times, when stressed.

Don't give people a hard time if they are unable to fulfil this role for you. Not everyone is great at it. Some people are incredibly inspiring, or dependable or funny, but not containing. Just work out who your 'calmies' are and be sure to use them and not the others when you're in need of containment.

Look at the people you know who appear to manage their emotions well. Ask them how they do it! I used to tell a story that my old boss was just genetically lucky and naturally calm. When I got to know her and once interviewed her for my old radio show 'Loved up on life', I learned that her seemingly natural chill was in fact testament to her commitment to regular practices of meditation, yoga, chanting, and being in nature. You can create harmony! You can find practices that support and empower you to contain your own emotions, too.

Sarah x

Getting stuck on the 'wrong' emotion

My wonderful therapist Morag helped me to understand how sometimes, depending on which emotions are common in childhood, or considered 'acceptable' we can get 'stuck' on the wrong one. For example, one family may allow anger but anxiety is frowned upon or viewed as 'weak'. Another family may not allow any expressions of anger, viewing it as too threatening – anxiety may be preferable.

I definitely witnessed anxiety and anger more often than sadness growing up. It makes sense when considering how stuck on anxiety I was for so long – perhaps because I didn't allow my sadness. Sadness feels very vulnerable to me and I'm still learning to allow it. Instead of crying in the bath with the door locked, I attempt to ask Neil for a hug. It's hard.

The reason you can get 'stuck' is that the true root emotion is healthy, it is supposed to motivate you to take action. Sadness is a signal to seek comfort, anxiety to seek safety, anger to take action. However, if you are scared of a certain emotion you can learn to feel the wrong one. Perhaps responding to a situation with a surprising 'go-to' emotion. I think for years after the abortion I was disconnected from my sadness, numbing out, never feeling it or processing it or seeking comfort. I got stuck on anxiety and constantly tried to seek safety, though there was nothing to seek safety from. You can see how this prevents you from reaching the equilibrium you would, if you allowed the true emotion.

These ideas were developed by Eric Berne who founded Transactional Analysis. They have helped me and my clients immensely over the years.

Brain development

When studying brain development and trauma as part of my professional education, I was fascinated to learn that our brains are not fully developed until way into our twenties. The basic structure is intact when we are born but the majority of development occurs during our first few years of life. The beneficial thing about this? We can adapt. Our brains adapt incredibly well to our environments. Compared to other animals, humans are born helpless, which means that our brains can shape-shift to serve us in whatever situation we find ourselves in.

You have probably heard the term 'use it or lose it'. This refers to how our brains grow in the areas we need them to most, and how the thoughts we think again and again become 'hardwired'. As discussed earlier, the old nature/ nurture argument is now considered, well, old. It is widely accepted now that, although genes may lay the initial mapping, it is a child's experiences, environment and relationships which shape the brain.

Our brains grow in a 'bottom-up' sequential order. First come the lower regions of the brain: the brainstem and midbrain. These parts govern the bodily functions necessary for life, called the autonomic functions. The limbic system (involved in regulating/managing emotions) and the cortex (responsible for abstract thought) come later.

When babies and children are neglected or abused, oftentimes this shapes their brains. Their brains become focused on survival. They can get 'stuck' in the lower regions of the brain so that the limbic system and cortex become compromised. This impacts massively on the development of the ability to manage emotions (limbic), and the ability to think and learn (cortex). As adults, people can get stuck in the 'fear' part of the brain, and can become hypervigilant to danger, even when there is no danger. Often, people who have experienced abuse or neglect can think

132

that they are threatened (misreading facial cues, for example) even when they are not.

Young people who have experienced what is called 'development trauma' cannot respond to therapy that is targeted at the cortex, the thinking part of the brain. A large proportion of therapy fits into this category. Instead, a different approach is needed. It is becoming increasingly common for a neuro-sequential approach to be adopted, which involves working from the 'bottom-up'. If stuck in the brainstem, we need patterned and repetitive rhythmic activity in the lower brain before moving up. We need to retrain the brain stem. This takes time and lots of repetition. In fact, to make any changes in our brains, repetition repetition repetition is required. I will be repeating repeating repeating this throughout this part of the book!

Even for people who have not experienced severe abuse or neglect, activities aimed at the lower regions of the brain can really help with emotional regulation. Polyvagal theory, discovered by Stephen Porges in 1994, has recently become popular amongst the therapeutic and self-development circles I'm in. Polyvagal theory talks about the different states of fight or flight and the role of the vagus nerve. I won't go into too much detail, but I'd like to highlight an aspect of polyvagal theory which many clinicians have found to be useful and effective: become friends with - become familiar with - your central nervous system.

The idea is to identify the practices that help your central nervous system to feel good. The work complements trauma therapist Bessel Van Der Kolk's approach. You have already seen this idea in action in my chapter on Dance. The key is to find activities that are rhythmic, repetitive and which also give us a visceral experience that contradicts our stories about ourselves. There are many practices that fit the bill, and I will outline some that may work for you in the upcoming chapters.

133

Another interesting truth about brains is that we tend to over-identify with them. Instead of witnessing our brains from afar, we think we are our thoughts, and we accept thoughts as facts. In fact, if we were to hold up our thoughts to scrutiny in an objective court case, we would find little conclusive evidence to prove that the stories we tell ourselves are true. Our brains are just like computers that have been programmed with tonnes of information. When we actually stop to tune into this information, we may find that we don't even agree or feel aligned with much of it. Some may be old, out-of-date information that we are still using. Our brains are excellent at keeping us safe and protecting us from danger, but we need to be careful about letting them run the show. Often, when we make decisions from our brains and heads, we are making decisions from a place of fear. We overthink things, fall into fearful thinking, scarcity thinking. We forget to make decisions from a place of love. I teach my clients how to separate from their thoughts and to make decisions from their hearts, from a conscious, loving, trusting and limitless place.

Further reading

Look up all of Bruce Perry's work on brain development

www.childwelfare.gov/pubs/focus/earlybrain/index.cfm (for a great outline of brain development and trauma)

Deb Dana – *The Polyvagal Theory In Therapy*

When joy isn't easy to access

For me, the shift from anxiety to joy was seismic and happened over a relatively short period of time That might not be how it goes for you. Do not make yourself wrong for not feeling joyful in life or if joy isn't easy for you to access. Do not make yourself wrong for not feeling grateful for your life. Gratitude practice really is a 'practice' and it's easier for some than others. It takes time. Don't shame yourself for being ungrateful or joyless.

As discussed throughout, some people have had experiences in life which are non-conducive to the development of joy. I am offering you all an invitation, though, to reclaim your joy. To commit to this as one of the most important things you could do in your life.

Your spirit, the deep down part of you that makes you uniquely you, is separate from your conditioned mind. You may have learned that it's not safe to connect with others, to relax or to celebrate yourself. Your brain, like a computer, has programmed itself to survive your environment and perhaps you would have been shamed or unsafe to celebrate yourself or life. As discussed in the previous chapter on brain development, maybe your resources were focused on keeping you safe and on identifying threats. I hope you understand a bit better now why it might be more difficult for you to 'just enjoy yourself' or to 'just let go' or to 'lighten up'. Why the things you see others achieve with ease might take a little more practice for you. It isn't a problem with you. You'll get there. You've not been doing anything wrong.

Time to reclaim your joy?

Now you are an adult, you can create safety for yourself. Re-read that sentence again if you need to. Let it sink in. You can slowly expose yourself to the things that you felt or still feel scared of. This technique, called graded exposure, is one of the most common techniques used by clinical psychologists for anxiety. The thing you fear may be human relationships and connection. You can choose to slowly connect with others in a way that feels good. You learn that nothing bad happens (or if it does that you can cope) then you can connect some more, perhaps with more people, or more deeply. You gradually expose yourself to the perceived threat until the 'fear' extinguishes. You can do this alone, or with support from friends, online communities, therapists, or coaches.

As explained in the chapter on brain development, you can create safety for yourself by nurturing your central nervous system; replicating the repetition and rhythm which is so important for the lower regions of the brain.

Here are some examples: using a rocking chair, a weighted blanket, dancing, singing, music, walking, running, being in nature surrounded by the beautiful repetitive patterns. These things soothe us in mind, body, emotion, and spirit. Consistent, repeated activity like this will change the structure of your brain. You *can* rewire your brain; it just takes repetition, repetition, repetition.

For people who may have experienced abuse, neglect or trauma and felt powerless, there is research to show that doing the 'opposite' bodily movement to the story provides a visceral experience that contradicts the helplessness. So, for example, if your story is, 'I feel so helpless', the opposite bodily movement might be to feel empowered in your body by practicing control. I have used this technique with coaching clients and for myself and it has been so empowering. When I found out about the link between these physical movements and the stories we tell, it made absolute sense. I could see how Nia, the dance form that I love, provided me with the perfect opportunity for these contradictory visceral experiences. When I was feeling helpless, having been unable to save my son from death, and joyless, in the depths of grief, and motionless and stuck, my body was able to feel powerful (martial arts kicks to amazing music!). My body was in action as opposed to stuck, and flowing as opposed to motionless. With regard to the polyvagal theory, as outlined above, I was able to move my central nervous system from 'dorsal vagal' - motionless, trapped, helpless and depressed – to 'ventral vagal': joy, curiosity, in the present moment, groundedness. Amazing!

I believe Nia could be especially helpful to someone who has experienced sexual trauma, whose joy of sexual intimacy has been compromised. Dancing in a safe environment with a beautiful community, gently (in a graded way as discussed) exposing yourself to sensual moves over time, can replicate the self-empowerment that therapy might attempt to instill. A 'pelvic circle' to sensual music… at first a little one, then maybe retracting, then as time goes on, as you feel safer and and your brain has learned that there is no threat, a full on sexy, sensual pelvic circle. It's a perfect way to reclaim sexual and sensual joy.

Many researchers talk about how difficult it can be to rewire the brain when the 'critical periods' of brain development have been compromised (resulting in developmental trauma). I adore the neuro-sequential model of therapy I have described, and the reminder as a therapist not to always use talking therapies, but I want to start a different conversation about this.

Yes, repetition repetition repetition *is* required in order to rewire the brain but it *is* possible. The thing is, when researchers talk again and again about how hard it is to rewire the brain post trauma, it leads to low energy. A mindset of 'I can change my brain, but it's going to be so much harder for me because of the trauma I've been through', leads to low energy. I wonder about a new story. Perhaps this new story could read like this:

'My brain is my brain. There is no point comparing it to someone else's. I know that my brain needs to grow in certain areas to support my development. I am so inspired by the many, many people who have achieved this. If I tell myself it's hard, those words will become my experience. If I tell myself that I can

137

100% shape my brain through daily activities and choices, I am going to feel full of energy to do this. When I don't manage, I give myself grace and self-compassion and love. I am powerful and I am not my thoughts, or my conditioned brain. I am more than that. I am my spirit which is deep within me and was untouchable by any abusive person. I focus on what I can do, not on what I can't do. I understand why joy has been hard for me to access; but I choose to reclaim this joy. I trust if I start off with small steps each day, it will pay off. I am the creator of my life and I can change my brain and become who I want to be.'

Further reading

Bessel Van Der Kolk – *The Body Keeps The Score*

Dr Joe Dispenza – *Breaking The Habit Of Being Yourself*

Please be warned, the start of Joe Dispenza's book feels technical, I found it challenging. Even if the start of the book feels complex, persevere, it becomes easier and there is so much to take from the book. I chose to trust that my brain would take in what it needed to.

Why 'Getting Rid of Anxiety' isn't my goal or
my marker of success

As a clinical psychologist, I often felt that people approached me with the aim of getting rid of their anxiety. They hoped I could help them to be free of it forever. They had received a diagnosis of 'generalised anxiety disorder' along with the message that it was something they needed to get rid of. It often felt like the goal was to go from 'disordered thinking' to 'normal functioning'. Now, I view it so differently; I don't think it is disordered to develop anxiety, and I want to help people do more than 'function normally'. Of course, there are some people who experience anxiety in such a debilitating way that being able to function 'normally' would be a beautiful achievement; but I want to invite you to crack your thinking around this wide open.

Many of us have experienced traumatic events in life. I have talked about some of mine; amongst some of the most traumatic are becoming pregnant as a young adult and deciding to end the pregnancy, having an abusive partner at the time, and losing Finn. 'Trauma' is used to describe what happens when something in life distresses a person to the extent that the emotions become so strong that the brain becomes overwhelmed. The brain can then be unable to process information in a usual way and can get 'stuck' in the traumatic memory, re-living it time and again. This can take the form of flashbacks, dreams, and re-plays. It can almost be like the person is 're-living' the memory. It can feel as distressing as it did at the time, because it is not processed. Trauma can also show up in the way we react to things, with trauma responses sometimes looking like emotional overreactions, hypersensitivity, or unusual sensory reactions. Trauma can be triggered without our conscious mind even realising what's happening. As Van der Kolk writes, '*The body keeps the score*'.

EMDR (Eye movement desensitisation and reprocessing) is a form of therapy that has been around since 1987, when Dr.

Francine Shapiro discovered that eye movements can reduce the intensity of distressing thoughts and feelings under certain conditions. She studied this scientifically and had success treating victims of severe trauma. EMDR has since been proven through wide research and clinical practice to be extremely effective (emdrworks.org).

From an anecdotal perspective, as a clinical psychologist I have never come across a form of therapy that is so widely popular amongst therapists and clients alike. It is quicker than most other therapies - and so effective. I received some EMDR after Finn died, when I was experiencing very distressing flashbacks of various images. I remain hugely grateful to the NHS clinical psychologists who saw me in Edinburgh.

I received 3 or 4 sessions and it was utterly unbelievable. The memories which once caused me such emotional and physical distress (horror, sadness, nausea, shock, disbelief) were processed in a profound way. I only just made this connection but interestingly, given the title of this book... when we broke down much of the distress in the therapy session, I found that it related to my fear of whether I had done *the right thing.* I was anxious after Finn died. Had I done the right thing? Had I done everything I could to help him, had I done everything I could to love him, had I done everything I could to save him? Had I done something wrong, had I made the right (complex) medical decisions?

Had I got something wrong?

This was such a deep belief below the memories. It made the situations anxiety-provoking rather than just devastatingly sad. I was able to love myself through it. To know that every decision I made was from a place of love; to process the horrific images and know that all that really mattered was the love. In a contained and safe environment, I could allow my brain to see and feel the images and feelings, without become so overwhelmed that my wee brain shut down.

The inspiring thing about EMDR is that it has the potential to really heal, not just to help clients to 'cope' with symptoms. Ricky Greenwald is a practicing clinical psychologist and works as a founder, executive director and chair of faculty at the Trauma Institute & Child Trauma Institute (childtrauma.com). He talks about how having role models who have survived trauma is great… but that he wants more. He wants role models who have *healed*.

I want to highlight something here; that we should be aiming for more than just coping with or managing symptoms. We must also learn to allow ourselves to heal to our own timeline, and trust that it might not follow a straightforward, linear trajectory.

We may heal from one trauma effectively. But life is messy; something may trigger anxiety for us, and this is OK. For me, it is about *allowing* ourselves to grow. I often use a visual of a squiggly wave-like line that goes up and down but always on an upward trajectory. It helps my clients have realistic expectations of 'expansion' and 'growth' and to resist that all-or-nothing thinking of, 'I'm feeling sh*t again, I'm back to square one' – because even when you go to the bottom of the wave you are in, you never go right back to the start.

We need to help people to aim high and have faith and high expectations of their healing and growth. It is important not to view anxiety as something that we need to 'get rid of completely'. As I discuss in other parts of the book, anxiety is just a feeling like anything, just like sadness, happiness, embarrassment. As long as we are in a human body and as long as we are living a full life, anxiety may well be part of our experience. It is not about getting rid of it but befriending it, telling a different story about it. I want people to allow their triggers; to have new ways of functioning. To feel that, despite any emotional experiences which may still be unwanted, you can still feel hopeful and joyful about your vision in life. To replace the shame with curiosity. To replace the resignation with hope.

When you feel like a 'failure at therapy'

For some people, Cognitive Behavioural Therapy (CBT) works. There is undeniable evidence for it. It didn't work for me, though. Instead, it made me feel that not only was I failing at life, but I was also failing at challenging my thoughts and developing rational 'balanced' thoughts. I just couldn't do it. It was deeper than that. I needed so much more.

I needed big changes, but no-one even entertained that idea with me, and I didn't entertain it either. You see, sometimes the anxiety is ours and sometimes it's not. Sometimes, it's a combination. When you spend your time in environments where there is significant stress and tension, it's easy to conclude that there is something wrong with *you*. But maybe there's something in the *system* or the *environment* that's not working; maybe the environment just doesn't work for you. Maybe the fit isn't right.

I know many people who feel like they've failed at mindfulness or meditation or CBT. At this point in your journey, after you've taken the most difficult first step towards doing things differently, it's so important to remember that therapy is a process. If you've tried something once and it's not worked or not felt right for you, try something different. There are about five gazillion different ways to meditate. Therapy with one therapist might not work... but a different therapist could help you change your life. Don't judge yourself for not 'getting the therapy right'. Try something different, keep going.

For me, what helped was discovering a psychodynamic approach, whereby through therapy we explored various relationships and dynamics from childhood and how these continued to play out in my adult life etc. But I'll reiterate that by far the thing that transformed my anxiety the most was *not focusing on it*. It was, instead, focusing on what I *did* want. On surrounding myself with other people doing the same; on being brave and doing things that scared me; leaning into the accountability that came with being part of a supportive group.

For the more acute trauma and anxiety, it was the EMDR which helped.

I also think it is important not to give your power away too much to your therapist or to the idea of 'therapy' and not to have unrealistic expectations of them. I once had a client who, at the start of his second session with me, asked why he didn't feel better. Perhaps I hadn't been clear enough about how these things take time! Bear in mind, too, that if you see your therapist or coach or have group coaching once a week, you have to be realistic about what this can achieve; it's the *action* in between sessions which can be the biggest game changer. For me, having the power of a big community was so important for me; to keep the momentum in making changes and to sustain the bravery to really do things differently, knowing that a large group of people had my back and would celebrate me along the way.

The tyranny of the should

I *should* be more loud/ quiet. I should be more sociable. I should be more positive. I should be thinner/ fitter/ more healthy. I should read more, I should be more creative, I should watch less TV, I should enjoy parenting more, I should be happier, I should be less happy, I should be more grateful, I should be more loving, I should be calmer, I should be kinder, I should be prettier, I should be stronger, I should be less bossy, I should be more confident, I should spend less money, I shouldn't want money, I should be a better friend, I shouldn't have done that, I should have worked harder, I should have got better grades, I shouldn't have had an abortion, I should have chosen a different path. I should have better general knowledge, I should be married by now, I should own a house, I shouldn't be so career focused, I shouldn't feel jealous of people, I shouldn't feel angry, I shouldn't feel sad.

Does this sound familiar to you?

Write a list of yours!

German psychoanalyst Karen Horney coined a phrase for this: 'the tyranny of the should.' She described how 'shoulds' divide our personalities into two selves: a real self and an ideal self. She explored how, when we fail to live up to the ideal self, we are split; conflict is created, and our inner critic has a field day. I often use this concept with my clients to think about how they could meet themselves exactly where they are: how could they better allow themselves to be exactly who they are in any given moment.

Albert Ellis also wrote about a similar concept: when we tell ourselves that we 'must' be a certain way or do a certain thing. He talked about how this creates demands on ourselves (and others) and fosters anxiety, guilt, shame, depression, self-hatred,

144

and anger. We criticise ourselves when we fail to live up to what we *should* do and what we *must* do.

Instead of telling ourselves that we *should* be a certain way or constantly comparing ourselves to our 'ideal selves', imagine if we *allowed* ourselves more? Imagine if we were able to accept ourselves in every moment. Imagine if we allowed ourselves to make mistakes, to be less than perfect? If we celebrated ourselves and others for being exactly as we are? *Imagine if we allowed the people around us to make mistakes and get things wrong?* This is a game changer in romantic relationships and in parenting. How much more harmony and peace could we create? How much more likely we would be, then, to actually *become* our ideal selves! From a place of joy and inspiration.

Stop shaming yourself in an attempt to motivate yourself to be a certain way and just let yourself be.

Brené Brown talks about 'pre-requisites' for self-worth. Imagine if we felt worthy for just being us. Imagine if we didn't have to prove our worthiness to ourselves or others.

Right now, as I write, I have had my first night away in a hotel *alone* for years! Oh my goodness, some solitude and space! Yes! Last night, I was in the hotel room. I wanted to make the absolute most of my time. I *should* be making the most of this time to myself. I should be writing my book. I should be journaling, I should be meditating… you get the picture. We create so much conflict when we resist what we are doing and tell ourselves we should be doing something else. I spent a bit of time reading and editing this book. Then I just wanted to watch TV. How many of you can relate to this? The need to just, guilt free, veg out and watch TV. I was aware of my thoughts, spoiling the experience, stopping me from 100% embracing what *was* happening and focusing on what I should be doing. I laughed and told that voice to 'do one'. I watched two episodes of *24 Hours in A&E* and it was glorious. Voice piped up again! 'Shouldn't you be watching something more uplifting'. *Should should should*, even when I do this work and teach it all the time. It's so ingrained!

Imagine if we could spot this conflict, the 'contrast' as Abraham Hicks calls it and just choose *again and again* to lean into the joy and the *pleasure* of whatever we were doing. Last night, I had nothing to do, no tasks to complete, a beautiful comfortable bed to sleep in. I felt totally safe and happy in my Premier Inn at Whitley Bay. It was amazing. I was able to lean into it and really enjoy it in the end. Partly because I could witness my thoughts without identifying with them like I would have done in the past. This sounds like a superficial example, but it illustrates the following point:

How often are you doing something yet telling yourself that you should be doing something else?

How can you love this familiar voice but become vigilant to it? How can you challenge it and instead choose something different?

And what about our expectations of other people? Of our partners? Friends? Children? Parents? Imagine if we could allow others to be who they are. It doesn't mean just being a doormat and accepting any behaviour but imagine if we could focus on what others *do* bring to our lives. Imagine if we could make clear requests of people rather than thinking about what they *should* be doing?

My partner should know that I need a rest and offer to help more, they should be more affectionate, should be better with money, should earn more, should be more driven, should be calmer, should be friendlier, should be more sociable, should be more _____. Does this sound familiar?

What about your children? My children should be better behaved, should be more advanced, should have less tantrums,

146

should be more grateful, should be less selfish, should be more _____.

I will continue to do this work for the rest of my life, but it has been completely transformative in *all* my close relationships, to *allow* the people I love more, to celebrate their strengths, to stop focusing on what they *should* be.

When you really allow yourself, it helps you to allow others.

When you feel like you are getting art or creativity wrong

Just imagine all the amazing art that has not been made or shared because artists or musicians fear that their creations are not good enough.

Isn't this quote from Kurt Vonnegut perfect?

'When I was 15, I spent a month working on an archeological dig. I was talking to one of our archeologists one day during our lunch break and he asked one of those kinds of 'getting to know you' questions you ask young people: do you play sports? What's your favourite subject? And I told him, no I don't play any sports. I do theater [sic]*, I'm in a choir, I play the violin and piano, I used to take art classes.*

And he went 'wow, that's amazing!'

And I said 'Oh no but i'm not any good at any of them'

And he said something that I will never forget, and which absolutely blew my mind because no one had ever said anything like it to me before.: 'I don't think that being good at things is the point of doing them. I think you've got all these wonderful experiences with different skills and that all teaches you things and makes you an interesting person no matter how well you do them.'

And that honestly changed my life. Because I went from a failure, someone who hadn't been talented enough at anything, to excel, to someone who did things because I enjoyed them. I had been raised in such an achievement-oriented environment so inundated with the myth of talent, that I thought it was only worth doing things if you could 'win' at them.'

Vonnegut's words resonated deeply with me. I used to write music in bands and was brave enough to form a band that solely performed songs I had written. I was inspired after the loss of a dear friend in a cycling accident. I wanted to honour my life, and really live it, because of my awareness that this privilege had been taken away from her. But, as I spoke about earlier, I was so scared of performing that I robbed myself of the joy, relying on medication, then berating and loathing myself for it.

Now, I still get stuck with songwriting. Frequently, I will sit down at the piano to write some music and after a short amount of time I get so frustrated at myself. I judge that what I've written is sh*t and I give up. Because I once wrote songs that I was proud of, I have high expectations. Because I have less time these days juggling parenting and work, when I do sit down I paralyse myself with this pressure to produce something 'good enough'. Luckily, my songwriting partner in crime Mark and I keep connecting and discussing this, and I know I will overcome it. But it's a work in progress.

I encourage you to share your art with the world. I encourage my clients to do the same, often, and it is such a joy and an honour to witness people allowing themselves to be vulnerable and then being celebrated in my online community for this and rediscovering their creative selves.

I need to take my own advice!

The law of attraction

As you have read, I was obsessed with anxiety. I thought about it constantly. I scanned for it. I tried to see if others were anxious. I talked about it. I made decisions based on how anxious I thought I was going to be. I turned down amazing opportunities because I wanted to hide anxiety.

I thought about it and focused on it *and time and again attracted more and more of it.*

Dear reader,

If this is you, I understand, it feels scary. We are hard-wired to focus on perceived threats, but this is not an actual threat, it's just your mindset. Start to focus on joy and love.

You can do it!

When I found dance through Nia, I met a community of people who seemed *happy*! They accepted me and loved me, and I loved them. They were committed to experiencing joy. One of the biggest focuses of Nia is on experiencing the joy of movement. Its guiding ethos is that *you cannot get it wrong*!

This is the same with life. Start focusing on what you *do want*!

What do you want?

What are your dreams?

Write about them, draw them, think about them, talk about them.

In the words of my glorious mentors, The Little Volcano:

150

Make your dreams bigger than your bullshit.

Make your dreams bigger than your shame around anxiety, bigger than your fear of anxiety, bigger than your fear of what others think, bigger than your stories.

What is going well in your life? Focus on that. Don't focus on what isn't going well.

Change what doesn't feel good. Leave the job you hate. Leave the partner. Leave the friends who you don't feel aligned with. Stop listening to the people who moan all the time. Stop moaning yourself.

Focus on what you love. Practice gratitude. Every single day. Think about what you have, allow your body to feel grateful.

Already today I have woken up in a comfortable bed. My toddler said good morning and asked me to sing the good morning song:

'*Good morning good morning, we danced the whole night through good morning good morning to you.*'

I have enjoyed two delicious coffees.

My husband is giving me some space to write.

My body is healthy. I had the best day yesterday with friends at Loch Ard, in a canoe and on a paddle board. There were swallows and herons, and the trees were beautiful. We swam in the loch and the rainfall looked miraculous on the water. We said hello to many strangers. It was heaven.

Dear reader,

Stop wasting your life focusing on what is not real. Your fear of anxiety lies to you. It tells you people will judge you, people will reject you, that you are worthless, that you are going to get something wrong, that you are going to do something so unacceptable that people will laugh at you, that you will humiliate yourself, that there is something wrong with you.

Tell it to f*ck off. Tell it that you are done. You have wasted enough of your energy on trying to spot the danger. Tell it enough is enough. Go and sit by the ocean and drink a flask of tea, or whisky or whatever you want. Listen to your favourite music. Do something you're scared of. Post a video on your Facebook page of you telling a joke or singing. Stop fearing other people's responses. Be yourself so that the people who are meant for you can find you! Start living this life. Be brave and vulnerable. Dare to create your absolute ideal life.

There is so much beauty everywhere. Focus on that, focus on what makes your soul light up, focus on what makes you smile, laugh, relax, focus on the people you love, focus on the joy.

Become as obsessed with JOY as you are with anxiety. When you find yourself focusing on anxiety, love yourself, forgive yourself but encourage yourself to look the other way. Become completely obsessed with creating and focusing on joy. Become completely vigilant to that negative voice rather than anxiety. Beat it. You can do it. Your focus on anxiety is what you need to be scared of, not the anxiety itself. Shift it! You can do it!

When you feel anxious, tell yourself I CANNOT GET THIS WRONG. Let go of fearing other people's judgements. If you can LOVE YOURSELF when you shake, when you blush, then you don't need to give other people's opinions a second thought (they aren't likely to even notice or judge you anyway). Never ever ever shame yourself for feeling anxious. Accept and embrace all of you.

DO the things you once avoided, once turned down but wished you could do. Do the things you tell yourself you can't do.

I love you. You cannot get this wrong.

Recently, I was asked to give a presentation on gratitude (I'm obsessed with gratitude practice) by my friend, for the civil service.

Previous me: would have immediately focused on anxiety and turned it down or planned to take propranolol and would have felt shameful about that from the go and the whole experience would have been a bit of a downer.

Present me: 'Oh my goodness, what an amazing opportunity this is! To talk to hundreds of people and spread love and joy. Even if one person in the group goes away and integrates gratitude practice into their life, that would be amazing. That could ripple into the rest of their life and affect their loved ones. This is so exciting - I want to do a wonderful job on this. They also want to pay me and a decent fee - wow, I'm so amazing at attracting abundance into my life.'

(Previous me snuck in): 'She did say there was an option to pre-record the webinar. I could just do that and then not risk me getting anxious in front of hundreds of people.'

Present me: 'Are you friggin' kidding, I CAN DO THIS, so what if I get anxious, I'm not gonna focus on that, I wanna go live to connect with people more, to share my energy LIVE. There could be soul clients who are destined to work with me more deeply (there were, by the way!) and this is the best opportunity to connect with them and impact their lives. Bring it ON!'

I did it. Beforehand I hugged Neil (I let myself be vulnerable!) and we both laughed at how scary it was. Of course, when the time came to go live, my heart was beating fast, and I stumbled my words for a few minutes BUT I DIDNT CARE! The information I was sharing was gold and I was thrilled to have that opportunity. Also, I got some amazing feedback, and they want me to return!

Gratitude

Gratitude practice has changed my life. It's part of everything I talk about here. It's part of shifting the focus from anxiety to beauty; choosing to regularly let your mind linger on the things you love, the glory of being human.

I've woken early this morning, up before my husband and child. I did a very brief meditation. It wasn't as long as I planned, and the old voice tried to sneak in. But I want coffee and to write this. I'll meditate later! I sit for a minute.

I'm grateful I took time to breathe - to think about my spirit being with me in all that I do today. I'm grateful for my coffee brewing, it smells amazing. I'm grateful the house is nice and tidy. I'm grateful my husband did the dishes last night. Oh my goodness, I'm *so* grateful that my friend who I was trying a new coaching technique on made me two pieces of art entitled 'magic is real' *and* sent me a significant amount of money as a tip for a programme I provided for them!

I'm *so* grateful to all my coaching clients for the honour of walking alongside them on their amazing paths. I'm grateful for the freedom and joy the money I earn gives me. I'm grateful for the little hedgehogs in our wildlife friendly garden. I'm grateful for my husband who is called the Wildlife Friendly Gardener! How cool is that!

I'm grateful for my beautiful home, for living by the sea, for the colourful buddleia and fennel blowing in the wind. I'm grateful for the *amazing* colourful blanket I'm under which my mum knitted me, using cotton to make it vegan. I'm grateful for my gorgeous floral dressing gown I'm wearing. (Oh my lord the coffee! Just had my first sip!). I'm grateful for the beautiful people on the 8 week online course I ran. I'm grateful for my two children; one in my heart and soul guiding me, leading me towards beauty on a daily basis and to the little bossy beautiful

155

hilarious silly one snuggled up to my husband upstairs. I'm grateful for my husband, his big muscly legs, his calm energy, our relationship, how we develop independently and as a unit, the love I witnessed between he and Finn. The sun is shining today, corona time is easing, restrictions are lifting, we were gifted lots of extra time with our little babe as we stayed at home. I'm grateful for the delicious aubergine pasta my husband made me last night. I'm grateful for this quiet time by myself before the world wakes up. I am grateful for Nia and for all the people who dance with me twice weekly!

Revisiting this months later, I am grateful that my business has grown beyond my wildest dreams. I've started to train people to become coaches in my 'Spectacular School'. I had zero plans to do this, but I responded to people asking me to provide this service and it has grown and grown. I am grateful that a lifelong dream of mine has recently been realised and we have bought a beautiful campervan. We have called her Peggy-Sue and she is beautiful!

I could go on and on and on…

Now go pick up a pen and do the same! Do it, do it!

What do you love?

We think so much about what we want, or what we wish was different, or what we lack. But what do you love?

You can find glorious, guided gratitude meditations, you can journal, you can just fall asleep thinking of the things you are grateful for from that day. You can make it a daily ritual of sharing these things with your partner or friend or children. You can take photos of the things you are grateful for. Just take your focus away from what you don't want and focus on what you *do* want!

We practice gratitude with our three-year-old. 'Isaac what was your favourite thing from today?' Yesterday's was eating an ice lolly. Then he asks 'what was your favouritest thing?', what was your 'nother favouritest thing?' Mine was eating curry on the beach! We took leftover takeaway for a picnic on the beach with close friends and Neil swam in the sea with the kids.

When you do this regularly it seriously transforms you. Your mood, what you attract into your life. It's like a glorious cycle - 'the better it gets, the better it gets'.

I have demonstrated how to tune into gratitude for current things in your life. You can also tune into gratitude for anything that has happened at any point in your life. Here are some more of mine:

-   The love and support of my whole family. Having a big family. Cousins, aunts and uncles, brother and sister-in-law, niece and nephew, parents, grandparents, Neil, parents-in-law, my children. Everyone.

-   My many gorgeous, interesting, and fun friends.

-   The lovely primary school I went to; the big sports fields and running around them in the summer.

-   Singing in Mrs McKay's class. Doing art with Mrs Garforth. Getting to take the crisps round the whole school to sell if you finished maths on time.

-   Going on a trip to London with the primary school and visiting an actual chocolate factory!

-   My first boyfriend Jevon Turner and the innocence and excitement of holding hands on another school trip in the sunshine and in my head thinking of the Beatles song; 'I Wanna hold your hand' and kind of feeling like I got it.

157

- Playing Sylvanian Families with my friends Louise Kelly and Laura Cunningham.

- Going wild swimming once as a kid with the Furneauxs.

- Having had so much freedom and the ability to travel and explore the world.

- How many people smiled at me when I was in India; and the beautiful family who we stayed with and the Mum who taught me how to cook some amazing food.

- The amazing activists who do so much work for animals or social justice for all.

- Our lovely neighbours.

- Strictly Come Dancing.

- RuPaul's drag race.

- Our friends in America.

- My friends Caitlin and Suzanne who came over all the way from America to meet Finlay when he was alive for that short amount of time.

- How I have never gone hungry, or not had access to clean drinking water in my whole life.

- How I have always had a warm home to live in.

- The education I received and the piano lessons I received and how this led to me being able to join bands and have the time of my life.

- My family who taught me about caring for everyone in society.

Research shows that writing down 5 things a day that you are grateful for impacts significantly on your emotional wellbeing. Gratitude has proven itself a compelling area of research. It has the power to transform your experience of being human.

Brené Brown has also conducted research with people who were experiencing a lot of joy in life and who were, in her words, living '*wholehearted lives*'. She wanted to find out what they were doing that was different to everyone else. She did not expect to find that the one thing differentiating them from others was that they all practiced gratitude. She talks about how gratitude has the power of transforming fear into joy. She gives the example of how, during joyful moments, people start to fear the moment ending, or fear losing the person they love. I bet many of you have looked at your child or partner sleeping and had the thought 'but what if something were to happen to them'. Brené explores how teaching ourselves to tune into gratitude in these moments can transform the foreboding emotions of fear into joy. She also talks about how joy is one of the most vulnerable emotions; it takes bravery to lean into the beauty of life, because we are not in control and we could lose those beautiful feelings. If we fall in love and let someone in, they could leave us and hurt us. If we have another child after losing a child, we could run the risk of more heartbreak and loss.

It is so helpful for me to revisit these ideas. I try to remember to tune into this perspective: 'How lucky am I to have someone in my life that I love so much that it makes the thought of losing them unbearable'. It's so preferable to, 'I couldn't cope if anything were to happen to them'. If I'm honest, sometimes I still get stuck on the fearful story. As I've said multiple times during the book, this work is ongoing. We have to do it again and again, and we can always make new starts, all the time, year after year, like the seasons.

It takes bravery to allow your heart to experience joy.

159

It takes bravery to love wildly and with abandon.

Having lost one of the people who brought me more joy than I had known and who I loved more wildly than I had done before, all I can say is that the joy and love were worth the pain.

Further resources

Look up Robert Emmons for more reading on gratitude.

Brené Brown also writes about the impact of gratitude on living 'wholeheartedly'.

Search *for 'Gratitude: The Short Film by Louise Schwartzberg* – You Tube' for a lovely inspiring 6 minute video.

Words words words

> *I just know that something*
> *good is going to happen. I*
> *don't know when, but just*
> *saying it could even make it*
> *happen*
> *— Kate Bush*

Words are so important; the words we use to describe ourselves and the things we say out loud about ourselves and others. I stopped talking negatively about others a few years ago. I slip up sometimes, but it does *not* feel good in my body when I do, so I immediately guide myself back on track. What happens after you stop speaking badly about others is *magical*.

I stopped calling myself anxious. I started paying attention to the words I used in life. I stopped paying attention to things that I didn't want to feel and started talking about what I *did* want in life. Often, we talk to ourselves in a way we would *never ever* talk to anyone else. It's almost like we *choose* to live with our *worst enemy* (our inner voice). If someone else criticised us the way we criticise ourselves, we would likely vehemently defend ourselves from such an attack. Nearly every person I have worked with over the last 20 odd years *chronically lacks self compassion*, has self-expectations that are ridiculous and talks to themselves with critical and shaming words: *I'm not clever enough, I look fat, I should lose some weight, I'm so lazy, I'm so selfish, I am not a good enough parent, I'm a failure, I haven't achieved enough, I don't earn enough money.*

Sound familiar?

Now imagine if someone else said this to you!: '*You are not very clever, are you! You look so fat today. You should lose some weight. You are so lazy. You are so selfish. You are not great at parenting, are you? You are such a failure. You haven't achieved enough. You don't earn much money, do you?*'

You wouldn't stand for it! Stop standing for it from yourself...

You have been conditioned by society to criticise yourself and to compare yourself to others and to try and live up to wildly high standards. As I explored in the earlier chapter about my relationship with my body, both men and women are told stories of what they need to do in order to be acceptable. We develop expectations of our body, mind, emotions, and spirit: hindering our ability to *just be.*

Let's start a revolution of self-love and self-acceptance. Start talking to yourself like you would to a loved one. Use words that *nurture and nourish* you.

What do you think the impact of these words are?

When it comes to self-compassion, many people I work with fear that, if they become too kind to themselves, they will lack motivation. This is not the case! When we beat ourselves up, our energy is *low - and* we teach our children or loved ones to do the same. Imagine motivating yourself from a place of joy instead. It is possible! And it makes life so much more fun. It increases your energy and enables you to do *more* not less.

Imagine the impact on your life and on your loved ones if you could start loving yourself and speaking to yourself in a loving way? Here are some examples of the ways I speak to myself now compared to in the past:

Previous me: 'you are such a failure, you are selfish, you are fat, you are ugly, no one will love you, you need to be different, why can't you cope with small easy things?, you are so self-obsessed, you are so weird, you are so anxious, you cannot show others how anxious you are.'

Present me: 'you have created the most amazing life, you are so great at prioritising joy, your body is amazing, you bring so much joy to others, you are so loved, you are so authentic, your anxiety and vulnerability are beautiful and make you so human and relatable, you have a need to be celebrated and that is a normal human need, it doesn't make you self-obsessed, others have that need too, you don't need to focus on other people's judgments of you, you are amazing, you are so fun, you are so kind.'

The words we use can literally make our bodies and our central nervous system feel under constant threat or attack.

The words we use can also make us feel safe, connected, loving and full of energy and enthusiasm.

Choose them carefully.

Simona's story

Simona suffers from arthritis and transformed her life by changing the words she used to describe herself. She used to label herself as *'weak'*, *'a burden'* and *'a failure'* before she examined her stories in transformational coaching. Now she tells herself that she is *'strong'*, *'fierce' and 'determined beyond belief'*. Rather than resisting her body and feeling angry with it, she developed a genuine respect and admiration for it. Simona went from a person full of negativity and self-loathing to a person who wakes up every day with a sense of purpose, excitement and gratitude: "I can only describe it as my pilot light being reignited. Happiness, confidence and positive energy just naturally radiate from me now. I don't have to act or pretend that I'm happy anymore, I really am". She now has her own transformational coaching company called 'Simona Murphy- Shining through pain'!

Meditation

It's 7.15am. I'm sitting in the garden whilst Isaac and Neil are sleeping. (We've been here before on the chapter on Gratitude…it's one of my favourite ways to carve out time for these practices). I aimed to meditate for 15 minutes. I did maybe 9 then felt inspired to write instead. In the past, I would have beat myself up with a big shame stick as to why I hadn't managed the full 15 minutes. I would also have told myself that I was getting too distracted; that I was *not getting it right*.

Now, I can observe my thoughts. I can be light with them. I can love them. I can encourage that critical part of me or anxious-to-get-it-right part of me to calm down. Sometimes I imagine inviting her to come and sit in an armchair by the fire and put her feet up. This process of witnessing thoughts and processes is a rich part of meditation for me: creating some space.

To meditate is to focus your mind purposefully for a period of time, either in silence and unguided, following the voice of a guide or using chanting. There are a number of forms of meditation, so I encourage you to try a few: mindfulness meditation, moving meditation, transcendental meditation, loving-kindness meditation (this is glorious) just to name a few! There are also thousands of beautiful guided meditations, which you can access for free online, from 5 minutes up to hours long! Meditation has been an absolute game changer for me. It is one of the main practices which supports my mental health. My daily practice has become non-negotiable. I now love taking a little time to still myself, though it took time to develop this practice. I have a naturally busy mind and slowing down is great for me (and I resist it at times). I have however learned to associate pleasure with meditation. It doesn't feel like a chore. It supports my joy and lack of anxiety beyond measure.

I also adore a beautiful little Abraham Hicks exercise whereby you tell everything in nature that it's your favourite.

165

Each flower in your garden: 'you're my favourite, you're my favourite'. And you look up to the sky and connect to something bigger than you and thank the universe for supporting you. I wonder if sometimes that idea of connecting to something bigger stops more people from embracing meditation. It doesn't have to be certain or complicated. Just an expression of acknowledgement that there is a bigger picture, even if we can't articulate the details of what that bigger picture might look like.

Meditation allows you to begin to build new neural pathways in the brain. It's like magic, really helping you to speed up the creation of the 'new you'.

Sometimes, people who have never meditated before can feel a bit overwhelmed. You might feel like 1) you don't know how to do it or 2) you are not the sort of person who meditates. But anyone can; it's just about slowing down and returning to yourself: coming home. It allows you to witness what is going on within yourself. It enables you to start or end the day from a place of stillness and calm. It's free. You don't need any equipment. It's accessible to anyone at any time.

You can start off really small. You could time one minute. These days, we are constantly bombarded with information, often glued to our phones, with incessant stimulation. I have witnessed the people around me finding it harder to read books, or to 'just be'. So be gentle with yourself, if at first meditation is unbearably challenging. For just *one minute*, get still, and follow your breath in and out. Try to concentrate solely on your breath. When your mind wanders off (which minds tend to do!) just be gentle, resist judgments and invite it back to your breath. Observe the space between your breaths. This space between your breath or between your thoughts is pure stillness. You can then gradually increase the amount of time that you do this. Or search for a 5-minute guided meditation to begin with and gradually increase the amount of time. Explore and discover what you love. It is such a treat to create this time for yourself. I loved something I heard recently when someone likened the cleansing impact of meditation on the mind to the impact of having a morning shower to clean the body. It makes so much sense to me, as well as cleansing our bodies on a daily or regular basis to do the same with our minds.

Further resources

Sarah Blondin meditations are some of my favourites. Search for the following:

Feeding the heart and caring for goodness

Remembering your trust

A call to presence (the home of your happiness)

Make it sacred

I also recommend Davidji's meditations.

A great place to start is by downloading an app like 'Insight Timer' – you can search for whatever you need on a daily basis. If you need calm, to release anger, to feel grounded or to quieten a busy mind and become present you can tailor your meditation to suit how you are feeling.

The magic of presence

The best way of expressing gratitude for life is to be fully immersed in the present moment. We often think similar thoughts over and over, again and again like a broken record of our past experiences. We *overthink* - and these thoughts create familiar patterns in our bodies and brains. These patterns can be soul destroying. We learn to *expect* things in life and then only see that which we expect to see, which prevents us from experiencing what is *actually real* in front of us.

Something can happen in everyday life that triggers a thought or a feeling. Suddenly, we are reliving the past. We make judgements of our experience, of ourselves and others and this can create suffering.

At the height of my anxiety, I was so lost in my inner world that I simply didn't notice what was going on around me. Before an event, I would anticipate feeling nervous at that event; I'd visualise it happening. Sometimes, when the event actually came around, I would cope better than I'd anticipated. Even then, though, I would be on guard, anticipating that anxiety could become uncontrollable at any given moment, and feeling like I had had a lucky escape when I left.

If my heart started beating fast, I would think 'I am so anxious', then I would become hypervigilant to these symptoms, attending to my body, and looking for danger in the environment. I would fear people's judgements and would be looking for cues of their approval or not. I was so focused on suffering that I was blind to anything else. I was unable to relax into the flow of life, to experience joy or connection in a way that I would have liked to. It was all I saw for years; I was totally preoccupied.

This process – of our thoughts creating suffering for ourselves – happens in real time. It isn't always extreme. Often, it's tied to everyday occurrences.

Sometimes, I get very stressed when Isaac refuses to get dressed to leave the house. I tell a story that 'this is *so* annoying'. I am judging the situation and it is this judgment that leads to me feeling stressed and tense in my body. Perhaps we are due to meet friends, then I tell a story we will be late and that this is rude, and I create more stress. I know I could start getting ready earlier to remove this stress, but life doesn't always flow that way.

When the above situation happens, I get lost in this thought pattern. It stops me from being present. From seeing what is real in front of me. From keeping calm. I then create more stress and tension which obviously doesn't help Isaac to want to get dressed.

There are frequent other examples in my own life. Something could trigger my grief or a reminder of Finn then I could get lost in my mind, reliving the past. Of course, at times I allow this, but other times I don't want it, I want to be present to the beauty of life.

I often observe that people are:

Not present to their precious and fleeting lives.

Not experiencing the beauty of the now.

Missing so much magic right in front of them.

They are creating suffering with their mind which keeps them either stuck in the past or anticipating the future. You all know the feeling of being with someone, but not really being with them, when they are lost in their world, untouchable. Hopefully, you all also know the feeling of being with someone who is completely present and listening intently to your every word. In the moment with you with all their heart and soul; there's nothing like it!

There's a beautiful meditation by Sarah Blondin called *'A Call to Presence'*. I listened to this once in the bath and something extraordinary happened. Sarah asks you to keep your eyes open at one point, and to witness what is surrounding you and what is sharing your environment with you; and to not be surprised by how quickly you are rewarded by the universe when you show up in this way. I noticed candlelight flickering across the wall which looked beautiful. The reflection of the water on the wall was also gorgeous (I don't think I had ever noticed it before). The window was open, and I saw something moving gently in the breeze. When I looked closely it was a little white feather stuck in a tiny spider web just a metre or so away from me. White feathers are one of the signs, along with red admiral butterflies, that connect me to Finn.

The moment was mysterious and moving and so symbolic to me: I could have been in that bath lost in my memories of the past or (like I did for 20 years!) anxiously anticipating the future, and I would have missed out. It also made me think about all the magic that I missed over that period of my life when I was so focused on the future because of my story that my anxiety was shameful. It made me think of all the magic awaiting me in my future as well. I want to be as present as possible, so I don't miss any of it.

When I heard Eckhart Tolle say, 'we are not our thoughts', it blew my mind. We over-identify with our thoughts, often taking our thoughts to be facts, without question, when in fact they are just thoughts. They come and go and sometimes they are even really weird! My experience with clients is that a great deal of people experience strange, intrusive thoughts from time to time. They often just represent our conditioning, or an interpretation of an event based on past experiences, rather than reality.

You can learn to be the witness of your thoughts; to create separation between *the real you* (your spirit, your inner being) and your thoughts. You can learn not to take them seriously, not to attach to them, to let them come and go. Meditation helps tremendously. It's about getting into the habit of resisting the invitation into the cycle of repetitive thoughts; resisting the hamster wheel of repetitive thoughts which lead you nowhere!

Non-judgment of self and others is something I strive towards. It is something I will be working on forever and ever but it is such a beautiful and spacious place to be when I am there. Just living in the moment. Experiencing life through my senses. Really experiencing the person sitting beside me - with an open mind, observing things about them, listening to their every word. Resisting judgments, resisting resistance!

When you think back to the happiest moments of your life, I bet you were fully present (and probably not judging anything). Some of my happiest memories which come to mind are:
Laughing my head off in a taxi with my friends Naomi and Tree in Brighton (howling with laughter requires presence!). Holding my Grandma's hand and getting totally lost in her warmth and softness and stroking her precious skin. Opening a chocolate bar as a child and sensing *everything* about it (the smell, the colour the texture of the foil). Yesterday, losing track of time for nearly 6 hours, playing in the snow with Isaac and our friends, sledging, witnessing him and his friends playing, pressing my hand into the snow. Feeling the warmth of the sun on my face. Being with a client and becoming totally present to them, listening intently and really hearing and feeling them, not attaching to the outcome, but just being with them fully. Not my wedding day, but the day before when I said to Neil that I wanted to tell him my speech there and then just the two of us, and I told him all the things I loved about him. Breastfeeding Finlay and him popping off every now and then just to smile at me; staring into his eyes and getting completely lost. My children's laughter and how that invites me back to the present. Cuddling Isaac at the end of a

171

busy day and feeling his skin on my skin and luxuriating in the warmth and closeness and love. I could go on and on.

Joy exists in the present moment.

Further resources

Eckhart Tolle – *The Power of Now*

Surrender

Surrender is one of the most powerful ways I have found of being in the magic of the present moment. When we attach to the outcome of *anything* it prevents us from being fully present. When, instead, I focus on being present to my life as fully as possible and leaning into the *joy* of life, then the magic happens. Let's be real, I still often get sucked into the past or future, but I just bring myself back again and again and again. You all know those magical days when you haven't made any plans and you get into a state of flow and then life delights you. A spontaneous connection with a friend that turns into a day of chatting and drinking tea or wine or an amazing conversation with someone, a friend or even a stranger on the bus. That state of flow is where the magic lies. When you can be fully present *and* be in a state of not forcing anything, not trying to control anything, just trusting!

When I think of surrender, the image that comes to mind is of me lying like a star face up in the sea, being carried about by the waves, allowing myself to be carried by the universe, held, supported, and trusting. Going with the flow. I am an absolute control freak in recovery, and I want everyone to know about this state, because it is where your happiness lies. There are hundreds of beautiful meditations about surrender.

Some of you will be very familiar with the term 'manifest' and others perhaps less so. Manifesting is linked to the Law of Attraction. It means intentionally creating what you want. Our minds are always manifesting something, because we are almost always thinking - where our focus goes, energy flows. That's where the power of changing our story comes in; the more positive our thoughts, the more positive the situation we manifest.

Surrender has been a huge part of my manifesting the life I really want. I invite you to get really clear and *really specific* with

173

regards to the life you want and how you want things to be. Write down what you want, feel it, celebrate it before it has happened. Then, surrender. You can write down what you want on paper and then burn it in a fire to symbolise releasing attachment, to symbolise surrendering. Leave it up to the universe (often the universe has better ideas than you do!). Then just be in the present moment, leaning into the deliciousness of life as often as possible. Watch the magic unfold.

Here are some of the ways I manifest:

- I oftentimes choose how I'm going to feel about something, the emotions I'm going to manifest. For example, 'Today is going to be easy', 'This morning before work is going to be calm and connecting' or 'My drive today is going to be straightforward and smooth'. It's so amazing the power of focus and intent

- Other times it might be an actual goal - like 'in January I want to manifest (enter a certain amount of money)' - it's absolutely incredible how often I get exactly what I have manifested!

- Sometimes I write things out on paper as I've suggested above - crucially I write down WHY I want the thing and also why I KNOW it's going to happen, connecting to the idea of faith

- Sometimes I manifest in groups, within the communities I am part of. We share with joy the things we want to attract into our lives and celebrate that they've already happened (before they've really happened - KEY to manifesting - feeling grateful BEFORE the thing has happened)... sometimes this involves dancing!

- Sometimes I intentionally become the version of myself that would attract the thing I want. I am a strong believer that the energy I put out is key - when I am joyful AND relaxed (not attached to the outcome) I manifest the most powerfully

- Sometimes I decide what I want to attract but also, like I said, let go and trust the universe... because sometimes the universe has even bigger and better plans than I have.

Further resources

Gabrielle Bernstein – *Super Attractor & The Universe Has Got Your Back*

Listening to Abraham Hicks helps me get into a state of surrender!

Celebration station

Do you celebrate yourself? Do you celebrate life?

In the UK and in my family, it is not really the done thing to celebrate yourself. It's considered much more usual and appealing to put ourselves down or be ever so modest. To dismiss our achievements. More than that, to take little responsibility for our achievements but full responsibility for our failings!

When we don't allow ourselves to celebrate ourselves or our wins, no matter how small, it stops us feeling *joy* and creating positive momentum. When we focus on what we get wrong and never focus on what we do right, it contributes to our anxiety and affects our mood. I say *celebrate the hell out of yourself!*

Many of my friends now come to me to celebrate themselves, which I am *all about!* I love celebrating! I celebrate everything. I'm currently wearing a necklace from Tatty Devine (giving these glorious jewellery designers in London a shout out for being amazing) that says *celebrate*. I bought *celebrate* necklaces for my whole team recently! Celebration is central to the work I do.

I think some people worry, 'how will I motivate myself if I'm too celebratory of myself or if I'm too kind to myself?' My experience? You'll be *more* motivated and everything you do will be from a place of *joy*.

What is the point in this life if you cannot enjoy the journey? If you're always focused on the destination. I say *celebrate everything*.

Absolutely everything.

Another mantra, apart from 'you cannot get this wrong', which has transformed my life is:

How is this perfect?

The words were first spoken by my mentors Kit and Rosie Volcano, or that's where I heard them anyway. I even commissioned an amazing piece of art, How Is This Perfect embroidered in colourful letters, so I can read it every day. When challenging stuff happens that is outwith your control, why waste energy lamenting it? How can you celebrate everything? How can you focus on the positive?

Someone forgot about a meeting with me last week!

Previous me: would have taken it personally, been frustrated at my time not being respected (I would have told a story about that anyway, which wasn't true), and would have wasted energy feeling annoyed.

Present me: *flowed*, celebrated that Isaac was set up with a film and ice-cream (I mean come on, he was ecstatic!) and used the time to do something else. Celebrated the time that had been gifted to me - focused on how it was perfect.

When you feel so desperate for something to happen that you are bereft when it doesn't, write about how perfect it would be if that didn't happen.

For example, I desperately want X number of clients for my new course.

How is it perfect if no one signs up? I will be given loads of extra time. I will have more space. Perhaps the universe has something even better in mind for me than I realise. I can spend time writing this book! I can spend more time exercising and getting fit and tickling and kissing my baby boy. I can cook up all sorts of exciting plans. I can use the time to really learn more and read. I can spend time catching up on a business course I'm taking.

See! You've just witnessed this in action! I just talked about something I really was willing too hard, and within 30 seconds I have now talked myself out of it and now I'm sort of seriously thinking that if no one signs up it will be perfect!

So many people I've worked with over the years take too much responsibility for the things that go 'wrong' in their lives, and dismiss the amazing things they have created. They wasted those opportunities for joy.

Celebrate yourself as a parent. Even if you don't think you're perfect (no one is), celebrate how loved you make your little one feel. Celebrate the ten minutes you played with them. Don't focus on the time you were distracted. Celebrate *anything* that feels good. Don't focus on what doesn't feel good.

Let your mind linger on how great you are doing.

An example from right now in my life? I've just arrived home from four nights at my parents' house with Isaac. We gave Neil a little solitude and I was able to see my folks and pals. Win win. On the drive home, I noticed my brain starting to mull over the ways I hadn't met my expectations of myself as a parent or daughter:

Brain : 'you didn't play with Isaac enough, too much screen time, you were too irritable with your mum'...

Present me: 'Woah woah woah, rather than focusing on the few things you wish you had done differently, think of all the things you did wonderfully! What about chasing Isaac around the garden, both in hysterical laughter? And making art together and Play Doh. What about taking him to the park and to the sand dunes and leaving your phone at home for uninterrupted time. What about you breastfeeding him and snuggling him at night and being happy and calm with him nearly the whole time. You read some lovely books to him and played imaginary games where you pretended to be a baby and he loved it! He was jumping off the sofa into your arms and having the best time!'

(Even now, writing all of that out makes me feel *so* much better.)

'And your ma? Which daughter doesn't get irritated by their mother? Rather than focusing on the couple of times you snapped, what about the fact you danced Nia together twice and had a great time. You did a lovely meditation together. You were so grateful for all the delicious food she made. You expressed gratitude for the care they took of Isaac. You're doing grand.'

Now, Celebration Station has become a regular feature of my online courses. During my four day online event 'BS to Bliss' as well as my longer courses, I dedicate a significant amount of time to celebration. Sometimes it feels like the easiest and lightest part of the course from my perspective, yet often it is one of the most profound experiences for people. I have seen people feel overcome with emotion when they have realised how little they have celebrated themselves in their whole lives. I have seen people celebrating and witnessing themselves in a totally different light (seeing themselves as warriors for having lived with chronic illnesses, or for killing it as single mums or for parenting during lockdown). It is so beautiful to go through this process in a group; everyone gets to celebrate everyone's wins. It requires vulnerability and it builds such trust. I have had people incorporate Celebration Station into their work, with kids or with their team members; and then report back to me on how powerful it has been.

I invite you to think. Where could you celebrate your wins more. Where could celebrate your partner, children, family, or work colleagues more? Just like gratitude, the thing about celebrating is that, once you begin to look, you'll see your reasons everywhere.

179

Nonviolent Communication

One of my favourite books is *Nonviolent Communication* by Marshall Rosenberg. Rosenberg was a clinical psychologist in the USA. He died on 7th February 2015, the day after Finlay was born. Nonviolent Communication (NVC) is Rosenberg's legacy, a framework for thinking about feelings and needs which I deeply believe has the power to change the world. Every therapist and teacher and parent should know about this framework; it is so simple yet utterly life changing.

Rosenberg discusses how, from a young age, we are conditioned to view the world in terms of right and wrong. Through fairytales, we learn that there are good people and bad people. Through films, we learn that there are wicked people and kind people. As we grow older, we are told that there are groups of 'others' who are wrong, which makes us feel that we must be 'right'. The dualities and divisions follow us into adulthood. We are bombarded with TV shows about people claiming benefits and told that they are in the 'wrong'. Or we are told that the rich people are wrong. Our values are constantly pitted against someone else's, and we are taught that there can only ever be one winner.

In arguments with our partners or friends, we think that we are right, and they are wrong. Or we shame ourselves, judging ourselves as wrong. We judge our behaviour: *How could I have done that?* We judge our feelings: *I shouldn't be so angry/ sad.* We judge our needs: *I shouldn't be so needy, I'm selfish.* Blah blah blah.

But what if no one is wrong? If everyone has their feelings and needs and everyone is right. What if, from their unique perspective in any given moment, each individual is right. If, with the information available to them at that time, with their lens and their history, they are feeling the only emotions they could feel in that moment. That premise is at the heart of NVC. It has totally transformed the way I relate to myself and the world around me.

I used to feel deep shame at how I talked to my husband at times. Sometimes, especially when tired, I would feel so angry about my needs not being met. I would tell myself stories: *if he really loved me, he would know how I felt and meet my needs before I even knew them.* Haha, that old chestnut! I essentially expected Neil to be a mind reader. It's embarrassing now to admit but, sometimes if I asked for help (which I found so difficult) and he didn't help me immediately, I would feel *furious*. What a catch I was!

In retrospect, I was behaving like a massive, weird toddler. I would snap at Neil and speak to him in a way that showed no reflection of how much I really loved and respected him. I just didn't have the knowledge or skills to understand or articulate my feelings or needs.

I would feel shameful afterwards for being like that and the cycle would continue. Usually, I would apologise for being snappy and underplay it to myself. We would go on to have a great time together that day. But the reality is that, had that pattern continued, it would have irreparably damaged our bond - and my love and respect for myself.

I want everyone to be armed with the knowledge I gained through NVC. We must become familiar with our needs and feelings. We must practice tuning into them so that we know when they're changing. It's *our* responsibility to communicate our needs or to meet them ourselves.

I use the NVC model (alongside teachings on co-dependency, boundaries, and various other methods) to help couples heal their relationships and learn to communicate in clear and loving ways. I have seen incredible changes in families, including children becoming better able to understand and communicate their needs and parents better able to listen well and really hear what is being said.

I learned why I was feeling angry with my husband. It was because certain needs of mine weren't being met. Basic human needs that we *all share*. When I understood this, I stopped feeling ashamed of myself. I stopped making myself the 'bad person'. I understood and respected my needs. I learned that it was *my* job to meet my needs - and not my partner's responsibility to read my mind and meet my needs! I was so empowered by this knowledge.

If this model were taught in schools all over the world, it would be an absolute game changer. Politicians need to live it! They need to start understanding their opponents' needs. We live in such a polarised world, where we view people with different opinions as 'other'. I have been guilty of it; making judgements about people who are less liberal than me. It is not helpful, though; we need to understand the needs and feelings of other people as much as we need to understand our own.

Every feeling shows up because a need is either being met or not. Right now, I feel engaged and inspired because my needs for intellectual stimulation are being met. This topic fills me with interest and passion. I feel eager to write about it because, by sharing this information, my need for connection with others is likely to be met!

When I felt angry with Neil and unable to understand what was going on, NVC enabled me to see things more clearly. I gained more understanding and compassion for myself. When I was up multiple times through the night, breastfeeding Isaac, and Neil was in the spare room getting lots of rest (haha! Who else knows the *who's most tired* game as new parents…), I felt angry, irritable, exhausted, depleted, and jealous. I judged myself harshly for feeling these feelings but NVC enabled me to develop an understanding of my feelings and behaviours, without 'right or wrong' coming into it. My needs for rest, sleep and equality were not being met. To be fair, Neil was amazing, but he didn't have boobs so the breastfeeding couldn't be equal! When I was able to understand this more clearly, I began to take responsibility for meeting these needs. Instead of hoping Neil would offer me a lie in whilst falling to his knees expressing gratitude, I would say to him, 'Neil, I'm exhausted, please could you take Isaac for a couple of hours so I can sleep before I start the day?' Most times, he was more than happy to support me in such a way. Ask and you shall receive. Definitely better than silently stewing and waiting for the other person to figure out what's up.

Before learning about NVC, I would sometimes knock on the wall in between Isaac's bedroom (where I was stuck) and our bedroom (where Neil was dreaming). I would be knocking to ask for help. If Neil didn't appear in a millisecond, I would be furious. But I learned that it was my responsibility to communicate my needs. I could get up, go through, and lovingly make a request of Neil for help, like an adult, rather than being furious at my unmet needs which he wasn't even aware of.

The beautiful thing about learning to communicate directly and lovingly is that not only do you develop a more loving, compassionate, and respectful relationship, but you also develop more respect for yourself and pride in yourself. This then has a ripple effect on the rest of your life. On your career, your friendships, your relationships with family members. It is so far reaching.

This is so applicable to anxiety and joy. Learning what your needs are - and which needs are unmet, or which are really important to you - can be key to creating a fulfilled life. Also, learning to lovingly communicate with others, leads to *total and utter joy*. Your trust in yourself increases, your trust in your ability to meet your own (and your child's or partner's) needs increases, and you feel stronger and 100% more able to cope with whatever life throws at you. These tools empower you to completely turn around your emotional world.

The joy of working with clients is that I get to witness this magic in action. In 2020, I was working with a woman (let's call her Helen) who was living with her partner and three kids (and dog and cat). Helen was struggling with low mood and was feeling unhappy in her relationship. She often argued with her husband and felt like neither of them understood each other at all. She felt that he judged her negatively; and she judged herself negatively, too. She beat herself up and shamed herself when anything went wrong in life and took zero credit for all the amazing things she had achieved. She and her partner were on the verge of separating. She was even picking out furniture for her new place.

Helen learned about NVC and discovered how to identify her feelings and needs. Most importantly, she learned how to communicate them. She also learned to stop judging herself for having needs, because she now viewed them as 'normal basic human needs'. We worked together on my 8 week 'Relationship Magic' course, exploring NVC alongside Boundaries and Codependency (next chapter!). In that short stretch of time, Helen was able to shift some long-standing patterns within her relationships. This is what she wrote about her experience:

'Relationship Magic in action. Two months ago, James and I were separating. I was looking for a new home, thinking about how we would co-parent our 3 kids and wondering which bits of furniture I'd get. Last night and today we have been planning our handfasting ceremony for next year! 11 years of relationship... blurred boundaries, f*cked up communication, major patterns of codependency and wondering what the hell was going wrong... rewritten in 2 months with Sarah's expert guidance and amazing coaching! It's really affected the kids too, they are communicating their needs and emotions to us and getting along better. The atmosphere in the house is so different. We can't wait to start 'BS to Bliss' together.'

She said even the dog was happier (but that the cat didn't give a sh*t). What a joyful environment they co-created, for everyone to enjoy together. Amazing what happens when we stray from the narrative of 'right' and 'wrong' that has been programmed in us from birth. When we meet ourselves and others exactly where we are.

Recognising, articulating, and standing up for our needs is not always straightforward but, as the following chapter by my dear friend Naomi demonstrates, it is always worth it.

Further resources

Marshall Rosenberg – *Nonviolent Communication* (I really recommend the Audible version – Marshall's voice is incredibly calming!)

There are several NVC resources for kids too, including You Tube videos

From Deaf Shame to Deaf Gain
By Naomi Preston

Last Sunday I got up and thought 'I'll have a lovely soak in the bath and have a go at guided meditation.' As restful music played from my phone, a gentle voice began to guide me towards calm and inner peace. Slowly, I felt the tension start to slip away. The bath was so hot that sweat began to drip into my hearing aids distorting the mantra and ruining the mood. Annoyed, but trying to stay calm, I dried off my hearing aids and, fashioning a makeshift headband from a flannel, started again.

'Bring your focus back to your breath...' intoned the voice in my ears but I realised that all that was going through my mind was 'what if you aren't really stopping the sweat? What if you slip into the bath and drown your hearing aids? What if the kids come in and splash you? You'll have no hearing aids, you won't be able to work tomorrow. Aaargh!!!'

I tried to focus my breath back on the meditation. Just as I was approaching peace, the door flew open and in barreled my son with his latest Lego creations. 'Look mum, this one is a ship, look it floats,' Micah shouted as he flung his ship into the hot waters. Hearing Micah, Mayumi burst in soon after and started shouting over and over for the TV. So much for relaxation!

After negotiating for them to leave, I tried one last time to get back to some form of tranquility but I was too stressed and couldn't be bothered continuing with the podcast. Damn these hearing aids and damn being deaf!

Although I didn't realise it until recently, I carried a deep-rooted belief that I should do everything that a hearing person does. When I couldn't, I would feel like I had failed. Not being able to listen to meditation in the bath because of my hearing aids, because of my deafness, would usually have made me feel like a failure. Then it struck me: I can have a bath in silence when my hearing aids are out. Real, proper, no interruptions silence. Perfect for relaxation. I took my hearing aids out, lowered myself into the steaming hot water and closed my eyes. I focused on calming breathing exercises and had a relaxing, meditative bath. Deafness 1 Anxiety 0!

I am a 45 year old wife and mother of two. I was diagnosed with severe bilateral sensorineural deafness when I was 5. Both my parents and older brother are hearing. Upon getting my diagnosis, my parents were worried as they had no experience of deafness. When the Local Education Authority recommended that I attend a special needs school catering for children with physical and learning difficulties, my parents refused. They did not see my deafness as a reflection of my educational ability. They fought to send me to the same school as my hearing brother. My parents believed that with support from a peripatetic Teacher of the Deaf, I was more than capable of attending the local primary school. They had decided not to treat me any differently to Colin because - apart from hearing - they reasoned, whatever Colin could do, Naomi could do too.

I am extremely grateful to them for this, as I firmly believe this attitude helped me to become resilient and determined not to let my deafness stop me from doing what I wanted to do. I wonder now, if this had the unintended effect of fostering the negative self-belief that I am at fault if I do not perform as well as a hearing person.

I enjoyed primary school, I had lots of friends and felt accepted. This all changed at secondary school. I went to a different school than most of my friends. I struggled to fit in and was often an easy target for bullies. I quickly disposed of my enormous and conspicuous radio hearing aid from around my neck, pretending that I could manage without it. I hated school. I felt embarrassed and ashamed of myself. I would often retreat to the toilets mid-lesson to cry and hide away. After particularly difficult days, I would cry myself to sleep wishing that I would never have to return to school. My brother would sometimes

187

catch me in tears and have words with (or beat up) the bullies. This felt great for a few days, but then the abuse would continue regardless. Children would whisper and then laugh when I'd ask what they said. In class they would deliberately call my name out until I turned around and then they would pretend they hadn't said anything and make a show of being hard at work. I was often excluded, and jibes were made about my looks, style, walk... anything, really. That's why it's hard to say I was bullied solely because of my hearing, as two friends from school also reported feeling like outsiders. When I finally left and arrived at college, I was so relieved to meet like-minded people who loved the same music as I did, shared the same sense of humour and interests as I did, and seemed to accept me for me.

Until I was in my twenties, I did not know any other deaf people. I was fully immersed in the hearing world. If I am being honest, I always felt like a defective hearing person. I rarely connected to any emotion relating to my deafness, preferring to brush things under the carpet and use humour as a tool of avoidance. I did this for so long it made me believe I was more accepting of myself and my deafness than I really was.

Whilst at college, I won a competition to work at *Just Seventeen* magazine on a fashion shoot. One morning I was sat at an empty desk in the busy open plan office taking in my surroundings. I was feeling excited and smiling to myself when the phone rang. My stomach dropped and the colour drained from my face. I prayed as hard as I could that someone else would pick up the phone, or that it would just ring off. Each ring seemed to last hours and I tried to pretend it was not ringing. The Fashion Editor shouted across from the adjacent desk, 'Do us a favour, answer that for us will you?' I did my default response of pretending that I'm not deaf and nodded, slowly reaching my arm out, still hoping that before I lifted the receiver up, it would ring off. My heart was beating so loud, sweat was dripping. The person on the phone uttered a couple of indecipherable words and hung up. I slid off the chair and went to the toilets to compose myself and hide away.

Later, when I returned, the Fashion Editor appeared agitated as the driver she had ordered was late. She asked me who had been on the phone. 'Oh it was a wrong number,' I lied. Fifteen minutes passed as we discussed the plans for the photo shoot when suddenly the office doors burst open and a receptionist came in distressed, shouting that a driver had 'just hurled a load of abuse' because no one had come down even though she'd rung up. The Fashion Editor shouted back at her saying that no-one had rung up. I went red as I realised it was my fault.

As always, I just acted like it didn't happen and hoped that others would play along. I did not engage in any meaningful or emotional way, I just told myself that it would make an amusing anecdote to tell my friends.

I was able to tell people I was deaf, and for them to see my hearing aids, but it was important to me to pretend that they worked perfectly. I would say it was like putting on a pair of glasses, magically correcting failings in sight. This is not the case, though. Hearing aids do not cure deafness. They simply boost losses in frequency to provide some clarity. With my hearing aids in, I am not a hearing person. So much of my hearing with hearing aids is guesswork based on the social context. I worked hard to appear hearing. If there was any hint of my deafness drawing attention to myself, I would feel ashamed as if my cover had been blown. I remember one time the flatmate of a friend shouting out that it was 'Naomi on the phone' despite never having met me before. Later I asked her how she knew it was me, and she replied, 'it was the deaf tone in your voice'. I was crushed.

I worked hard at college and was accepted at Stirling University to study Japanese. But this success was no shield to my shame. I experienced the familiar burning cheeks, increased heart rate and shaking body when Support Services left 'DISABILITY SUPPORT' leaflets in my letter box. It was like a neon sign shouting out to my peers that I was disabled, different, less than. Shame would wash over me. I threw the

189

leaflets in the bin, not looking at what support was available, then the horrible feelings went away. I had tamped them down, repressed them and locked them away.

However, in my final year, I had to give in and contact the Disability Support team. I decided to seek help when in a Japanese listening mock exam, it was impossible for me to separate speech from the 'realistic' cafeteria background sounds. I had to fill in a volume of paperwork, get proof of my deafness from my audiology department and make a number of time consuming and difficult phone calls - all taking time that my peers were using for study - before 'support' finally came through. It was agreed that I could have 15 minutes extra listening time on top of the hour allocated for the exam. I was devastated! How was that going to help? All that hassle sorting the paperwork and the discomfort of having to engage with DISABILITY SERVICES and they finally offered me useless and impractical support. I should have just spent more time in the library! There was no time to appeal. I could not have a transcript as this would make it like a reading exam rather than a listening exam. Kindly my tutor let me listen to the tape a few times so I could try to familiarise myself with the speech patterns and subject matter. But this did not make it an even playing field with my hearing peers. I had such a headache after concentrating solidly for such a long period of time, I was convinced that I had underperformed. I returned to my room and cried with exhaustion, filled with an overwhelming sense of failure.

Somehow, I completed and passed my degree in Japanese Studies with a 2:1, but to this day I have no idea how I actually did on that exam. I guess it's not important now, but this and other experiences of so-called support did little to encourage me to ask for help, to draw attention to my deafness, to remind people that I am not like them.

I am a people pleaser and I have realised recently that I do not want people to be inconvenienced by my deafness. Reflecting on this, I think it feeds into the pretence that I'm just like a hearing person: asking people to recognise my deafness destroys this facade. Recently I have begun to wonder if I internalised subtle messages from experiences in my life. I once asked a tutor if he could refrain from walking around the classroom as he spoke. I explained that I couldn't lip-read him if I couldn't see him. He said that's how he liked to teach and wondered if I could re-position my desk. OK!

At primary school when taking part in class assemblies, I was told to speak up for the audience. A teacher told me to take my hearing aids out to remind me to speak up because without my hearing aids I could not hear myself speak properly. Ignoring the dubious logic of this approach, it meant more importantly that I could not hear the other teachers and children, meaning I always missed my time to speak unless others made excessive physical gestures. I felt lost, humiliated, and foolish.

There were times I was quick to take advantage of the positives of teachers not really knowing how to handle my hearing or hearing aids. One day a week, half the class would do art and the other half extra maths. I used to lie to the teacher that I had an earache or a headache because of my hearing. This meant I got to do art most weeks! It may well explain why, as an adult, numbers are not my strong point.

On leaving university I spent 10 years working for Deaf charities and services. This was a revelation to me. Most people involved in those environments were deaf. Deafness was the norm. Colleagues were deaf, clients were deaf. Our needs were considered and catered for, without even having to ask!

I was introduced to amplified and text phones, note-takers, lip-speakers, and specialist equipment. I met confident, articulate, and proud deaf people. Deaf people who were not afraid to ask the non-deaf world to accommodate their needs. It was liberating. I was able to access proper support and not feel ashamed about asking for it.

During this time, I attended a college that specialised in Deaf studies and was overcome by how much easier it was to access learning when the materials were delivered in an accessible way. Lessons were conducted with a transcript on a screen, note-takers present and regular breaks offered. I was no longer missing large chunks of learning. I wasn't putting my head down to furiously scribble notes only to look up moments later having lost track of what the tutor was saying. I did not have the confidence to ask them to repeat what I had missed. In this new environment I got to make contributions, join learning discussions, and learn at my pace. Finally!

I learnt British Sign Language and learnt about Deaf culture. I worked as a volunteer on the National Deaf Children's Society Deaf Role Model Project, sharing my experiences as a deaf person in hearing world. I got to take my husband and children to hotels the length and breadth of the country as they heard, often for the first time, my experiences. As a role model I often had worried parents and scared kids asking me questions, the same questions my parents had asked and questions I had asked myself.

'Can I go to university?'

'Yes.'

'Will she get a good job?'

'Yes.'

'Will he have friends?'

'Yes.'

'Can I fall in love and have a family?'

'Yes, yes emphatically yes!'

I could help others to feel better about their deaf futures and this had the knock-on effect of highlighting the positives and the achievements in my own life.

I slowly learnt that it was my responsibility to speak out about my needs. It is also the responsibility of others to play their part in effective communication. Understanding this has enabled me to develop the confidence to be assertive about my needs outside of the deaf world. However, there were still a few setbacks along the way.

About 10 years ago, I started to experience pain in my hip and leg. This deteriorated to the point of chronic pain and poor mobility. Despite repeated visits, my GP and physio told me it was weak muscles. I accepted their opinion and thought it was my fault for not exercising enough. However, whenever I tried to exercise, I experienced excruciating pain and would seize up or fall. I was unable to properly play with my children, I could not go on walks with my husband or exercise with friends. When we went on trips away, I would frequently have to stop and rest as my hip would seize up. It was eventually discovered that my hip cartilage had wasted away due to arthritis. I had a hip replacement a couple of years ago.

Using crutches and struggling with mobility flared up that old sense of being different, disabled, disadvantaged, and redundant. Now I had mobility *and* hearing issues. I felt anxious about going out. I began to think that people were looking at me and judging me. 'Look at that poor disabled woman with hearing aids and crutches.' Eventually I received a hip replacement and hope returned. We celebrated my recovery with a 'Hip Hop Hip Op' party and over 50 of my family and friends and I danced the night away. I was back and ready to take on the world as a physically able deaf confident woman. Then Covid struck...

I was surprised by how lockdown increased my anxiety and caused a prolonged dip in my mood and confidence. However, it does make sense when introduction of masks took away half my communication coping strategies in one fell swoop. Even pre-Covid, supermarkets were difficult places for me due to the background noise. Over the past year, I have had more shop assistants and fellow shoppers than usual shake their heads in exasperation at my lack of response to their requests. Bumping into people I know is a bittersweet experience. On the one hand I'm so happy to see people I know face to face, but on the other it's so stressful trying to decipher what they are saying. I realised I was resorting back to my old ways of pretending, trying to mirror responses (difficult when half their face is covered) and giving a half nod and smile usually with a non-committal 'mmmm' as a proxy for understanding.

Covid also meant that almost overnight, everything switched to telephone or online. So, as well as all the uncertainty, stress, and adjustment that we have all had to endure, I was disadvantaged at work. I was excluded from continuing a work-related post graduate qualification at the same pace as my cohort. Whilst I am extremely grateful for the flexibility and the support that my work place and university has given me, the self-expectation and belief that I should operate and function as effectively as a hearing person was firing on all cylinders!

My employer had not yet managed to set up an online platform, so initially all work in my role as a therapist was moved to telephone as face to face appointments ceased. As I could not manage on the telephone, I was unable to put into practice any of the teaching I had learned, and I began to get that familiar sense of feeling like a failure, comparing myself unfavourably to my hearing peers and rapidly losing confidence. It was at least 3 months before I could start offering therapy again when an online platform was finally launched at work. However, there were inevitable teething problems. Often the picture was out of sync with the sound so I could not lip-read, or the screen would freeze and the sound would continue, leaving both the client and I frustrated and not making any progress. My manager fought for me to have access to a platform that recorded and had live transcripts. However, the transcripts were often nonsense, and made work ultimately more stressful.

During lockdown there were many reports of Zoom fatigue and, although concentrating in this way is not new for many deaf people who rely on lip-reading, the pressure to ensure I missed nothing amplified this fatigue tenfold.

On one occasion we had to observe a fellow supervisee's therapy and, because the video platform had no recording facility, I could not fully participate. All supervision (a crucial time for support in my stressful role) was moved online. Sometimes I would turn my camera off, overwhelmed by frustration, and cry. I would share my feelings with my colleagues who were all wonderfully supportive, but I imagine they felt at a loss as to what to do when all our efforts to overcome barriers seemed thwarted and futile.

What I am thankful for, though, is that this experience gave me an opportunity to recognise all those horrible feelings I used to get at school as they came flooding back. This time, rather than continue to brush them under the carpet, I wanted to address them and an online self-development course I was undertaking was the perfect place to do this.

I was able to uncover those shoulds relating to my participation and achievements and to work on challenging and being more flexible with them. I was reminded of what I gain from being deaf, rather than focusing on what I lose. This has been very helpful in relieving anxiety and increasing my mood and joy.

I'd like to share some of these positives/gains with you.

1.   I get to fall in love with my favourite songs twice.

I cannot make out words in songs so it's always the music itself that I first like. I used to love it when Sarah and I would listen to music over and over and she would write down the lyrics or I would lip-read as she sang along. This could be a double-edged sword as there were numerous times when I discovered the actual lyrics were awful, nothing like the ones I had swirling around in my head! My husband Mark now does the honours – usually it's to his own songs as I rarely listen to any music not made in Seattle after the 1990s!

2. I don't get ringing in my ears at loud gigs.

At gigs I can go right to the front, stand by the speakers and not suffer with ringing in the ears that my hearing friends report. In fact, after a gig is the time when I have the best hearing out of us all.

3. I can hear you in a different room.

Modern technology enables me to hear people even if they're in another room, something hearing people can't always do. I'm also looking forward to getting Bluetooth hearing aids so I can stream music directly to my aids.

4. I experience true silence

I remember going to a temple in Japan and sitting with my friend. She said it was so rare to experience true silence, so peaceful and relaxing. I thought, I can experience that pretty much every day when I take my hearing aids out. Perfect after a long stressful day at work.

5. I can sleep through anything

If there's a storm, it never disturbs my sleep.

I rarely have sleep disturbances, no matter what is going on in my life. I've always wondered if it's because I'm not disturbed by external noises.

I got rid of my baby alarm alert for deaf people, as I realised instinct woke me up when my children wanted to be fed or changed during the night. This was such a relief as the alarm was

196

so sudden and loud it would make me, my husband and daughter scream out with fear when it went off!

6.   I can turn my hearing off

When it's busy in the office at work and I need to focus on my notes before my next patient, I can switch my hearing aids off and not get distracted by the background noise.

7.   I find it easy to be in the present moment

I think this is related to my communication needs. I have to lip-read and focus and therefore must be very visually connected and aware of who and what is happening in front of me.

8.   My mishearing makes things more interesting

My deafness has made so many conversations ridiculous and hilarious. At work I just have to crack up when my manager is talking about 'collating the outcome measures' and the transcript of the conversation on Teams reads that she has been talking about 'inflating dancing frogs of leather'.

In comfortable social situations with friends I've known for years, it feels absolutely safe to ask, 'Who's Justin Dunn?' when someone had described someone as 'just so young'. It's OK for us to all laugh, as it is funny. However, when it's a new social situation, or an educational or professional setting, it can be very anxiety-provoking making a contribution and participating when you are not sure how much of the discussion you are correctly picking up.

When I went to university in Stirling, it was a melting pot of different accents and I was on high alert! The anxiety was ramped up – and it took a while for me to tune into the Scottish and Irish pronunciations and lip-patterns. I think in terms of anxiety adrenaline reactions, I was definitely in freeze mode. I thought that my 'hmm' and gentle nods feigning understanding went by unnoticed, so I found it hilarious when some people with whom I shared a kitchen in halls told me that they initially thought I was a foreign exchange student as communication was so stilted.

The reality is I am a deaf person in a hearing world. I am in situations that generally demand that I hear to the capacity of a hearing person. This means that when I'm in the company of others, I'm always scanning and hyper-vigilant to check if someone is talking and that I'm not missing something. I can also start to worry that other people will think I'm rude if I don't respond, or unintelligent if I respond inappropriately. Being aware that you don't have all the same information as everyone else can feel unsettling and that sense of frustration, hurt and failure is never too far away. All of this is just so exhausting and draining.

Other people, even coming from a well-meaning place, can also add to the anxiety. I can recall numerous times when I've asked others what has been said and I again don't hear what they've said, they'll say 'Oh it doesn't matter.' Even when I insist I want to know, they'll say, 'Oh it's not interesting, it does not matter'. This feels dismissive as *I* want to be able to decide if it's interesting or not and this takes away my power to be able to that. I remember when I'd given birth for the first time after a long labour and no sleep for over 24 hours and I was so worried that I would fall asleep and not be able to hear my daughter cry. I was already upset as I didn't realise my husband was not allowed to stay, so I asked the nurses if they could keep an ear and eye out to wake me up if I fell asleep. However, they just said, 'we'll take care of her for the first night and bring her to you if she cries'. They put her in a room full of empty cribs and said, 'Our office is just next door to her.' I was outraged and insisted that my daughter would be better off next to me and I spent the whole night with my chin resting on the side of her cot with my hearing aids turned up full to make sure I could attend to her if she cried. I was knackered!

Things like this make deafness related anxiety and exhaustion inevitable. However, Covid and my learning from the self-development course reminded me of my responsibility to ask for what I need and to educate people if they exclude me, intentionally or not. This feels scary and vulnerable, but the pay-off is always worth it. It's my responsibility to take the time out and the rest I need to replenish from the strain of listening, rather than pretend I'm hearing.

This book is all about changing the way we think about anxiety and helping us to access the joy in our lives. The recognition of the belief I held, that I should achieve and function as a hearing person, has enabled me to let go of the anxiety I was experiencing. I realised that it was within me to make the shift to a more constructive mind-set. I am lucky, I have always found it easy to lean in to fun and now I can look outward rather than inwards. I love time with my beautiful family and friends, reading, listening to music, going to gigs, sitting in my garden, taking beach walks, playing Bananagrams, consuming anything to do with Japan, practising Yin-yoga (Thanks Charlie!), eating and drinking, enjoying hot baths (without meditation!) and feeling the sunshine on my face (rarely in Cumbria!). Being freer from anxiety and accepting and appreciating my deafness has given me the headspace and more time to connect to the joy in my life.

Further resources

An introduction to Deaf Gain, Dirksen Bauman & Joseph Murray:

https://www.psychologytoday.com/gb/blog/deaf-gain/201411/introduction-deaf-gain

My reflections on Naomi's chapter

It feels different reflecting on Naomi's chapter because we are such close friends, we were together all the way through university and our lives continue to be beautifully entwined.

Naomi is such a beautiful person and friend - she is one of the funniest people I've known and so caring and fun. People just love her. She has supported me through some of the hardest times in my life. She was my main support after the abortion - once I remember lying in her bed and she just held me whilst I cried. Then again at Finn's funeral and throughout everything - she was one of my main supports. Mostly, though, we just have lots of fun and laughter together, and talk about music and the things and people we love.

Naomi is just Naomi to me. I don't think of her hearing. I think of her beautiful nature. It's so interesting reading her chapter. It makes me think of how, perhaps, this perspective isn't always as beneficial as I'd thought - and how a narrative I told wasn't necessarily the most helpful. I would always compliment Naomi on how she just gets on with life. It is interesting to think about how at times this may have been in part due to Naomi denying her true feelings, struggles or needs in relation to her hearing.

It has been beautiful to witness Naomi on a journey of voicing her needs more, of accepting herself more and of releasing anxieties. I am also in awe of her strength and resilience - it's so easy to forget the energy drain involved with disabilities or with having a marginalised identity. As Naomi says, it's fatiguing. I can take for granted how society and services, education and shops for example, are set up to cater for me and not for every body.

I love how Naomi celebrates the positives as well - what a gift she has been to help other families and young deaf people anticipate positive and joyful futures. Some of the most joyful times I have ever known have been shared with Naomi. As I said at the start of the book, the world opened up when I met her and connected with someone on such a deep level. It's interesting that despite Naomi's hearing loss, the main thing we connected over was our love of music. I've never known anyone more 'in the moment' than Naomi or who flows with life more. I'm beyond grateful that our paths crossed and that I have been able to better understand Naomi's needs and feelings over time - as she has done, too.

Boundaries and Codependency

Since I have started saying a guilt-free 'No' to things I don't want, my joy has grown exponentially. When you allow yourself to say no to things you don't want, you create space and energy for the things you *do* want. It really helped me when I started this process of saying 'No' to things, not to focus on what I was saying no to, or missing out on, but to focus on what saying 'No' enabled me to say 'Yes' to! Previous me constantly abandoned my desires and needs to please others and transforming this has been key to my joy.

When you focus on and take responsibility for *your* emotional world instead of constantly worrying about other people (Previous me!), you become more authentic. When you stop feeling like you must be everything to everyone, you can actually offer more to others. When you stop taking responsibility for others (madness-inducing because you are not in control of others!), you become more aligned with who you really are. Furthermore, you can do all the above from a place of love and joy. The feelings of obligation, which can easily turn into resentment, disappear.

Sometimes, we feel there is a template for being the 'right' kind of friend, partner, daughter or employee. We must be kind to others. We must help other people. We must please. We must think of other people's needs before our own. This idea was deeply ingrained in me with my Catholic upbringing, not just through the behaviour of those around me but in the religious teaching itself. People who sacrificed their own needs, who always prioritised the needs of others, were referred to as 'saints'. This happened recently at a funeral I attended - 'She was a total saint'.

But what about when we put other people's needs first and neglect ours and then resent them? Does that serve anyone?

202

The form of codependency that I witness most often in those around me and in Previous me, is perhaps one of the less extreme definitions (there are many) – it is when we try to constantly take care of or please *others* and neglect to take care of ourselves, or even notice or have any awareness of our own needs.

Some of you may resonate and recognise this within yourself, and also recognise patterns in who you are attracted to – perhaps people who are very needy or even addicted to substances. Co-dependent people can often try and control the other person's behaviour or can feel like they need to act like a performing seal to cheer the other person up if they are angry, they can feel responsible for the other person's distress and they can spend all their time trying to look after or 'change' the other person instead of focusing on themself.

Are you the friend that people always come to for advice and help? I am (or at least used to be) an emotional sponge! An empath is someone who has the ability to sense the emotions of others. Like many empaths, I have a tendency to be codependent. Empaths often not only sense but feel responsible for other people's emotions. As described, they focus on helping others, seldom focusing inwardly to look after themselves. The healing for codependents comes from focusing inwards and finally looking after their own needs.

What if '*getting it right*' looked like - lovingly and firmly - having boundaries about what we were willing to do or accept in life? What if you could say 'No' with zero guilt, knowing that you are not responsible for the happiness of other people.

When you feel that pull to try and rescue someone and put your needs aside, can you try this instead? Can you trust someone else's 'higher self' and trust the universe instead of diving in? Sometimes, others will expect you to be the one who meets their needs, or the one who is responsible for their emotions, especially if these patterns have been the status quo. But you can learn to be boundaried about what feels good; to listen to your inner guidance system and to honour your needs.

It is quite disempowering to assume that other people cannot meet their own needs; that you are responsible for them. I used to do this a lot in friendships, and a few of them sadly ended in disaster. Looking back, I wish that I could have known what I know now and been able to communicate my feelings and needs more effectively. I ended up befriending people and then trying to 'help' them to feel better. I lacked a boundary about my personal time and would agree to do things with people that I didn't want to do, out of fear of upsetting them. I would take on too much responsibility for their wellbeing then feel like my needs were being neglected in the friendships, creating that old 'victim' 'persecutor' 'perpetrator' triangle!

Learning about my co-dependent tendencies has been such a gift for me. I feel so much free-er and more authentic. These days, I only agree to do things I really want to do, things that are a 'F*ck yes!' for me! I don't feel guilty for saying no to people. I don't do things I don't want to do. I don't resent people! I am learning not to take on responsibility for my husband's feelings. Sometimes we both struggle when the other one gets angry; we often want the other one to 'just stop' being angry or we fear that we have been the cause of the anger, rather than allowing the other to express and feel it. Anger is such a necessary and healthy emotion, and we're learning how to let that expression fully take place, to complete the function that anger serves in the body.

Much like geographical boundaries delineate a separation between one place and another, boundaries in this context can be summed up as:

Knowing where you end and others begin.

For people who have never considered this, the implementation of boundaries can quickly have a profound effect on their relationships. Jenny is a client of mine who just completed the four day 'BS to Bliss' relationship challenge. She talked about how, before she learned about boundaries, she had no concept of where she ended and her partner began. For example, she had an idea of what she wanted to happen in the morning, what time she wanted him to get up out of bed and the order of things that were going to happen. Instead of clearly communicating her feelings and needs and making direct requests, she would feel furious at him and lash out. This, of course, ended in both of them feeling terrible. It triggered some traumatic childhood memories for him and resulted in him stonewalling (refusing to communicate) for two days. She then felt guilty. She learned about healthy boundaries and was able to recognise how her partner was separate to her. He had his own feelings, needs and desires. She was able to allow him to make his own decisions and not to expect him to fit in with her plans. This enabled her to really listen to him and hear him. Both of them ended up feeling more understood.

Just like my NVC example, you can imagine the pride that Jenny will feel when, knowing what she now knows, she is able to communicate lovingly and better respect her partner's boundaries and needs. This will likely result in her being able to feel proud of herself, which will have a ripple effect on other areas of her life. I am excited to see how things progress for Jenny as she has signed up to do more work with me and to train as a coach herself!

Boundaries are not always easy to implement. You may not always receive the reaction you hoped for. It can catch people unawares when you suddenly stop doing what you have done forever, or implement new boundaries, or begin to show up differently in the world. A few months ago, I found out someone had said that the way I show up online is 'false' and that it can't be authentic. This cut deep! One of my main goals in life is to be as authentic as humanly possible. They also criticised an online course that I run.

I felt so hurt. Have you heard that quote about 'not taking things personally', even when someone insults you directly? Ideally, we should keep it about them and not us. I took it way too personally, rather than just keeping it about them and feeling sad that they couldn't believe that my joy was real.

I want to be loved, though! Haha! By everyone! Which is not realistic. What is realistic is me working on *my* love for myself; practicing unconditional love for myself and unconditional alignment. Rather than focusing on approval from others, we need to develop a *stronger sense of self* - so that we don't take things personally. I used to take so many things personally which, the occasional misstep aside, no longer bother me at all. It's such a relief.

I show up in a *very* joyful way online. For years and years, I would downplay my joy so as not to make other people feel bad (co-dependent!). I would ask someone, 'How are you?' If they replied, '*oh not amazing*' or '*not bad*' and asked how I was, I wouldn't tell the truth and say I was doing great. I would say '*oh you know, been better*' or '*not too bad*' or I would talk about something a bit negative and moan with them, even though it felt awful in my body. I was not honouring the boundary between the two of us; where they ended and I began. Clearly, if someone was going through something really challenging, I would be attuned and sensitive and wouldn't just bang on about how great things were with me, but you get the idea!

So, the interesting thing is that *now* when I show up full of joy, this is me showing my real self *more*, stepping into authenticity more. As a culture, we have a problematic relationship with joy - and with joyful women in particular. As I referenced in the chapter on my identity as a woman, our society feels more trusting towards men who are confident and joyful but *less* trusting towards confident and joyful women. How unsurprising yet annoying. That obviously makes me want to exhibit *all the confidence and joy*!

My dad is an introvert, calm and generally quite reserved. Growing up, I longed for his approval. I think he struggled with my joy. I wonder if this is why the comments from this person cut so deep. Perhaps those comments brought back deep-down stories that *I'm getting something wrong*, a deep anxiety for approval. Of course, as a kid I really did need my parents' approval for survival, I couldn't have hacked it on my own. But I don't need everyone's approval anymore, I need a stronger sense of self. I decided to reframe what had happened. How were those comments perfect? Well, my business is growing rapidly and I'm going to be receiving more feedback (both positive and negative). I'm grateful for the opportunity to witness how personally I took something which had nothing to do with me.

The same week that this happened, *another* person sent me a message to say that they had been feeling down lately and feeling jealous and even angry at me for being so openly joyful. My joy triggers something for people. I'm most often triggered by something that I feel jealous or envious of or by someone who exhibits behaviour that reminds me of something that I don't like about myself. I view it as a gift to be triggered by someone! - it provides me with more insight into what I want! It's valuable information that I need to *do* something to create the thing I want or to heal. It's so interesting, as I edit this chapter months later, this very person signed up for my 8 week course, and just this week posted a video in our private group saying how she is feeling *so happy*! She told the group how previously she felt triggered by my joy and thought to herself...

'How can she be that happy? Surely she can't be that happy all the time?!'

Then she wrote that she now feels like this too! She celebrated how great and joyful she had been feeling! She said that previously she had felt stressed 80% of the time and happy 20%

of the time but that this had now flipped and she may even feel happy more than 80% of the time! She is a beautiful example of someone who shows up and puts all the methods I teach into practice. I'm so proud of her!

Back to when I felt hurt by their triggers - it does boil down to the whole point of this book, doesn't it? When we feel criticised by others, we feel like we are getting something wrong. Or we might try and make the other person 'wrong' to feel better about ourselves. But what if both of us could be right. What if we were all doing our best with the information available to us? What if this person finds it hard to access joy? Or what if they had just been feeling a bit down? Perhaps they couldn't connect with someone who is so *in your flippin' face joyful*. That would be fair enough. They are not wrong for feeling whatever they feel about it. With the information available to them, maybe they are doing their absolute best.

This isn't about me and the person who criticised my course and online presence, or me and the woman who emailed me. This is between *me* and *me*. This is about my love and approval of myself. This is about me knowing deep down that I am not doing *anything* wrong openly sharing love and joy. This is about me choosing to continue to prioritise and seek out joy every day because I know from experience that this life is fleeting and precious and when things are good I wanna *celebrate* that!

It's about me having a healthy boundary in terms of where I end and where other people begin; and not over identifying with other people's judgments of their version of me.

Where do you need to establish healthy boundaries?

To care less what people think?

To say 'No' more, without feeling guilty?

To honour your needs and time more?

How much more joy could you create if you allowed yourself to say no to things that make you feel sh*t?

Further resources

Melodie Beattie – *Codependent No More*

Faith Harper – *Unf*ck My Boundaries*

The drama triangle I reference was created by Stephen Karpman

Nature

As my connection with nature has strengthened over the years, so has my connection with joy. Nature slows me down, fills my body with a soothing frequency and puts things in perspective; it helps me feel connected to something bigger than me. When Finn was terminally ill and deteriorating, I used to make tea and go to watch the sunrise on the beach before he woke. It nourished my soul and reminded me of the beauty out there in the wider world. The sea soothed my mind and restored my energy. It enabled me to keep going. When he died, we returned to our favourite place for natural beauty. We travelled to New Zealand, the bright blue of Lake Tekapo, the snowy mountains and glaciers, and the tracks of Abel Tasman. One morning in Abel Tasman, there was a dawn chorus at around 4am. It was absolutely unbelievable. I could cry calling it to mind. I couldn't believe my ears. It was like the most sophisticated, mysterious, and intricate symphony written by some genius.

I've become fairly outdoorsy of late! Is that just part of growing older? We own paddle boards and go canoeing with our friends. We go to the beach nearly every day. We have a lovely garden. Living close to the sea has been such a gift these last 6 years. There was a beautiful poem about nature and grief that someone sent us when Finn died. It described how soothing it is to go down to the river, to get close to nature, and that creatures aren't worried and in a state of anticipation, they're in the present moment. Nature has been so supportive of me over the last decade.

Connecting to the mystery and allowing myself to feel in awe of nature is vital to me. When Finn died, I felt so connected to a sense of wonder. In his interview with Barack Obama, David Attenborough said that his favourite part of nature was the underwater world and that if he could show anyone anything it would be that.

I suppose this is the sort of wonder, beauty, and joy that people miss out on when they are constantly worried about keeping themself safe; when their bodies are in 'fight or flight' trying to protect themself. How much beauty have you missed out on when you have been consumed by a focus on anxiety?

I long for every reader to let go of the fear. To let themself wonder at this amazing universe and to use their energy to create a joyous existence here in this incredible natural world we are part of. To be open to the miracles of nature.

You don't need to trek in a different country or buy a wetsuit or schedule a weekend hike to incorporate a nature practice into your daily life. It can be little and often, slowly taking a bit more time to see the natural beauty that's already there on your doorstep. Together, my friend Aline Hill and I have run 'Self-compassion and Gratitude in Nature' courses, and I want to credit her with the following tasks which she has taught.

Task 1. Find a spot in nature and time 5 or 10 minutes. Just sense what is there. Try to take your mind out of it and just experience what you can feel, see, smell and touch.

Task 2. Find a spot in nature. Find one thing to focus on. Stay with it for as long as you want then notice something else and stay with that for as long as you want and repeat for 15-20 minutes or for however long feels good (remember you cannot get this wrong!).

Here is an example of what this looks like for me:

Go to the beach. For one minute, observe the ripples in the sea caressing the sand. For a minute, follow some birds flying in the sky. For two minutes, close my eyes and feel the wind on my face. For 30 seconds, sense the cold in my body. For two minutes, watch the clouds moving across the sky. For a minute, watch the crows or the seagulls on the sand.

211

Task 3. Embody what you see in nature. You might see the clouds slowly moving across the sky; close your eyes and imagine feeling light and floaty and embody what that would feel like. Then perhaps imagine the flow of the sea and embody what that might feel like to you.

When we feel disconnected from nature, sitting indoors and looking out, we cannot connect to any of the benefits or joy that might be waiting out there. When we look out of the window and see it is raining, it's a leap of the imagination to think of ourselves jumping joyfully at the sea's edge as the rain peppers the sand. When we see that the sun isn't shining today, it can be hard to imagine the enveloping, cocooning joy of walking in a forest. We need to get out there to feel it. Begin at your doorstep and take it from there.

Further resources

Some of the nature practices I have described were adapted by my friend Aline and inspired by the work of Joseph Barrett Cornell.

You can find out more about the work Aline does here:

www.forestschooltraining.co.uk

Ruth Allen – *Grounded: How connection with nature can improve our mental and physical wellbeing*

Your body

The difference in my anxiety now that I take better care of my body and nourish myself more is huge. I drink less, meditate daily, and eat *relatively* healthily. Nowadays, I drink one cup of coffee in the morning. I try to make sure I get lots of sleep.

Looking back, my anxiety was at its worst during the period of my life when I would drink excessively and occasionally take recreational drugs. I would act in ways when I was under the influence that I would never act when sober. The substances helped me feel better in the short term but in the long term were so unhelpful. With alcohol, I used to call it 'beer fear' or 'booze blues'... that awful feeling the day after drinking when you can't quite remember what you did but you're convinced it was probably shameful and embarrassing. In my journey, my emotional and physical wellbeing have always been entwined. My transformative experience of Nia shows how caring for my body was central to my healing.

When I look back, I can see how my body was so often in that state of fight or flight. As I've said, with fight or fight our bodies prepare to fight or run away - and when we don't do either of those things we can be left with excess adrenaline in our bodies. Moving our bodies and releasing adrenaline can help us to complete the cycle and return to feeling calm again, creating equilibrium.

How to begin to look after your body in more healthy ways? Move your body - dance, walk, run, cycle, row, hike, do whatever *feels good*, but move your body! Nourish your body. Honour your body. Be grateful for your body. Celebrate your body.

Don't punish your body with exercise - celebrate your body with exercise. Meditate on how grateful you are for your body. Rewrite old stories that involve body negativity.

As with nature, new habits don't have to be monumental or daunting. Begin by connecting with your body in little ways, through your senses. Try the following exercise:

Step 1. Put on some beautiful music which conjures up positive emotions then call to mind some of your favourite sights or write them down. What do you love to **look** at?

My sleeping baby is right next to me. What an amazing sight. How lucky am I to have eyes that can witness all his little creases and curves and softness.

I love to look at wide open horizons, the sea, flowers and trees. I love hydrangeas, fuschia, poppies, wisteria, lakes, rivers, birds. I love sunrises and sunsets. I love seeing people really smile and connect and I adore seeing joy in people's eyes, seeing their laughs, observing their little ways, their little idiosyncrasies. How amazing are our eyes? I love looking into my husband's eyes, sharing a quiet moment, his smile. I love art! I love looking at beautiful paintings and I love watching musicians get totally lost in their music and their worlds.

Step 2. What about your ears? Call your favourite **sounds** to mind or write them down.

I love listening to the wind blowing in the leaves, rainfall. I remember us driving back from Liverpool as a kid after visiting the grandparents, late at night in a sleeping bag all snuggly warm listening to rain falling on the car roof. I love the sound of my babies' voices. I love the sound of my parents' laughter. I love the sound of the violin, the piano, the cello, the human voice, especially harmonies. I love the sound of hedgehogs eating; we had some in the garden with babies recently… the sound they make when they are eating! Cats purring, dogs doing those cute noises asking for something. That dawn chorus in New Zealand. Miraculous!

Step 3. What about **scents**? Call them to mind or write them down.

Freshly baked bread! The smell of chips and vinegar from a chippy. Lavender, my favourite smell of all time. Lemongrass. That smell when it's been raining... there's a word for it... petrichor! The smell of babies' heads. Freshly cut grass. Mint. *Coffeeeeee*! An outdoor fire...

Step 4. What about your favourite **tastes**?

Coffee (again). Fresh bread, homemade pizza, olives, avocado, basil, garlic. Thai food! Yum! Mum's homemade cashew nut roast, Grandma's lentil bake, my husband's sticky tofu, and salt and pepper chips, fresh fruit! Raspberries, blueberries yum yum yum! Cherry Bakewell cake, a nice glass of wine or a gin & tonic...

Our bodies are supposed to experience pleasure. They deserve it!

For years during my worst anxiety, I didn't really pay attention to all of this glory. My body felt like a cage I was trapped in. I didn't feel much pleasure. I didn't feel relaxed or at home. Each time I exited a social situation, my body felt relieved, like I had always somehow *just* managed to escape. Life felt constantly threatening.

It doesn't feel threatening any more - it feels amazing, enticing, exciting. I feel *alive*. I felt almost dead inside for years. I went through the motions, but I didn't allow myself to feel. I hated my emotions. I hated my body for how it reacted to my emotions.

I love my husband's take on how life is supposed to be this incredible sensual experience. He believes, and acts accordingly, that we are supposed to be fully present to our senses, and to witness and *sense* the beauty of nature.

Start a mission today to learn to *love* your body. Be grateful, be light. Don't take it too seriously. Remember how debilitated I used to be by my fear of blushing? These days, I don't think people will even notice. I smile and relax and love myself and *allow* myself. We are entitled to feel embarrassment and it makes us so beautiful, human, and vulnerable *just like everyone else*.

Another interesting thing to mention about the body is mindset about exercise. I meet so many women who exercise almost as a form of 'punishment' for the food they have eaten, in order to get the shape of their body 'right'.

What about exercising to nourish, celebrate and love your body? This is the reason I love Nia so much. I don't even view it as exercise. I do it because it feels absolutely amazing to my body, mind, emotions and spirit.

I implore you to find a way of moving your body that feels *fun,* that you look forward to, that enriches you spiritually and emotionally. This holistic way of 'exercising' is *sustainable!* If you have never found a way of moving your body that you love, keep looking! It could be cycling, trampolining, dancing, running, hiking, walking; joining a group to enjoy these things alongside other people. It could change your life.

Further resources

For more of an insight into my husband Neil's perspective on a sensory experience of life you can listen to an interview I conducted with him during my time at Wellbeing Radio:

https://podtail.com/en/podcast/wellbeing-radio/dr-sarah-madigan-loved-up-on-life-episode-5/

Sonya Renee Taylor – *The Body Is Not An Apology: The Power of Radical Self-Love*

Comparanoia.

If I had a pound for every person I've met, worked with or read about who thinks that everyone else has their sh*t together and that they are a failure, I'd be a billionaire. We can make up stories that say *'look at how amazingly everyone else is doing'*. Or we can recognise those stories for what they are: completely unfounded.

Everyone experiences all the emotions! *Everyone feels fear.* Everyone feels shame. Everyone feels sad. Everyone feels angry. *You are not alone.* There is nothing wrong with you.

I used to think that *everyone* was coping so well with anxiety and that I was such a failure. I used to constantly look at people who were seemingly coping well in life and use it as proof of what a failure I was.

Sound familiar?

Everyone has their thing. They might be incredibly anxious about something you find really easy. They may feel sad rather than fearful. They might be happy and loving life *and* this still doesn't mean there's anything wrong with you. People could look at me and compare themselves to me when I'm public speaking - and have no idea how much anxiety used to swamp me.

Stop comparing yourself to others.

I used to undermine other people's struggles and tell a story they weren't as bad as mine because there was something wrong with me. I've had tonnes of clients do the same thing! Literally hundreds if not thousands of clients.

It's time to stop this *story* and get real.

There is nothing wrong with you.

'Comparanoia' is when we compare ourselves to others and feel paranoid that we are not as good or worthy (Davide Di Georgio).

If we knew *we couldn't get it wrong,* we wouldn't need to compare ourselves. We could celebrate others and ourselves, trusting that we are all enough.

It is almost like we believe there is a finite amount of *enoughness.* If someone else is great, then it impacts on me and makes me less great. What if we trusted there was an abundance of love and worthiness, everywhere; that we can all be loved and worthy!

I wonder about the role of social media in all this. Did people still compare themselves to each other before the days of Instagram? I'm sure it still happened; we are a competitive species by nature. But social media is a good place to begin to clean up these stories. Let's start celebrating ourselves and others more. Let's only follow people on social media who *light us up*! Those who inspire us and fill us with joy. Let's remember that when people share snapshots of their lives, they are just that. It's never the whole picture.

People used to comment on how amazingly Neil and I were doing after Finn died. I mean, we did and are doing amazingly *and* there were horrific times. I didn't take photos of those moments and share those moments, though. I don't want to focus on or spread distress. People generally share the good stuff, and that's *not all the stuff.*

Start honouring yourself and your life more. Start celebrating yourself more. Stop comparing yourself to others.

We can all be winners!

It's important to take it a step further. Our patterns live in the body. There is no point in challenging our stories without thinking about the role of our body. It can also speed up any healing when we target the body and the nervous system as well as our mindset. Our social media consumption affects not only our state of mind but also our bodies and it can be helpful to understand how 'comparanoia' impacts the autonomic nervous system.

I have talked about how the body prepares itself for survival by either fighting, running away, or freezing. To remind you, polyvagal theory is a theory of the ways the autonomic nervous system works. What I find helpful is how it outlines a hierarchy of the three biological pathways of 'response' that our bodies exhibit. It highlights how we move in and out of 'engagement, mobilization and collapse' in response to our daily experiences. They hold that the stories that we tell (I have spoken a lot about stories) are created in autonomic states and that 'state creates story'.

When we compare ourselves to others, a number of things happen. We can lose hope, become self-critical and tell a story that 'I'm never going to measure up.' This is a story of disconnection and it immobilises us. It is a form of self-sabotage and means that our bodies go into a 'helpless' state where there is 'no point in taking action, because I'm not good enough'. I'm sure you can think of times in life where you have experienced this. This is referred to as 'dorsal vagal collapse' in polyvagal theory.

When our autonomic state becomes more mobilised, and we want to take action but we still don't feel good enough, we may start to feel competitive with others. We may judge and criticise others (and ourselves) and tell a different story: 'I need to be better than others'. We are taking more action than when we are in 'dorsal vagal collapse' but our bodies are still feeling threatened and in a state of separation from others. This is referred to as 'sympathetic mobilization'. We feel as though we need to protect ourselves.

When we are living life from a place of '*I cannot get this wrong*', we are more likely to be in connection with others, with stories of connection rather than protection or disconnection. We are able to connect, cooperate and collaborate. We have self-compassion, compassion for others, and tell a new story along the lines of 'I'm curious about the world and my place in it'. We don't feel the need to run away, or fight, or freeze. We don't immobilise. We don't compete. We can celebrate ourselves and others. Everyone can succeed!

Further resources

Deb Dana - *Polyvagal Flip Chart – Understanding The Science of Safety*

What if it goes right!

Stop focusing on what could go wrong. Become obsessed with what could go right. Choose to view everything as working out perfectly. The quote above my desk reads, 'Things are always working out for me.' It keeps me focused on the joy of possibility every day.

Do not engage in 'catastrophic thinking'. It will come up. Choose not to partake. Yesterday, I was speaking with my parents. I had arranged a retreat with clients. Complications had arisen because, well, Covid times. We were trying to work out what to do; do we cancel or go ahead? My mum expressed her fear that the people who'd booked to come on the retreat might sue me if I cancelled. Catastrophic thinking alert! To be fair, she didn't realise they were my friends. Dad also thinks that basically everyone is gonna get scammed by dodgy people online. Fear can be contagious! I took a deep breath.

Don't engage.

You can choose to trust that things are going to work out.

You can choose to trust the universe.

I disagreed with my folks, made a gentle joke then swiftly changed the subject!

Remember the saying I told you about towards the start of the book? *'Worrying is like praying for something bad to happen'.*

Imagine all that energy going into something positive? Letting yourself see your dream vision for life?

I was once talking to someone about self-compassion and they said, 'I just don't think I've got time for it.' I asked, 'Do you find the time to beat yourself up?' They laughed. Direct your thoughts in a different direction. Become totally vigilant - not about avoiding anxiety but about focusing on joy. About choosing joy. About leaning into what could go right, what could be perfect. Visualise it, expect it and celebrate it even before it happens.

Cognitive Behavioural Therapy

Although CBT wasn't what helped me transform my anxiety, I have worked with hundreds of people who have benefited from this extremely well evidenced approach, so I wanted to take the time to outline how you can put it into practice. There are many branches of CBT but I am just going to outline what I think will serve you best, from my experience both as a clinical psychologist and as a transformational coach.

The 5 systems model can be helpful for illustrating this approach and the relationship between thoughts, feelings, behaviours, physical feelings and the environment. It looks like this:

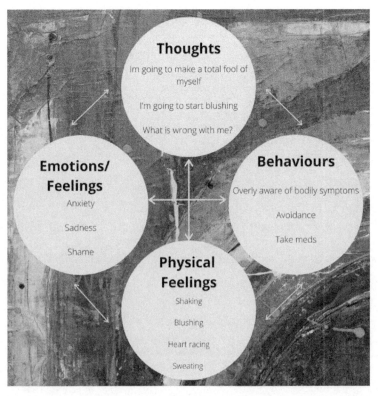

The 5th system is the **Environment - in this case, for previous me, it could be almost any social situation.** The idea is that all of these areas feed into each other and exacerbate the other area. So, one negative thought could elicit a small amount of anxiety. Then the anxiety makes the thoughts become more negative. Then these thoughts make your body respond with more severe physiological symptoms and the thoughts become more negative. This affects your behaviours and feelings even more and it's one *vicious cycle of anxiety and shame!*

This model is helpful to understand what is happening, but it didn't help me to turn my anxiety around. The diagram above is a very typical example of how my thought process used to look. Now, though, my system looks radically different:

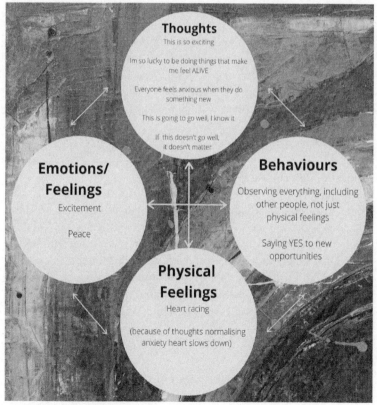

Thoughts

This is so exciting

Im so lucky to be doing things that make me feel ALIVE

Everyone feels anxious when they do something new

This is going to go well, I know it

If this doesn't go well, it doesn't matter

Emotions/ Feelings

Excitement

Peace

Behaviours

Observing everything, including other people, not just physical feelings

Saying YES to new opportunities

Physical Feelings

Heart racing

(because of thoughts normalising anxiety heart slows down)

It can be really helpful to have an understanding of what your body is doing. When I feel anxious these days, I thank my body for trying to prepare me for fight or flight. And then I tell myself I don't need that part of me anymore. As I said, I imagine that part of me sitting by a fire and putting their feet up and *chilling out!*

It can also be helpful to think about how you can turn the vicious cycle around into a more positive one. For example, if you engage in behaviours such as dance and meditation, this leads you to release more positive feelings and physical sensations. This then leads to more positive thoughts and you can create a different *and glorious cycle of joy!* You can create momentum in the opposite direction.

In my experience, CBT can be extremely helpful for *some* people. In case this is you, I am going to take you deeper with this and outline how you might want to have a go at using it to challenge your thoughts or to change your behaviour. There are two methods often used by therapists; one is called 'thought challenging' and the other is called 'behavioural activation'.

Thought challenging

I have friends and clients who have found huge value in this exercise. Take a piece of paper and write down a list of the thoughts that are leading you to feeling anxious. After you have made a list of the thoughts, you decide which thought elicits the strongest emotion. Underline that thought. Rate on a scale of 0-100 how much you believe that thought. Write down the emotions that it brings up for you. Here's an example from my life:

I hate presenting
I am so scared I will make a fool of myself - 90%

People will judge me
I will look so unprofessional
Maybe I will take medication to help

Emotions it brings up - fear, anxiety, shame, hopelessness

Then it's time to become an investigator. You have to find evidence for and against this thought. Let's call it the 'heavy thought'.

Evidence *for*
I once did a presentation before and got so nervous I had to leave the room

Evidence *against*
There are many other times when I have coped with presentations
Even the time when I didn't cope, nothing bad happened, people were just really understanding
I had a lot going on at that time and it's understandable I felt anxious
Most people feel anxious during presentations
Often, I feel worse beforehand then once it starts I just get into it
If I appear anxious maybe rather than people thinking I'm a fool, they might think I'm more relatable
I have done loads of things in my life that made me anxious and been OK
It doesn't really matter to me if people judge me negatively anyway
I can cope with physical sensations, they won't harm me, they may peak but then they will subside
I always feel great afterwards
When I focus on what I'm doing and not on how I'm doing it, it really helps

Then you develop and write down a more balanced thought. It often looks like a combination of both the evidence for and against. Rate how much you believe this new balanced thought. Then you write down the emotions this brings up. Something like this:

Balanced thought
Even though that one time I had to leave the room, there are numerous other occasions when I have coped with presenting. It's normal to get nervous. I can cope with physical sensations of anxiety. I will focus on the presentation and on the message and not on my anxiety. I will feel great afterwards and I will celebrate. This is a great opportunity to share knowledge with people and develop my confidence. - 70%

Emotions this brings up - excited, hopeful, calm.

You can also re-rate how much you believe the original 'heavy thought'. Maybe it would go down from a 90% to a 30% or something.

When using this model with clients, I would go further and ask:

What do you *want* to feel?
I want to feel inspired, alive, fun, joyful…

What 'stories' would you need to tell to feel those feelings?
I have such great ideas to share in this presentation, people are going to love what I'm going to share. My positive energy will be contagious.

How do you want the presentation to go?
I want it to be interesting and fun and engaging.

What would you have to believe about yourself to create this?
I am powerful and confident and able. I am inspiring. My passion is contagious.

What actions are going to support this?

I will dance in the morning before the presentation to get in a good frame of mind.

I will start visualising it going really well. I will imagine people smiling and telling me how much they loved it.

I will imagine the positive ripples from the presentation spreading out.

I will imagine me feeling excited and happy.

I believe so much in the importance of focus. Of not only balancing out anxious thoughts or stories but developing new and more positive ones. Taking it one step further, not only to balance out the anxiety but to empower yourself to create the ideal outcome.

Further resources

For more info on the 5 systems model I reference, look up Chris Williams - *Overcoming Depression: a 5 areas approach.*

Lucy's story

I will now share a case study to illustrate someone else's journey in overcoming her fear of getting things wrong. Lucy is a client of mine and has been for the past 18 months on and off - she is now training to be a coach with me too! She is in her forties and is a Mum of two gorgeous kids. She is a great example of someone (so many of my clients share this!) who previously had a deep fear of getting things wrong.

This would play out in Previous Lucy in the following ways:

- She would receive an email or text and assume that she had done something wrong! Before she'd even read the message, she would get a sinking feeling that she was about to be 'told off' or made to feel bad.

- As a parent she would constantly worry about getting it wrong.

- She wouldn't try new things, for example hobbies or sports, out of a fear of getting things wrong whilst learning (i.e. not allowing herself to be learning!). She feared the humiliation of looking silly and of others judging her.

- Because of these beliefs, she attracted people into her life (and put up with them!) who felt critical of the way she did things and who did want to 'punish' her for doing this wrong.

This is how things now look for Present Lucy:

- Lucy identified the one activity when she has never felt wrong – dancing! She now chooses to do more and more of it, which she says helps with everything. 'Somehow, dancing has always saved me. I knew I could not get that wrong. I spent some heavy years dancing in dark and sweaty drum & bass nightclubs where people really didn't care what you were doing and I felt completely at home, as though I was my true self. I will literally dance anywhere I am and never care about getting it wrong. I only do what makes my body feel good'. Whenever Lucy wants to feel better she dances - it is one of her main ways of accessing joy and it also helps her to embody the belief that 'I cannot get this wrong'.

- Lucy now has distance between herself and her story of 'I cannot get this wrong'. Through coaching she has shined a light on it, she is aware of it and this has empowered her, and enabled her not to act it out - she is now conscious and can choose something different.

- Lucy says that the belief still crops up, but she can override it now.

- Lucy uncovered that beneath her fear of getting something wrong was a belief that she wouldn't be loved. She tells herself a new story now that she is lovable no matter what.

- Lucy no longer views herself or her actions in a black and white way. She celebrates experiences and learns from them. She gave me the example of an interview that she'd told herself she 'got wrong' because she didn't get the job. Lucy now reframes the experience, celebrating how it worked out perfectly because it led her to the job where she met my husband and then me! And how she is now creating the perfect job for herself as a coach!

231

- Lucy has an underlying new belief that she is good enough. Making mistakes or getting things wrong no longer confirm her belief that she isn't good enough. She has freedom! She allows herself to make mistakes and loves herself and her imperfections. She says, 'everyone is human and we are all doing the best we can'.

- With her kids, she no longer slips into 'I've shouted at the kids and this means I'm a terrible Mum'. Instead, she is forgiving of herself. 'I was angry, annoyed, that's cool, I'm human!' She no longer judges her actions as 'not right, not good'.

- With her own parents, she also feels less fearful of their judgments of her as wrong, and so she is more able to enjoy her relationship with them.

- Lucy also no longer judges herself for spending money in a way she used to.

Being a parent

It's likely that nearly every single parent in the world worries if they are getting it 'right'. Becomes wracked with guilt over long work hours, too much screen time, shouting at their kids, not feeding them healthy food. The list is endless, no?

Imagine if we told ourselves as parents that we were getting it perfectly right. We were not getting it wrong.

Imagine if, instead of beating ourselves up and then probably feeling terrible and missing out on golden opportunities of connection and fun with our kids (thereby in a sense creating what we fear), we instead leant into the absolute deliciousness of our lives and time with our kids.

Imagine if we trusted that we were enough. That our love for them was the main thing. That the other stuff was OK. That, actually, our kids do not need perfect parents. Imagine if our expectations of ourselves were loving and realistic?

Dear parent,

There is no such thing as getting it right as a parent. You are doing your best. Trust me and child development specialists: YOU ARE ENOUGH! You are good enough!

You do not need to be perfect. It's not what your children need.

Child Development specialist Suzanne Zeedyk writes,

'In the face of unremitting demands, failure is inevitable'.

You cannot succeed as a parent all the time. You cannot get it right every time and it's not what your children need you to do

233

anyway. It wouldn't prepare them for life. They need to learn how to manage disappointment, anger, and frustration, which they can practice with you, when you fail them by limiting their chocolate intake...

They don't need all the things you beat yourself up about not doing. They just need your love. They need YOU to feel like you are enough. To trust that you are getting it right enough of the time!

They need your joy more than they need you to be perfect. They need you to show them how to create joy. They need you to love. To love yourself, your life, them, to celebrate it all. To seek out JOY every single day, in the tiny things and the big things, but mainly the tiny things (and on the days when that's not possible, to be gentle with yourself and trust).

They need you to engage with life, to seek out the beauty. To take adventures. To remember what you love. They need you to pay attention to when your body feels great, and do those things! Again and again! They need you to allow yourself to be imperfect and to love yourself anyway. They need to learn compassion for themselves and others.

They need you to get it wrong and make mistakes. They need to be angry at you. They need to fall out and then learn how to repair. They need you to get it wrong again and again and to say sorry.

They need you to be gentle with yourself on the days that you don't feel joyful and to model how to care for yourself during these times. They need you to love yourself unconditionally.

It is time to end the generational trauma that has likely been passed down to you for generations, to heal the ancestral wounds, to release shame, to learn to love MORE, love better, love love love.

Months after writing this chapter, I had an outing at the park and want to share with you an example of my *parenting expectations* in practice…

Oh, my goodness. Today I got into such a tiz at the park. 'Comparanoia' kicked in big time. My dear friend was teaching an outdoor Nia dance class. It was a gorgeous sunny day in late September. There were 7 or so women and a bunch of kids all running around and playing together. There was also a big pond, *which stressed me the f*ck out!*

The kids were running around freely. There was another wee one of a similar age to Isaac. His Mama didn't seem worried about the pond.

Cue inner dialogue: '*Why am I worried about the pond? Why can't I be a relaxed chilled earth mother like Lynsey? Why can't I relax? I have paid a tenner and all I'm doing is running around after Isaac for an hour. I'm pretending to be a monster having fun but I'm only doing it to stop him from going in the pond. I'm so anxious. For f*ck sake. Lynsey's kids are gonna be so well adjusted, they are also having the best time. I am disrupting Isaac's fun and I'm probably going to turn him into a nervous wreck! All the other mums are probably judging me and wondering why on earth I can't just chill out, they are looking at me and judging! I want to run away, this is sh*t.*'

It was day 1 of my period and it was also the day after the anniversary of Finn's death. So, I probably wasn't in my most relaxed state. The tense, anxious, resistant state I was in gained so much momentum. I just kept making myself worse and worse. Instead of just allowing myself to do what I felt was appropriate in that situation, I judged myself so harshly and resisted all the emotions.

After the dance, we sometimes have a relaxed picnic together in the park. I made my excuses and headed to the play park just to get away from the pond and away from people and to escape my fantasy of being judged (they weren't judging me). I phoned my husband and Neil said, '*Yeah, I have noticed other parents are more relaxed than us and maybe it's something we need to think about.*'

I wasn't in the place to hear this. I absolutely do reflect on the impact of Finn's death on my parenting, and I want to consciously make efforts not to give Isaac raging health anxiety. But I just needed some love. Neil then had to go because he was waiting on a work phone call. How was that perfect? It probably diverted us away from an argument! I desperately called Naomi, for some reassurance. It was exactly what I needed. I'm so lucky to be so supported by patient, wonderful friends.

'Sarah, trust yourself. You know your child. I would have been the same if Micah was three years old because he would have jumped in! You know Isaac. Don't worry about it'. Instantly, my body relaxed and I started to feel so much better.

'Yeah, you're right, it's not the end of the world, is it.'

She basically spent 5 minutes loving on me and understanding and making me feel like I *wasn't getting it wrong!*

It is fascinating writing this book and thinking about how deep this idea that we are getting it wrong goes. I knew that was at the bottom of it that day. A fear that I was getting it totally wrong, doing the wrong thing, making the wrong decisions, failing Isaac, being a sub-standard human.

Naomi in her inimitable Milton Keynes accent that sounds Cockney to me: 'Anyway darls, I mean it's not like you were barking at him and telling him that something *awful* was about to happen was it, don't worry about it'....

Me: 'Naomi! Wanna f*cking bet!? Haha! That is exactly what I was doing.'

236

Hilarity ensued, we laughed our absolute heads off and that release was exactly what I needed.'Naomi I literally did, I was shouting at him and telling him to stop going near the pond, I threatened and bribed and told him I would eat all the chocolate and not leave any for him if he didn't stop going near the pond!'

I was desperate! Powerless! Using anything I could think of! I was also telling him that he would drown and it would be awful. I maybe even used the word awful. OH GOD.

Isaac was then upset obviously, I was a wreck and the beautiful, sunny, cold morning we had had on the beach which was so calm and carefree felt like a lifetime ago!

Naomi reminded me of an article by Suzanne Zeedyk. I had interviewed Suzanne about it on the radio. 'Sarah! It's OK to not be perfect! It's OK to 'get it wrong.' Like Suzanne says, *making up is more important than messing up.*'

I talked to Isaac about how tense and worried I'd felt in my body, and how that made me grumpy and made me shout and that I was sorry. I also talked to him about how important it is not to go to the edge of the pond. He had obviously worked out how much power he had over me with regard to the flipping pond and was running away, standing at the edge of it and staring at me! He probably felt like a powerful emperor. There I was, this quivering wreck threatening to steal his chocolate if he didn't do what I told him.

Naomi and I laughed about how maybe my neuroses would make Isaac really interesting and lead to him writing some interesting music one day. It was just the conversation I needed to get some distance from the situation and to be able to shift from a stuck place of beating myself up and hating on myself.

Again, a few weeks later I am editing the book and re-reading this chapter and thinking about how, despite all the times Isaac has too much screen-time, or I shout at him, or I'm distracted, or

I am not fun enough, or I am boring and too controlling… he thinks I'm the best.

Last night as I put him to bed, we were snuggled up. Then he did his usual routine of prolonging the waking hours, so I turned my back to him and we lay there. Then he said (makes me teary),

'Mummy, I like you so much.'

Further resources

This is the fabulous article by Suzanne Zeedyk regarding how we don't need to be perfect parents, and our children don't even need that!:

https://suzannezeedyk.com/fed-up-of-being-cooped-up-in-lockdown-with-the-kids/

You can also access an interview that I did with her about this article here:

https://www.facebook.com/wellbeingradio/videos/9206448 68395312

Honest conversations with our children

I have worked with many parents and have witnessed many conversations between parents, or had friends come to me directly to ask for advice about tackling challenging topics with our children. Most parents want to protect their children which is really natural. It is an instinct to protect children, to guard their innocence. Throughout my work, I have found it helpful to share the following idea with parents:

When you are too fearful to talk about something, this is scarier for the child than if you were just to talk about the thing.

Often, I will talk to parents about how best to broach difficult subjects such as divorce, death, grief, harm, illness. What I have said time and time again to people is that, in some ways, it matters less what you say, it just matters that you are saying something; that you are not avoiding.

When we avoid difficult subjects, this is what children do: they know something is wrong because they can sense your fear, but they assume it must be really bad if you are not talking about it and they fill in the gaps with their fantasies.

Conversely, when children pick up that you can cope, that you can talk about it, that you can deal with it, even if you choose the wrong words, or bumble your way through a difficult subject, it is *incredibly containing* for a child. It also stops you feeling stressed about not having said anything, or not knowing what to say, and you can preserve this energy.

It is obviously important to speak to children about topics in a developmentally-appropriate way, in language that is clear, unambiguous and that they understand. For example, not to talk about topics that are too adult or scary or to talk about death excessively around them, and not to talk about your own death excessively. Only last week, Isaac asked me and Neil when we were going to die. We had been watching the film 'Up'. I said, 'it's such a long, long way away that we don't need to worry about that for now'. I didn't change the subject or say that it wasn't going to happen. I just said that it was going to happen a long, long way away so that he didn't feel scared about it.

We also, of course, have talked to him a lot about Finlay. We don't avoid talking about him, Isaac knows that he died. We have been careful to make it clear to Isaac (and at the time of Finn's death, to the other children in our life, his cousins who when he died were 12 and 7) that most children are healthy and it is really unusual for babies to die, but that sometimes it does happen. It was important for his cousins to know that it was not something they needed to worry about, but that it was really sad that it was happening to Finlay.

Helping children to embrace 'difference': moving away from fear

Some conversations don't relate to a big upheaval in a child's life, but to the ongoing parental role of helping our children to find their place in the world. This chapter links directly to the discussions about joy in the face of discrimination. How do we best equip our children to celebrate the diversity of the world around them? How do we speak to them about difference as it relates to either themselves or to people they know? How do we move the next generation away from the fear that we've been conditioned into?

During my training as a clinical psychologist, I interviewed young people in foster care as part of my doctoral thesis. There had been anecdotal evidence that for young people in care *'feeling different'* was a significant issue, but no systematic research had taken place around this. I interviewed nine 12-16 year olds who were in foster care in Scotland. The process was such a privilege and a challenge. The point of this research was to help the adults around these young people to connect with the textures of the emotional experiences these young people were having. It was also to think about how, more widely in society, we could take collective responsibility for their emotional wellbeing. The goal of my thesis all those years back mirrors the goals of this book: to help people develop understanding and compassion, towards themselves and also towards others.

My research confirmed that *'feeling different'* was a major concern for these young people. 8 out of 9 of them talked openly about experiences of being 'made to feel different', of attempting to hide the fact they were in foster care from other people, of experiencing and witnessing people being bullied for being in care and for also feeling different themselves. Interestingly, underlying a lot of this was an apparent lack of awareness about what care was. One young person described getting bullied for being in care and then feeling guilty for having previously bullied someone for being in care, and not having really known what 'in care 'meant. Many of the young people said that other people just did not understand. This is an area we must pay attention to: to help other young people understand their peers from a young age; not to fear the difficult conversations; not to model avoidance.

Bruce Perry & Maidi Szalavitz talk about how our stress responses mean that we are much more focused on threat rather than on safety/ acceptance. This was apparent with the young people who were fearful of other people's responses to their foster care status and who were also dismissive of the times when people had responded well. They focused on possible threats. It is also relevant in terms of everything I am writing about in this book; all of us fearing *getting things wrong*. It relates to my fear of 'getting it wrong' bringing racism or discrimination into the book. No doubt I will have got it wrong in places, but I am more focused on the healing and beauty that could come from the book rather than the fear of making mistakes. People fear what it *means* about them as people when they mess up. They focus on the fear of being labeled as 'racist' or 'discriminatory' and this prevents focus on possibility; on being open and learning and understanding.

We need to model to children that it is OK to get things wrong. That it is OK to make mistakes and not to know things. To learn and then do better next time. To make brave decisions from the spaciousness of the heart; from a place of love and trust. We need to teach them not to make decisions solely from the brain, from a fearful place. Our brains are great at keeping us safe but sometimes we need to aim higher.

Re-reading my thesis now, in relation to this book, is fascinating; it is so relevant when considering our ability to create joy as individuals. One of the main things I talked about in the thesis was about how identity development is not solely an internal process; it is dynamic, fluid and it happens within

242

interactions, within relationships. My research confirmed the previous finding about how identity is socially bound. One of the young people actually said, 'if people say you're different, you're different'. As a society, our tolerance (or lack of) of 'difference' impacts on other people's experiences of themselves, and on their emotional worlds; on their experiences of anxiety and joy. This is especially true for young people who are going through a really important stage of identity development; whether they are in care, or a person of colour, or if they identify as LGBTQ+. How they are received by the world – by their peers and by the adults who interact with them on a daily basis - *matters*.

I wrote another article about 'making sense', where I explored how the young people talked about attempting to make sense of their foster care status. This, my supervisor Kate Paton and I suggested, could be considered as an extra development task of adolescence for kids in care. The energy it must take to make sense of all these experiences - on top of the energy to predict / be hypervigilant to other people's responses to foster care - no doubt impacts on young people's ability to concentrate in school; to relax, to have fun, to enjoy. So much of their focus is on keeping safe, and this prevents the central nervous system from connecting in a way that fosters those desirable states of joy. I imagine it is similar, the draining of energy and the strain on the central nervous system, for people experiencing other forms of discrimination.

But how do I talk to my child about people who are different to them? I don't want to *get it wrong*!

Although it feels like a dark subject, I will definitely be talking to Isaac about how some mummies and daddies can't look after their children well enough for various reasons. I will talk to him about how some children need to be looked after by other people and that some of the children in his class will probably be in this situation and that it is called being 'in care'.

243

I will talk to him about how some children haven't been given enough love. I will talk to him about how it can be harder for these children to love, and to form relationships; that it is harder for some children to keep calm and it is important we don't judge these people.

I will talk to him about the importance of being loving and kind to all children and to not fear those who are different to him. I will teach him the importance of the words he chooses to use, and the impact that these words can have on the people who hear them.

I will talk to him about how some of the children in his class may have a disability. They may have additional needs on top of the same needs that he has. That sometimes those children may behave in a way that draws attention to them and that kindness in words and actions towards these people are really important.

I'll explain that every single body is different and that doesn't make one body better or worse than another.

I'll teach him about tenderness and kindness to self and others, that it only ever takes one person to give another person hope and that he might never know when he is that person in someone else's life.

I will continue to talk to Isaac about racism. I will talk to Isaac about the racism in society and in policing; I will do it in a developmentally appropriate way but I won't shy away from these subjects.

Psychologist Bruce Perry once talked to one of his client's classmates about the impact of abuse and neglect on his client's brain. This had such a huge impact on the child's experience of school. His classmates actually understood why some of his behaviours were out of the ordinary and were able to access more empathy and understanding for him. Children cannot do this alone. We need to guide them. Pretending not to notice

244

difference helps no one. Teachers and parents all need to talk about the difficult subjects that we all too often avoid out of avoidance of pain and discomfort and due to a fear of 'getting it wrong'. It is better to try, to fear the shame of someone telling you that you got it wrong, than not to try at all.

Further resources

Perry & Szalavitz - *The boy who was raised as a dog: what traumatised children can teach us about loss, love and healing*

Perry & Szalavitz - *Born for love: why empathy is essential – and endangered*

Helping our kids to GET THINGS WRONG

Watch a little one learn. They try try try and try again. When children are really young, they don't care if they get something wrong. They just go again. We all started out like that.

Then, at some point for most kids, they become aware of being 'right 'or 'wrong'. We correct our children a lot. We take over when they are taking a long time to do something or when they are not doing it right. We step in to help them get it right. We then send them to school and there are more obvious 'right ' and 'wrongs'. As was my initial experience, significant praise and reward is given to the people who get things 'right'.

How can we help our kids to love themselves through making mistakes?

First and foremost? Love ourselves, model self-love, model allowing ourselves to try new things, model not caring about what others think, model trusting SELF and being in alignment with your values and letting go of the rest. Model making mistakes. Model taking risks.

Let kids help and let it take ages to complete a task. Encourage and praise them. Praise and celebrate the learning and the process not the quality of the outcome. (I'm working on this!).

If they ask you a question you don't know the answer for, tell them you don't know. Allow them to see you not knowing things and getting things wrong.

Also, on the days when you can't do these things, go easy on yourself.

Writing this book, with its focus on love and trust, led me time and again back to the adults who played the key roles in my own upbringing, to my own parents and grandparents.

I asked my folks to tell me about which areas of life they feel fearful in, and which areas they feel more trusting in.

It was so interesting. I feel like I learned a lot about my Mum. It gave me compassion for her with regards to her work-related anxiety. She said that she doesn't remember significant anxiety until medical school which, she said, was extremely stressful; anxiety and shame were used as a sort of method of teaching. Sounds terrifying. She also talked about the anxiety related to being on call and having to go out to people's houses in the middle of the night, not knowing what to expect, questioning if she could cope and feeling scared. Remembering life with a newborn baby, I can understand that stress of not knowing if your sleep is going to be disturbed or not.

Interestingly, Mum also talked about health anxiety with regards to me and my brother Chris. If we had a slight temperature as children, she always thought it was meningitis or something. I had always presumed that, being a doctor and all, she must have been calm about all things medical. It's hard to know what I would have been like without having had a terminally ill child. I always put some of my Isaac-related health anxieties down to what happened with Finn, but perhaps I would have been like that anyway, just like my mum!

It gave me great compassion with regards to that phone call I talk about in the chapter about 'containment'. I bet my work-related incident triggered a lot of fear and shame of my Mum's which she probably wanted to protect me from. I can't help but wonder about her predisposition to feeling anxious, though. Mum was raised by a woman who lost her own mother as a tiny baby (as a consequence of her birth), and who was very preoccupied with approval from others. My Grandma wanted to prove herself and her worth and focused on status. Mum also

247

talked about being bullied for having a funny accent, having moved from Liverpool to Canada and back. Those experiences of being bullied for being 'different' run deep, don't they? Interestingly, Mum, although super sociable, said that she dislikes big gatherings; not because they make her anxious but because they are boring!

Dad talked about feeling fearful of (in his words), in no particular order:

-   socialising (worse in formal settings)
-   forgetting names
-   eating out with young children
-   children's and grandchildren's future
-   singing/ playing in public
-   public speaking
-   being caught out generally, particularly by authorities
-   forgetting things when traveling
-   making mistakes professionally
-   being the centre of attention
-   confrontation
-   addressing issues with people

He then said that he would have to get back to me about his 'trust list' in 2 months, then joked about it being very short. Then he sent me this:

I trust myself, Liz, my children. I trust I'll be OK. I trust things I've tried and tested. I trust things in retrospect usually.

We often joke about how dad always dreads things then is pleasantly surprised by how they actually are. He often anxiously anticipates the future. In some ways, my husband Neil is similar to Dad. Even though Dad has a good deal of fear/ anxiety, he also has such a beautiful calm energy. Neil is the same. I once tried to explain 'mindfulness' to Neil:

248

Me: 'It's about being in the present moment and really deeply experiencing it. Not living in the past or anxiously anticipating the future, being really present to what is actually going on around you and sensing it deeply.'

Neil: 'Doesn't everyone just feel like that?'

Me (who had spent 20 years anxiously anticipating the future): 'NO NEIL! NO, THEY DON'T!'

I can see where both of my parents and their relationship with love and trust and anxiety have impacted on me. I adore big social gatherings though, unlike both of them. I think I definitely inherited or learned Dad's sort of social anxiety, although this laid fairly dormant until after the termination. I also love being the centre of attention! Although do I? I actually hated that on my wedding day.

And while we're looking at shared traits, how might my parents have been shaped by their own upbringings?

Grandma Joan was my mum's mum. Little grandma Joan was anxious. One time, she took a Valium because she was so anxious about watching my grandma Maisie iron clothes. They were both in their 80s and Maisie especially was a bit shaky. Joany obviously felt unable to speak up so she snuck off and took a friggin' Valium.

I've always laughed about this, but really. It's interesting, isn't it; she couldn't cope with the intense feelings. She always told me to 'float' if I felt worried. I wonder if she was referring to dissociation. Dissociation is when we disconnect from the present moment in an unconscious attempt to avoid distressing or traumatic feelings. You may have noticed people 'drift away' at times, mid conversation, or stare out of the window. This could just be them feeling bored (!) or it could be dissociation.

Grandma Joan was a beautiful woman. Soft and cuddly to me. Gentle and sweet; she was so loving. She was also critical. She was fixated on status. But I understand why. Her mother died when she was two weeks old of sepsis following complications caused by her birth. Imagine carrying the weight of that. Imagine the yearning. She told my mum about it, once; the yearning for her mama. Poor baby.

She probably yearned for her mother's approval. Like she yearned for validation and approval through status. I wonder what kind of story she told about herself with regards to her mum? What a challenging thing to live with. Her dad then died when she was 9. Grandma Joan loved us all, and she was also conditional at times with approval. She didn't feel good enough. She needed her family to be 'good enough' so that she could feel enough too, by proxy.

Dear grandma Joany whenever you are. I love you. I'm so sad your mama died and you never knew her smell and softness and embrace. I understand you looked for that love where you could. You criticised others because you felt critical of yourself. What a weight to carry. I actually felt so loved by you. Thank you. You had bought your little black wellies for our wedding on the Isle of Mull and you died just two months before. On my drive to the beach in my wedding dress, if I'm honest I just thought of you. I missed you. I wish I could snuggle you up. I hope the love of us all made at least part of your heart feel more than good enough. I heard about how amazing Aunty Gert was (Aunty Gert was Joan's Mum's sister, she brought my Grandma up after her dad died when she was orphaned at 9), *and I always admired how you just felt lucky for her love. I suppose if any of it had been at all different, I wouldn't be here writing this. I'm so glad you met grandpa Kev, he was one of the most positive people I've ever met. He adored you. I remember him showing me a photo of you, just so full of love and admiration for you. He asked me if I had ever seen anything more beautiful. I remember it like it was yesterday. I'm so glad you knew that deep love and approval from him. Thank you for your important role in my life. Hope you're snuggling up to my Finny somewhere in the sky. Sarah xxxxx*

There were definitely lots of messages about not getting things right. I think my mum carried that. There were definitely many messages about making sure things were done a certain way.

I would love these ancestral wounds to be healed now, for these feelings of 'not enough-ness' to end with this generation. I want to heal all this trauma so that it ends here.

'Ancestral wounds' have become a somewhat hot topic in the self-development world. It is also important to remember the ancestral strength and power that we inherited. I have a team of strong, loving, and powerful people behind me. I'm so lucky. Joan, thank you for passing lessons on gratitude and love and acceptance. How strong you were.

Grandma Maisie

This one, my dad's mum, was a warrior, too; so strong. She was hilarious. One time I ate some toast and left a tiny bit of jam on the side of the plate. There was one blackcurrant. Grandma Maisie said (insert Liverpudlian accent),

'Ey?! What did he ever do to you?!' Ha!

I used to phone her every night as a kid. I remember the old Huyton phone number 0514491740. I used to tell her about Mrs. Black, my teacher who was stern and uptight, and would compare me to my brother and ask why I couldn't be more like him (more quiet, shy, hard-working, well behaved).

Maisie used to threaten to come and wait for Mrs. Black at the school gates. She said, 'God didn't give you a mouth to sit there like a lemon, girl, use it!'

She encouraged my rebellious side. She snuck me sweets. She made me feel so, so, so loved. She made me feel like I couldn't get anything wrong in her eyes.

She also had a sharp tongue. It wasn't straightforward for my Mum, I acknowledge that, but Maisie adored me and she made me feel like there was *nothing* wrong with me.

Like I said, my dad was an introvert and I think at times struggled with my free and uninhibited nature. Mum wanted me to do ballet. I hated it and once wet myself in class and kept *not* getting moved up a class. She wanted me to wear pretty clothes. I remember a horrific velvet dress with shoulder pads that I wanted to throw on a bonfire.

But when I worried I was too much, Maisie told me to *be more*. She was like a little angel to me, who told me I was getting it just right.

When Finlay was diagnosed with a terminal illness, I was standing in the middle of the Meadows, a huge park in the centre of Edinburgh, close to the hospital where we'd just received the news. I called Maisie. I told her Finn was unlikely to live past his 2nd birthday. Her response, 'well, my love, we'll just have to make sure we give him the best two years ever.'

With those words I felt calmed. I felt contained. I felt like I could do it.

We had an end-of-life meeting for Finlay which I felt furious about. It was brilliant, though, amazing NHS. They asked me to imagine any regrets I would have about Finn's life. I said, 'I tried to take him to meet my grandma Maisie in Northwich but he was too poorly. And she's too poorly to visit him.' The nurses wanted to make it happen. I thought it was impossible.

They suggested hiring a private ambulance, I told Maisie, she texted back. 'Piss off. I'm not getting in a bloody ambulance, I'll make my own way up'.

There was no way she could do that. But she did take a load of morphine and my uncle Phil drove her up the motorway and met mum and dad who brought her to meet Finn.

It was one of the best days of my life. She stayed a few nights. She bathed his face with cotton wool buds. She fulfilled her parenting role towards him, and me. Her presence made me feel safe and stronger. She smoked ciggies in the back garden and met our gorgeous elderly neighbour Anna, who we miss.

She sang songs. She was *loud*. She took up space, it was perfect. Finn was scared of loud noises, but not of Maisie. He was fascinated. He knew she was his. One of us. She was my soul mate.

She couldn't make it up to the funeral, but I went to see her with Finn's ashes and they had a cuddle. She found out I was pregnant with Isaac before she died. She stroked my belly and was delighted. She guessed the babe was a girl. Because she was close to the end, we thought maybe she had psychic powers. My aunt and her bezzy mate Margy suggested having a gender scan before the funeral just for a laugh. I did and we saw that little willy straight away.

Isaac is loud and strong like Maisie. Maybe she passed the baton on to him. Everyone deserves a Maisie. Someone who threatens to come and beat up anyone who dare suggest they are getting something 'wrong'.

Maisie, thank you for helping me be myself.

Thank you for being loud.

Thank you for taking up space.

And giving me permission to do so as well.

She was so wise. She had a hard and abusive childhood. A violent father. She confided about so much to me. What a treasure and gift that adult-to-adult friendship we developed was. She was my home, my sanctuary, she made me laugh more than anyone, and I miss her so.

I dreamt a couple of nights ago that I was giving her a foot rub. What I wouldn't give.

When she was dying, I wanted so badly to go be with her. We have such a big family that I didn't want to overwhelm others or her. Thankfully, not long before, we had enjoyed a weekend just the two of us. I had tried and failed to take her to the shops in the wheelchair but we kept getting lost. We laughed so hard. You can imagine the hassle she gave me. October 2016. Just before I got pregnant with Isaac.

I texted Aunty Margy who was with her whilst she was dying and told her to tell her from me...

"Tell her to let go. Tell her ilymtylm. (Our secret code for I love you more than you love me). Tell her to go and snuggle my baby Finn and look after him.'

The world without that voice, that loud Scouse voice, is not the same.

But what about when parents weren't good enough

Some parents really fail their children. I worked with these children for years as a psychologist, children with the most harrowing of backgrounds. In these circumstances, it was my experience that actually often the parents aren't given enough accountability during the conversations with the children, due to the lack of ability of the system to sit with the pain of what happened. Sometimes children are told by health professionals *'your Mum was poorly, she did love you.'* This is not what a young person who has been physically or sexually abused by their parent needs to hear. When children think that their parents were just poorly and that love equals abuse, how distressing and confusing. It leads to children internalising the pain and abuse and thinking that it was their fault. When it wasn't.

Whatever led to the parents becoming abusive, it is absolutely imperative for children to know this: that is *not* what love looks like. That it was *not* what they deserved or needed. There may well be reasons why their parents developed such barriers to parenting in a way that was 'good enough', but these children need the workers around them to be able to sit with the reality of how absolutely awful that level of abuse is. It reminds me of racism; if people *deny* the pain, it cannot heal. The system needs to acknowledge it.

It is also my belief that these young people or adults who have been in these circumstances absolutely can rewire their brains (as discussed in the chapter on brain development) and learn how to love themselves and overcome anxiety. I understand wholeheartedly that some people who have had traumatic childhood experiences may not relate to my experiences of life and family that I've thus described. I want you to know that I feel you and see you and I absolutely accept my privilege. I know that for some people whose brains are more hardwired to anxiety due to growing up (appropriately) feeling terrified for whatever reason, this is more challenging than I will ever know. I do believe and know though that there is still so much hope for transforming your emotional and psychological world. I have seen it firsthand many times within the world of psychology and in transformational coaching with some of the amazing people I have met.

Sometimes I think the institutions around people can make them feel further disempowered. People are given labels and diagnoses and told that there is something wrong with THEM.

They are made to feel that *they got something wrong.*

I think instead of being told they are damaged or made to feel like they are a lost cause they should be told this…

'You had parents who absolutely did not meet your basic needs. This is not OK, it's not what you needed, and it wasn't good enough. You appropriately developed ways to cope, your brain was so amazing and adaptive and clever and became really good at being hypervigilant to danger. You are so strong for surviving this. Now your brain is overly hypervigilant to danger when danger is not present. You absolutely can overcome this, though. You don't need to feel like a damaged person who will always need the care of mental health professionals (and if you do need this help forever, that is OK too). But remember the power is within you, it is not outwith you.

Remember you can rewire your brain. Your brain keeps re-wiring all the way through your life. Empower yourself, know that you are the person that can help you the most. Meditate daily, do activities that bring you joy and make you feel relaxed. ALSO take the medication if you want to and if it helps, see the psychiatrist or psychologist if it helps, read all the self-development books, know that your life is in your hands and you can and will feel better. Make it your life's mission to feel better, to love yourself so deeply, to honour yourself and to help yourself heal from the pain.

Learn to trust people again, learn to believe in love again. It is real. It is there for you to receive when you let yourself. Connect to other people, there are so many people out there with similar experiences, healing themselves and working hard on feeling better. Find them, make connections, this will help you endlessly. The internet is your friend! There are support groups all over the world.

None of it was your fault. You did not get anything wrong. Every child, no matter how challenging their parent's or caregiver's circumstances, deserves love and understanding.

You can be the person that ends the generational trauma so that it doesn't continue to get passed down to your children and their children. Remember you are so powerful and I believe in you.'

Power is such an important word. It is my experience that people give this power away. Not only to health professionals but also to the parents who didn't love them or did not care for them. It is common that neglected or abused children put their parents on an untouchable pedestal. This is something to be mindful of and to work at. *You* can be the person that gives yourself the love. *You* can heal and create the life that you really want. You can be the powerful creator of your life and your emotional world.

Further resources

For anyone who wants to read more about how to create new pathways in the brain, refer again to:

Dr Joe Dispenza – *Breaking the habit of being yourself*

It will help you feel that you can change. A lot of your personality is just learned, thoughts that you have thought again and again become traits. You can choose who you want to be and become that person!

Doing the best we can with the information available to us

I've mentioned how, whilst studying for my doctorate in clinical psychology, it was common to discuss all the ways our parents failed us. Nowadays, my approach is a little different. It is important to acknowledge those areas that need healing. But, at the same time, what feels much more empowering for me and much more aligned with my spirit, is to tell a different story:

They did the best they could with the information available to them.

I learned of this idea during my coach training with The Little Volcanos. The truth is, I used to waste energy wishing my parents had been less critical or wishing Dad had found me less annoying, but to be honest a few things have shifted that. Firstly, there is nothing like becoming a parent to help you develop gratitude, understanding and compassion for your parents. Wow! What a relentless and challenging task. As I've discussed, it is impossible to 'get parenting right'! My parents were also younger than I was when they had kids; it helps me realise that they were just kids, doing their absolute best. And their best was amazing.

As well as this, I discovered what happened when you place the beautiful emphasis on living your life at 'cause rather than effect', i.e. taking full responsibility for your life and not blaming others. This perspective just feels so empowering and aligned in my body. I am a 40 year old woman. I take full responsibility for my life, for my emotions, for my choices. I have nothing but gratitude for my parents. I was so privileged to have such dependable, loving parents and, if I'm honest, I sort of cringe at the privilege I had, and the times I spent focusing on where they got it wrong. All of them, all of their human-ness, led me to be who I am today and I have been beyond lucky with the two little peanuts (that's what I call them) I was assigned at the parenting allocation meeting.

Like I have said, some of you reading this may feel that your parents failed miserably at meeting your needs; not only failing to meet them but perhaps actively being the people neglecting and abusing you. This is different; and I know some people who have chosen to end their relationships with their parents. I want to acknowledge that it might not be possible for some of you to get to this '*they did the best with the information available to them*' place. You *can* take steps to empower yourself, though. If you are still having flashbacks and reliving your trauma, you can have EMDR to help heal yourself. You can receive support to process your childhood in a way that empowers you to be fully in the present: to think about the parts of you the abuse could never touch; your essence. You *can* work to develop a mindset that supports you to create the life that you want. I just want to send you love and acknowledge that your mindset might look a lot different to mine, and I honour that.

In moving towards collective healing and collective joy, it is vital that we keep space open to hear and truly feel the experiences of those whose lives differ greatly from our own. To meet people exactly where they are on their journey. We have spoken about discrimination, and about agency, and about parenting. But what happens when all three meet at an intersection that is out of your control. While I was writing this book, I kept thinking of my friend, Faten. This is her story, translated into English. And, because it is so important to honour people's voices in their truest expression, I have included Faten's original story, too, written in her own words in Arabic.

From the memories of a Syrian woman
By Faten Almregawe

Do you know how it feels to start a new life at the age of 30?

In a new country that is different from the country where you were born in every aspect, including language, culture, religion, traditions and laws. I used to always describe myself as someone who is afraid of new beginnings! But I never expected to go through this experience.

I am Faten from Syria. I arrived in England on 26.3.2019 without family or friends. I was with my husband and two children, we were on our own.

Syria is a country with jasmine trees everywhere, it is the cradle of civilisation and includes the oldest capital in the world (Damascus).

I was born and grew up in my amazing city Homs. It is the third largest city in Syria and is located in the middle of the country which gives it a very important commercial advantage, and the river 'Assi 'goes through it. It is home to many archaeological sites such as the Citadel of Homs, Al-Zahrawi Palace, Tadmur Ruins and many more.

Historically, it used to be called Emesa and some of today's residents of my city give their girls this beautiful name. Homs used to have seven gates after which its streets were named.

I grew up in a well-known district of Homs. My family was very large and loving. I grew up with the help of my grandmother's advice, the kindness of my grandfather, the affection of my aunt and the company of my cousins. I had a happy childhood and when I went to school my heart was filled with great joy and big dreams that my father gilded. The years passed by and I grew up surrounded by love.

262

I married and made a beautiful family. I gave birth to two children and settled with my husband in our home. I always wanted to learn new things and used to look everywhere for new training courses that would benefit me, my children, and my life so I did a first aid training followed by a nurse training for beginners.

My husband supported me in doing what I wanted, so did my family. The days passed by, peacefully. Every day we made new memories and had new experiences. We visited most Syrian cities, and every city had its own character that made it special but they all had in common their authenticity, heritage and history.

My eldest child was 5 years old and my youngest was 3 months old only when we heard the first gunshot in our city and near our house which was located on a main road. They were occasional gunshots but enough to fill my heart with terror, the news was spreading as quick as lightning, and suddenly I received a call from my father who talked to me with his warm voice to help contain my fear. A few days later the number of gunshots had increased to a point where we were not able to recognise where they came from, and to add to this, we started hearing the sounds of canons close to our district, destroying houses and causing bloodshed. Before the war, we used to associate the sound of canons with happiness because we heard them during the month of Ramadan only, at sunset, and they were used to announce that it was time to break the fast and start our evening meal. The situation had changed from a state of safety to a state of unlimited fear.

Between the ruins of our souls, we found time to laugh and tell jokes, and one evening, we sat for dinner with my husband's family and at the first bite of bread our house was shaken. For a few seconds I felt there was no ground under my feet. The electricity was cut off and there was silence and darkness. I hugged my children without thinking, as if they were my soul. A minute of silence passed during which our laughter stopped and we stopped talking, it seemed to me like a year. I realised at that moment that a shell had fallen very close to us. The electricity came back and I saw my children and husband only.

I asked myself, 'where is everybody?'

Everybody had dispersed to other rooms in the house to seek shelter under the furniture. We calmed each other down and went back to eating dinner, then we started joking about how we were scared and how some of us ran and others crawled. At this moment I realised how much strength and toughness everyone has and how that helped us face all this fear by laughing and joking, and I realised that we are people who love life and hang onto it.

The situation became worse each day. My husband was kidnapped and this knocked us sideways until he was brought back to us. After surviving the kidnapping and coming back to us, he stayed with us for two weeks and then left the country because his life was in danger. After that, we had to leave our house because it was no longer safe for us at all to live in it and on the same day everyone fled our beautiful city.

We lived in a house that was unfit for human habitation for a month and then we moved two times afterwards because the war was following us.

A year and four months after the war had started and after I had been living away from my husband for ten months, I was no longer able to continue living this way on my own.

My father drove me and my children to the border with Jordan, which is a five-hour drive from our city. When we arrived, my first thought was how am I going to live without breathing the air of Syria, away from my land where the earth is mixed with the blood of martyrs, the good people, and many historical heroes, doctors and philosophers?

How will I embrace and feel that I belong in a new country? But I found consolation within myself and I talked with everything around me... the trees... the people and even the stones telling them that I will be back to my country. And here I am now writing to you from a place that is very far from Syria, the country that I left 9 years ago.

My father hugged me and bade farewell to me with words interrupted by tears and smiles. He had as much strength as an old olive tree that had lost the branch that is closest to its heart.

I left my family with who I lived for 21 years behind me. There are no words to describe the amount of pain that I felt because of leaving them. My father was and still is like Oxygen to me, he provides me with life, and my mother provides me with safety persistently and all the time. My siblings are like wings to my soul. There are not enough words to describe the support that my family gives me.

We faced many problems and barriers, and it would take a long time to describe them. I was finally able to join my husband in Jordan. The decision to leave was not easy at all, in fact, it wasn't a decision, it was rather an order that we were obliged to do because we feared the war that didn't have mercy for anyone. I never expected to leave my city for it's part of me and I am part of 'her'... I never expected to leave my country.

We lived there for eight years during which we built a new life and made many friends. We had challenges and good days. But most importantly we were safe. The days passed by, so did the months and the years, and our children grew.

One day, we were invited by the UN to travel. We thought primarily about our children getting a better education and perhaps me receiving treatment for my illness (Crohn's disease) as we faced significant financial and emotional difficulty to receive treatment for it in Jordan.

I experienced an array of emotions when I left Jordan. Even though it wasn't my country, it is the country that protected our souls and where we made many memories.

It was going to be the first time I boarded a plane and my heart was racing. I was scared of leaving Jordan and of being on a plane that is about to set off, and at the same time I had to be brave for my children. I embraced their hands and their little bodies and at the same time I needed to be hugged and needed warmth.

It was an amazing sight looking at Amman, the capital of Jordan, becoming smaller as we rose up in the sky until we couldn't see it anymore. We spent five hours between clouds, enjoying the different colours of the sky around us. There were a lot of tears mixed with emotions as we left 8 years during which we had made friends, visited many Jordanian cities, and made new memories…

The war indeed drains your soul and forces you to do things that push you beyond the limits of your capabilities. As we approached London, we enjoyed looking at the details of the vast surface of green lands and then we landed at the airport. We took many pictures and shared them with my own and my husband's families.

We had another long flight to Newcastle and then we boarded a small bus that took us to Cumbria. It was a very long and tiring trip, but we enjoyed observing the new and old buildings and all the details around us, the little and the large ones.

We arrived at our new house at 10 o'clock at night. It's our house but we didn't choose its location or furniture, and my husband and I did not argue about what colour we wanted to paint the living room, but we arrived at our house that was safe and that was enough. A staff member from the council and an

266

interpreter welcomed us because we do not speak English. I felt a little bit unattached from everything around me.

I had a lot of concerns after our arrival. I want my children to maintain their religion and Arabic language and I want to go back into education and work, and of course I thought about my husband and how he will find work, given that we did not speak English.

The days passed by quickly and we started to settle in our new home. We visited the schools where our children were going to be registered. The schools were beautiful and organised. I felt happy for my children because we came to this country for their sake. The schools were very different to what had been assigned for Syrian refugees in Jordan. Unfortunately, they had to go to school in the evening there and they did not integrate with the Jordanian children, and this is because the Jordanian schools lacked the capacity to take more children from both the Syrian and Jordanian nationalities. They went to school for three hours only, from two until five in the afternoon, and had condensed classes and one break. The time was considered late for them when they returned home after school during the winter season. But the only other alternative we had was sending them to private schools that had tuition fees affordable by a small proportion of the Syrian people only. Despite this, I believe that they welcomed the Syrian people well and did what they could do with what they had.

Do you know why I felt consumed by sadness when I visited the schools here? Because I couldn't stop thinking about the children in my country.

Where and how are they studying?

Are they able to finish the lesson without thinking of the loud noise of the military aircraft hovering in the sky? Are they able to control their reactions when the walls of their classrooms shake because a shell fell in the back street? The war is stealing our children's safety and happiness over and over again.

The agreement with the schools was made with the help of an interpreter and we had to put them in two different schools, one primary and the other secondary. This was the first difficulty they faced in their new country.

In fact, these were some of the most difficult days for our family because our youngest child who was eight years old could not accept the new reality and used to cry every day asking us to go back to Jordan. I felt my soul shattered when he cried, and I used to always reassure him that better days are coming and that he will make new friends and will feel settled soon.

It is not easy when one has to convince their children of something that they are scared of themself. But I used to try to pretend to be strong because everybody needed my strength as a mother.

Fifteen days after our arrival, my son started to cry and my attempts to soothe him failed miserably. He cried and sobbed more and more every day and he said one simple statement that really shook me, 'I want to go back to Jordan... I miss my friends a lot... I miss our house.'

I reassured him and said to him that everything will be OK. His crying was more like sobbing with gasps. I felt as if they were happening to me and that stopped me from being able to breathe. How I felt his pain! He cried for two hours or more and then I started to cry when he told me that he wanted to stop crying but that he couldn't. We cuddled then fell asleep that night.

The next day we woke up early with a new hope and many smiles. My children put on their school uniforms. They were very elegant, and everyone was happy that they were going back to school after a break caused by our travel arrangements and journey.

Their father took them, and my prayers accompanied them. I felt stressed out. They are shy and do not speak English. What if they wanted to go to the bathroom?

What if they felt scared, hungry, or uncomfortable! How would they tell their teachers?

These are simple things if you look at them from a distant position but if you come close you will feel what we feel and what we think of and you will know that we are struggling to learn the things that are basic routine to you.

The days and months passed by and we started to settle down. We learned the English language. Volunteers who work with a refugee support charity visited us and some of these volunteers became our close friends. We became familiarised with the area where we live, and I started a hair and beauty training course alongside many other activities. I like to improve myself and learn new things. My English language improved to a level where I can communicate my ideas with other people even though I reached the ninth grade at school in Syria. However, by practicing reading, which is also one of my hobbies, I was introduced to many other people and visited many countries in my imagination and waking dreams. This improved the level of my cultural knowledge.

My husband thought about work and started looking for a job that is suitable to his limited English language skills, but he didn't find any work unfortunately, so he decided to start his own business, but he faced challenges too. There were many new decisions that we had to take, and we couldn't understand the information surrounding many of these decisions. We tried asking our friends however no one could explain them clearly to us because they are laws related to refugees at the end of the day. He had difficulty funding his small business too because in our religion we are not allowed to take a loan with interest, and this has many logical reasons and explaining them would require a long essay.

Then I had an idea to start my own small business from home. This would help with generating income that would cover our needs and we could help each other. My business idea was preparing Syrian food from my home and the idea occurred to me when I noticed that many of my friends appreciate the food that I cook. However, we faced issues related to legislation again and we couldn't understand most of the laws. We were scared of doing something that would be against the law of the country that is hosting us. We asked to meet with the JobCentre and to have an interpreter so that we can decide whether or not we can carry out our business idea. Once again, everything was cancelled unfortunately including our meeting with the JobCentre because of Covid-19.

At this stage I felt desperate because we would like to depend on ourselves and generate enough income to cover our needs however the challenges stopped us, but I will always have hope that better days are coming. I spoke with my friend Sarah who invited me to attend Nia dance lessons with her and this allowed me to process my emotions and change my perspective.

These are beautiful days and I want to make the most of them. I did a Maths course, tried to improve my English language, and passed the theory test. I couldn't allow the lockdown caused by the virus to stop my life.

My family are doing well and my children like their schools. They receive education as they should do…

My husband perseveres with learning the English language…

I dream of making a beautiful life and I trust in God that my destiny holds beautiful things for me.

If you happen to see any one of us on the street, please smile for you don't know how painful it is for a migrant to feel unwelcome, and you don't know that smiling in our religion is a gift, this is what the prophet Muhammad (PBUH) said, 'smiling at your brother's face is considered like charity.'

We live with the hope that keeps us going despite the greedy war that destroyed our country in the present, and the country's history and its future.

Written by Faten Almregawe
Translated by Lina Harb Tyson

نستطيع القيام بمشروعنا أو لا . للأسف مرة أخرى تم إلغاء كل شيء و المقابلة مع مركز العمل بسبب كوفيد 19.

في هذه الفترة شعرت ببعض اليأس لأننا نحب الاعتماد على أنفسنا و كسب المال لتغطية احتياجاتنا و لكن الصعوبات لا تترك طريقنا لكنني لم و لن أفقد الأمل أن القادم أجمل. تكلمت مع صديقتي سارة و دعتني للقيام معها بدروس (NIA) و التي غيرت الكثير في نفسي و استطعت أن أفرغ الكثير من الأحاسيس من خلال القيام بها .

إنها أيام جميلة و لا أريدها أن تمر عبثاً . قمت بدورة رياضيات و حاولت إتقان الانجليزية بشكل أوسع و نجحت باختبار القيادة النظري . لم أستطع أن أسمح للحظر بسبب الفايروس أن يتسبب بايقاف حياتي .

عائلتي و أطفالي بخير يحبون مدارسهم و يتعلمون كما يجب.....
زوجي مستمر بتعلم اللغة الانجليزية.....
أحلم بتأسيس حياة جميلة و كلي ثقة بالله أنّ لي مع القدر شيئاً جميلاً .

إذا صادفت أحدنا في شارع ما من فضلك ابتسم فأنت لا تعلم كم من المؤلم شعور الشخص الغريب عن البلاد التي يعيش بها بأنه غير مرحب به . و لا تعلم أن الابتسامة في ديننا صدقة ذلك ما أخبرنا به النبي محمد صلى الله عليه و سلم) : و تبسُّمك في وجه أخيك صدقة.(

نعيش بالأمل الذي لازلنا بسببه نستمر على الرغم من أنف الحرب الجشعة التي دمرت حاضر بلادنا ، تاريخها و مستقبلها .

كُتبت بواسطة فاتن المريجاوي.

272

إنها أشياء بسيطة إذا نظرت إليها من البعيد و لكنك إن اقتربت ستشعر بنا و بما نفكر به و ستعلم أننا نخوض معركة مع الحياة كل يوم لتعلم الأشياء الروتينية الأساسية لك كشخص يعيش في الأساس هنا .

مرت الأيام و الشهور و بدأنا بالاستقرار و دراسة اللغة الانجليزية و زارنا أشخاص ينظمون مجموعة تطوعية لمساعدة اللاجئين و أصبح البعض منهم أصدقاء مقربين لعائلتنا. تعرفنا على المنطقة التي نعيش فيها بشكل أفضل و بدأت بالقيام بدورة شعر و تجميل و الكثير من النشاطات . أحب التحسين من ذاتي و تعلم أشياء جديدة دائماً.

أصبحت لغتي مقبولة أتحدث و أستطيع إيصال أفكاري للآخرين بالرغم أنني لم أدرس إلا للصف التاسع في سوريا، و لكن بممارسة هواية القراءة تعرفت إلى الكثير من الشعوب في خيالي و زرت الكثير من البلاد في أحلامي و ارتفع سقف ثقافتي لمستوى جيد .

فكر زوجي بالعمل و بدأ يبحث عن شيء يناسب لغته الانجليزية المحدودة و لكنه لم يجد عملاً مناسباً

للأسف، فقرر أن يبدأ بعمله الخاص و لكنه أيضا واجه صعوبات كانت القرارات كثيرة و جديدة علينا و لم نستطع فهم الكثير منها .حاولنا أن نسأل الأصدقاء و لا أحد يستطيع شرحها بوضوح لأنها في النهاية قوانين تتعلق باللاجئين . واجه صعوبة أيضا في تمويل مشروعه الصغير لأنه في ديننا من غير المسموح الحصول على قرض بفوائد و ذلك لأسباب منطقية يطول شرحها .

ثم خطر في بالي القيام بمشروع منزلي صغير يساعدنا في تمويل احتياجاتنا و نتساعد بالقيام به . كان المشروع عبارة عن تحضير طعام منزلي سوري و فكرت بذلك عندما لاحظت إعجاب الكثيرين من أصدقائنا بالطعام الذي أحضره . و لكن مجدداً وقفت بوجهنا القوانين التي لم نستطع أن نفهم أغلبها و لخوفنا من القيام بأي شيء يخالف قوانين البلد الذي يحتضننا طلبنا اللقاء من مركز العمل بحضور مترجم للغة العربية لنستطيع تحديد إذا كنا

في اليوم الخامس عشر بعد وصولنا بدأ ابني بالبكاء و بدأت محاولاتي بتهدئته و لكنها باءت بفشل ذريع و ازداد بكاءه و كانت جُملُه هزيلةً تهز الروح(: أريد العودة إلى الأردن .... اشتقت لأصدقائي جداً ... أفتقد منزلنا)

أخبرته أن يهدأ كل شيء سيكون على مايرام !

لم يكن بكاءً كانت شهقات تمنع الهواء عن صدري!!

يا إلهي ماهذا الألم المعدي؟ دامت نوبة البكاء ساعتين أو أكثر و بالنهاية بدأت أبكي عندما أخبرني أنه يريد إيقاف بكاءه و لكنه لا يستطيع و نام في حضني في تلك الليلة .

صحونا مبكراً في اليوم التالي مع أمل جديد و ابتسامات كثيرة . ارتدوا زيهم المدرسي كانوا أنيقين جداً و كانت السعادة تملأ المنزل ابتهاجاً بعودتهم إلى الدراسة بعد الانقطاع الذي سببه السفر و تحضيراته .

أخذهم والدهم و كانت دعواتي ترافقهم و التوتر يملأ خافقي .لديهم شخصيات خجولة و لا يتحدثون الانجليزية، ماذا لو أرادوا الذهاب إلى الحمام؟

ماذا لو أحسوا بالخوف أو الجوع أو عدم الارتياح ! كيف سيخبرون معلمتهم بهذا؟

هل تعلم ما الذي احترق داخلي عند زيارة المدارس هنا؟

لم أستطع منع نفسي من التفكير بالأطفال في بلدي .

أين وكيف يدرسون؟ !

هل يستطيعون إكمال حصتهم بدون التفكير بصوت الطائرة الحربية في السماء؟

هل يستطيعون التحكم بردات فعلهم عند اهتزاز جدران صفهم بسبب قذيفة سقطت في الشارع الخلفي؟

إنها الحرب مجدداً تسرق أمان وسعادة أطفالنا .

تم الاتفاق مع مدارس الأطفال بمساعدة مترجم واضطررنا لوضعهم في مدرستين منفصلتين ابتدائية ومتوسطة وهذا كان أول المصاعب التي واجهتهم في بلدهم الجديد .

في الحقيقة كانت من أصعب الأيام لعائلتنا لم يستطع ابننا الصغير الذي يبلغ ثماني سنوات تقبل الوضع الجديد و كان يبكي كل يوم مطالباً إيانا العودة إلى الأردن .كانت روحي تتمزق لبكاءه وكنت دائماً أخبره أن القادم أجمل وأنه سيكوّن صداقات جديدة و سيشعر بالاستقرار قريباً .

من الصعب أن تقنع أطفالك بفكرة تخيفك، و لكن كنت أحاول ادّعاء القوة فالجميع يحتاج قوتي كأمّ .

275

كان لدينا رحلة طويلة بطائرة أخرى اتجهت إلى نيوكاسل ثم استقلينا باص صغير ليوصلنا إلى مقاطعة كومبريا . كانت رحلة طويلة جداً ومتعبة ولكننا استمتعنا بمراقبة الأبنية القديمة والحديثة، و كل التفاصيل الصغيرة والكبيرة على الطرقات التي مررنا بها .

وصلنا إلى منزلنا الجديد في العاشرة مساء . منزلنا الذي لم نختر موقعه ولم نختر أثاثه ولم نختلف أنا وزوجي على لون طلاء غرفة الجلوس لكننا وصلنا إلى منزلنا الآمن وهذا كان يكفينا . كان في استقبالنا موظفة من البلدية ومترجمة لأننا لا نتحدث اللغة الانجليزية . أحسست بالقليل من الاستغراب من كل شيء حولي .

كان لدي الكثير من المخاوف بعد وصولنا . أريد لأطفالي أن يحافظوا على دينهم ولغتهم العربية وأريد لنفسي العودة للدراسة والعمل وطبعاً التفكير بزوجي وكيف سيجد عملاً . ونحن لا نتكلم الإنجليزية .

مرت الأيام سريعاً وبدأنا نستقر في بيتنا الجديد . ذهبنا لزيارة مدارس أولادنا لنسجلهم بها . كانت مدارس جميلة ومنظمة شعرت بالسعادة العارمة لأطفالي لأننا في الحقيقة أتينا إلى هذه البلاد لأجلهم . كانت المدارس مختلفة جداً عما تم تخصيصه للاجئين السوريين في الأردن . للأسف كانت مدارس مسائية الدوام ولم يتم دمجهم مع الأطفال الأردنيين وذلك لعدم مقدرة المدارس الأردنية استيعاب عدد الأطفال من الجنسيتين السورية والأردنية معاً وكان الدوام فقط ثلاث ساعات من الساعة الثانية حتى الخامسة مع تكثيف الحصص واستراحة واحدة.

كان وقت عودتهم يعتبر متأخراً في فصل الشتاء ولكن لم يكن هناك بديل آخر إلا أن ترسلهم إلى المدارس الخاصة التي لن يقدر على تكلفتها إلا فئة قليلة من السوريين ومع هذا أعتقد أنهم استضافوا الشعب السوري بطريقة جيدة وفعلوا كل ما يستطيعون فعله .

276

و جاء يوم و تمت دعوتنا للسفر بواسطة منظمة (UN)

انحصر تفكيرنا بمستقبل دراسي أفضل لأطفالنا وربما مكان أفضل للحصول على علاج لمرضي(داء كرون) الذي واجهنا الكثير من الصعوبات المادية والمعنوية لعلاجه في الأردن .

كانت تملؤني أحاسيس كثيرة عندما غادرت الأردن حتى إن لم يكن بلدي فهو البلد الذي حمى أرواحنا في حرب بلادنا ولنا فيه الكثير من الذكريات .

ستكون أول مرة أجرب بها ركوب الطائرة كان قلبي يخفق بشدة خوفاً من مغادرة الأردن وإقلاع الطائرة و بنفس الوقت كان علي أن أمثل الشجاعة أمام أطفالي .كان علي احتضان أيديهم وأجسادهم الصغيرة في حين احتاجت روحي لحضن كبير دافئ .

كانت تجربة رائعة مشاهدة عمان عاصمة الأردن تصغر كل ما ارتفعنا حتى غابت عن نظرنا.

قضاء خمس ساعات بين الغيوم والاستمتاع بالألوان المختلفة للسماء حولنا ، الكثير من الدموع والمشاعر المختلطة لترك ثماني سنوات من الأصدقاء والرحلات وزيارة الكثير من المدن الأردنية، وجمع الكثير من الذكريات المبهجة والحزينة، لترك حياة كاملة وراء ظهورنا، الكثير من الابتسامات لبدء حياة جديدة وجمع ذكريات جديدة...

نعم إنها الحرب تأخذ من روحك الكثير وتجبرك على فعل ما لا تطيق ولا تقدر.

بدأنا نرى الكثير من الأراضي الخضراء عند الاقتراب من لندن استمتعنا كثيراً بتفاصيلها وهبطنا في مطارها .التقطنا الكثير من الصور لنشاركها مع عائلتي وعائلة زوجي .

سوريا بعيداً عن ترابها الممزوج بدم الشهداء، و الصالحين، و الكثير من أبطال التاريخ و أطبائه، و فلاسفته ؟

كيف سيكون تقبلي و انتمائي لبلد جديد ؟

و لكني واسيت نفسي وتكلمت مع كل شيء حولي ... الأشجار .... الناس و حتى الحجارة قائلة سأعود قريباً يا وطني .و هأنذا أكتب لكم من البعيد جداً عن سوريا التي غادرتها منذ تسع سنوات .

احتضنني والدي و ودعني بكلمات تقطعها الدموع تارة و الابتسامات تارة أخرى . كان قوياً كشجرة زيتون عريقة كسرت العاصفة غصنها القريب من القلب .

تركت عائلتي التي عشت معها واحداً و عشرين عاماً وراء ظهري تركتهم متألمة لفراقهم بشكل لا يوصف . كان أبي و لا يزال أوكسجين حياتي و لم تمل أمي من كونها جسر الأمان لي في كل الأوقات . إخوتي أجنحة روحي لا تكفي الكلمات لوصف عائلة داعمة مثلهم.

مع الكثير من المشاكل و العقبات التي يطول شرحها استطعت أخيراً اللحاق بزوجي إلى الأردن . لم يكن قرار الرحيل سهلاً أبداً بل إنه لم يكن قراراً بل أمراً أجبرنا على فعله خوفاً من الحرب التي دهست الجميع بدون رحمة.

لم أتوقع للحظة واحدة أن أفارق مدينتي، فأنا جزء منها و هي جزء مني لم أتوقع أن أفارق بلدي . ....

عشنا هناك ثمان سنوات أسسنا فيها حياة جديدة و أصبح لدينا الكثير من الأصدقاء . واجهنا المصاعب و مررنا بأيام جميلة . و لكن الأهم من كل هذا أننا كنا نعيش بأمان، و مرت الأيام و الشهور و السنين و كبر أطفالنا .

278

في فمي اهتز منزلنا .لثوان شعرت أن لا أرض تحملني ... انقطع التيار الكهربائي و عمّ الظلام و الصمت معاً . احتضنت أطفالي بحركة لا إرادية و كأنهم الروح . مرت دقيقة من الصمت أوقفت ضحكاتنا و أحاديثنا أحسست أنها سنة لا دقيقة و في هذه اللحظة أيقنت أنها قذيفة سقطت قريبة جداً منا . عاد التيار الكهربائي و لم أجد في الغرفة سوى نفسي ، أطفالي و زوجي .

و طرحت أول سؤال أين الجميع ؟

كانوا متوزعين في غرف المنزل محتمين بأثاثها . هدأنا من روع بعضنا و عدنا لتناول العشاء و عندها بدأ الحديث الفكاهي عن خوفنا و ركض البعض و زحف الآخرين .و هنا أدركت كمية القوة و الصلابة التي يحملها كل شخص منا ليستطيع مواجهة كل هذا الخوف بضحكات و مزاح و أيقنت أننا شعب يحب الحياة و يتمسك بها .

كان الوضع يزداد سوءاً في كل يوم . تعرّض زوجي للاختطاف تمزقت أوردتنا لحين عودته . و بعدما نجا منها و عاد إلينا بقي معنا لأسبوعين ثمّ غادر البلاد، فقد باتت حياته مهددة بالخطر . اضطررنا بعدها لمغادرة منزلنا لأنه لم يعد آمناً أبداً و في هذا اليوم هجر الناس جميعاً مدينتنا الجميلة.

عشنا في منزل لم يكن مهيّأً للسكن لمدة شهر و غيرنا بعدها منزلين لأن الحرب كانت تلحق بنا .

بعد سنة وأربعة شهور من بدء الحرب و عشر شهور من دون زوجي لم أستطع إكمال الطريق لوحدي .

أوصلني والدي إلى الحدود السورية الأردنية التي تبعد عن مدينتنا خمس ساعات بالسيارة . عندما وصلنا فكرت كيف سأقدر على العيش بدون هواء

ترعرعت في أحد أحياء حمص المعروفة بين عائلة محبة كبيرة جداً . كبرت بنصائح جدتي و لطف جدي و حنان عمتي و صحبة بنات أعمامي . ذهبت كل يوم إلى المدرسة تملؤني بهجة عارمة و أحلام كبيرة جمّلها أبي في عينيّ ، و هكذا مرت السنين و كبرت و الحب يحاوط أطرافي جميعها .

تزوجت و كونت عائلة جميلة ، أنجبت طفلين و استقريت في المنزل مع زوجي . كنت لا أحب التوقف عن التعلم أبحث هنا و هناك عن تدريب جديد أقوم به يفيدني و يفيد أطفالي و حياتي فقمت بتدريب اسعافات أولية و بعدها بتدريب تمريض للأشخاص المبتدئين.

دعمني زوجي كما دعمتني عائلتي بالضبط للقيام بما أريده . و مرت الأيام ساكنة نزوّدها كل يوم بالذكريات و التجارب الجديدة . زرنا أغلب المدن السورية و كانت كل مدينة لديها شيء يميزها عن باقي المدن و لكنها جميعاً اتفقت على العراقة و الأصالة و التاريخ .

كان عمر أطفالي خمس سنوات و الصغير كان يبلغ ثلاث أشهر فقط عندما سمعنا أول طلق ناري في مدينتنا و على منازلنا التي تقع على الطريق العام . كانت طلقات عشوائية و لكنها كانت كفيلة أن تملأ قلبي بالرعب و كانت الأخبار تنتقل بسرعة البرق ليفاجئني اتصال والدي بصوته الدافئ يريد احتواء خوفي .و مع الأيام تحوّل الطلق الناري إلى طلقات كثيرة لا نستطيع تمييز مصدرها و لم تنتهِ القصة هنا بدأنا نسمع أصوات المدافع قريبة من أحيائنا تهدم المنازل و تريق الدماء .المدافع التي لم نكن نسمع أصواتها إلا في شهر رمضان و نطير فرحاً لأنها تعلن وقت إفطارنا و بدء تناولنا للطعام.

تغيّر الوضع من الأمان إلى خوف لا ينتهي .

بين ركام أرواحنا كنا نجد وقتاً للضحك و المزاح و بينما كنا نجلس ذات مساء لتناول العشاء مع عائلة زوجي و مع أول قطعة خبز وضعتها

280

من ذكريات امرأة سورية.

هل تعلم ماهو إحساس أن تبدأ حياة جديدة وأنت بعمر الثلاثين ؟

في بلد جديد مختلف عن بلدك الذي ولدت به بكل شيء (اللغة،الثقافة،الدين،العادات،القوانين) كنت أصف نفسي دائماً بشخص يخاف من البدايات الجديدة ! لكن لم أتوقع أن أمر بهذه التجربة .

أنا فاتن من سوريا وصلت إلى إنجلترا في 26.3.2019 بدون عائلة أو أصدقاء كنا وحدنا أنا وزوجي وطفلان .

سوريا بلد الياسمين ، مهد الحضارات و فيه أقدم عاصمة في العالم دمشق.

ولدت و كبرت في مدينتي الرائعة حمص ، ثالث أكبر مدينة في سوريا و تقع في وسطها مما أكسبها موقعاً تجارياً مهماً جداً و يمرّ من خلالها نهر العاصي . تحتوي على الكثير من المعالم الأثرية مثل قلعة حمص و قصر الزهراوي ، و آثار تدمر والكثير أيضاً .

قديماً كان تدعى ايميسا و البعض من سكان مدينتي يسمون بناتهم اليوم بهذا الاسم الجميل .كان في حمص سبع أبواب و سميت الأحياء بأسماء أبوابها .

My reflections on Faten's chapter

Faten has become a good friend of mine. My mum befriended Faten, as they both live in my hometown Barrow. Mum was involved in the refugee support group. I am so happy that Faten has connected so strongly with my family and more latterly with me and my friends.

She is so open-minded, warm, and kind. Before lockdown I loved drinking delicious Syrian coffee in her living room with her. I loved the beautiful jumper she bought for my son one Christmas. I love her boys, they are unbelievably beautiful.

As I am sure you found, it was heart wrenching to read Faten's words, and to be faced with imagery and descriptions of her pain. I am reflecting on anxiety in this book, yet the causes of most people's anxieties are a far cry from Faten's - war, bombs, prolonged separation from family, kidnapping - unimaginable horror.

Yet Faten and her family are now within our communities. The world is such that, at times, people are unable to stay in the countries they love with the people they love. Through no fault or choice of their own, they are forced to leave.

You likely live nearby to someone who has experienced similar trauma to this. I hope so much that this story, a story that often remains unheard, helps you to get close to Faten's experiences, to really imagine and feel what she is living with now from day to day.

We have been separated from our loved ones in various capacities over the last year during Covid. People have found this distressing and have missed their loved ones. Faten has now been unable to see her parents and family members for 9 whole years - I cannot begin to imagine the pain of this.

Faten lives with the trauma of the memories from her past, in her mind and body. As well as this, though, there are the barriers to joy, and causes of anxiety within our community. Faten talked about the anxieties of leaving a country she was familiar with, of boarding a plane, of needing to be the 'adult' and comfort her children whilst simultaneously longing for someone to comfort her.

And now in England, she talked about the anxieties associated with creating a new life. Fear of how her children would settle into new schools. My three year old recently started nursery, and it is hard enough for any parent to leave their child in a new environment, let alone with the barrier of language to content with. As well as this, Faten spoke of the desire to find work for her and her husband - this was the cause of anxiety, which she overcame, only to meet more barriers in terms of the rules and regulations around starting a business selling her delicious food.

I am happy to report that since Faten wrote this chapter, her husband Mahmoud has set up a business which is doing really well. I am celebrating their perseverance so much.

It is interesting to consider the 'physical' safety that coming to the UK provided, yet I wonder about the emotional and spiritual safety.

Faten speaks of the joy of the beautiful and organised school - and how this was bittersweet - because she was unable to fully enjoy, given her preoccupation with the children in Syria and what they were experiencing. To find joy and happiness in a new country with lots of her family in other countries, with less physical safety, sounds like a complex experience.

On reading Faten's words, I don't want you to tell a story of 'Wow I have nothing to complain about, I shouldn't feel anxious about my life'. When we shame ourselves for our emotions they don't go away. Brené Brown talks about distress, and how when we compare our struggles to another and minimise our pain, it doesn't make the pain go away, it just adds shame. Having empathy for ourselves enables us to release shame and meet ourselves exactly where we are.

In the chapter about talking to our children about difference, I explore how I believe it is important to help our children understand and embrace 'difference' and how we need to model and help children not to fear those who are different. Faten also talks about a very simple and easy way that you could add to her feelings of joy: to smile. When you see someone who looks different to you in the street, invite yourself to lean in, to smile, to say hello. Now you may have more of an idea about what they may be living with and the barriers to joy they may be facing, and oftentimes triumphing in the face of!

Further resources

To help children understand some of the emotions that refugee children may be experiencing, the following books, both by Francesca Sanna, are beautiful:

The Journey and *Me and My Fear*

Alongside *My Name is Not Refugee* by Kate Milner

And for older kids:

The Boy At the Back of The Class by Onjali Q Raúf

For an overview of how mental health stigma can present within refugee communities, and an insight into building capacity and challenging stigma & discrimination, Mental Health Foundation with See Me and Scottish Refugee Council have published the following briefing: Search online for 'Refugees, Mental Health and Stigma in Scotland'.

A CALL TO ACTION

What about when we actually do get things wrong?

Before we start planning the action we are going to take, I can hear some of you screaming, 'But what about when we *do* actually do something wrong'? And 'what about when others *do* do something wrong'? The point of this book is to encourage a new and different stance, one of less judgement. As I have explored in chapters on Shame and Guilt, all that happens when we judge ourselves is that we feel shame. This represents self-sabotage. It doesn't actually motivate us to take responsibility and do something different. Often, all it does is lead us into 'victim' energy: 'I'm so rubbish', or 'I'm always messing up' energy which prevents us from actually taking responsibility. I encourage that when you *have* done something out of alignment with your inner guidance system, you acknowledge this, but instead of the old pattern of shame, approach it from a less judgmental stance. Take full responsibility (this may involve feeling some pain or grief) and then re-commit to doing something different in the future.

Just the other day, I was talking about someone I love, not in a nasty way, but in a way that did not feel aligned with my inner guidance system. It was not a criticism so much, but it was a judgment of this person. At first, I got swept up in guilt, but very quickly I could ground myself, understand why I did this (I was trying to make sense of something with a friend) but I then committed to myself not to do this again and moved on.

When we fail to keep our word, we can choose to take responsibility, and communicate with others directly and lovingly. We can say sorry and make amends, but with an 'adult' energy rather than a 'victim' energy.

Then we can do something different next time.

286

And how about when others get things wrong?

Again, I would invite you to think about the stance of judgment that you find yourself in when assessing other people's actions. What does it do for you? How does it impact your energy to be in a place of judgment of others? As we explored in the NVC chapter, people take action based on their feelings and needs. We all share the same basic human needs, and when we can understand someone else's motivations, it really helps us move out of judgment. For example, I used to judge my husband for continuing to smoke. It really annoyed me. My focusing so much on something I was not in control of only wasted my energy. Not only this but, because of his strong need for autonomy, it probably made him smoke more! It was actually on our second ever date in 2013 that I asked him, 'Do you have any plans to quit smoking?' He had just finished smoking a cigarette but immediately lit up another and looked me right in the eyes. 'Nope,' he said. It actually attracted me to him, that he knew his own mind and was resistant to my suggestion. He did eventually give up and started 'vaping'. I still kind of wish he didn't vape because of my fears about how it impacts his health, but I no longer focus on it or try to change it.

There are times when people do horrific things in life, too, things that feel really 'wrong'. You may feel very resistant to challenging your stance of non-judgment around certain things (as do I). I do wonder though, if we were able to understand the needs of people who commit horrific acts of violence, whether we might better prevent them. Perry and Szalavitz in their book *Born for love; why empathy is essential and endangered* explore how lack of empathy impacts on child development. Children can learn to associate fear and distress with human relationships. Some never experience tenderness or care, leading them to struggle with empathy. We can judge such a person as a 'monster' for committing a violent crime, or we can think about how as a society we can look after vulnerable parents who are not able to meet their children's needs or how we can help men to talk more openly about their emotions. We can begin to try to understand the needs of people instead of passing judgement. Marshall Rosenberg talks about how NVC has successfully helped communities come together even when there has been longstanding conflict.

Empathy involves an action of understanding someone else, of being sensitive to and vicariously experiencing the feelings, thoughts and experiences of another. Szalavitz and Perry in 'Born for Love' explain how this 'soft skill' can be pushed aside for more rationality. This reminds me of what I have written throughout the book, with regards to thinking from the constriction of the mind, or feeling from the spaciousness of the heart. Szalacitz and Perry conclude their book by asking:

'Will increasing empathy solve all the world's problems? Of course not. But few of them can be solved without it.'

They call for individual and community action; more face to face interactions, increased neighbourhood participation and volunteering, high quality childcare and paid family leave to name a few. As Faten, who was forced to seek refuge from the trauma of war, says at the end of her beautiful chapter, a smile at a stranger in the street holds *such power*. We need to model this open heartedness to our children. We can jointly create loving and safe communities when we open our hearts to others and teach our children to do the same. We can start to move forward peacefully when we consider the needs of others and resist judging them, and when we encourage our children to do the same. We can stop labelling those in society as 'wrong' just because they are different. We can learn more about those we don't understand. We can acknowledge our own fear or defences and instead choose to take action from a place of love and empathy. We can create connection instead of separation, within ourselves and within our homes, our towns, our countries, and our precious world.

So, as we reach the final pages of this book, what is my Call to Action? When you act out of alignment, don't waste energy shaming yourself. Take responsibility and choose to *do something different* next time. When others wrong you, communicate your feelings, needs and boundaries clearly and try to understand their feelings and needs too. More broadly, try to extend this stance of empathy and compassion to others, too. Model this to the people in your life, including children. Do all of this even - perhaps most importantly - when it challenges you.

How about taking it one step further? How about trusting ourselves fully, absolutely; knowing that our bodies will tell us if something feels right or wrong. Trusting the direction we want to go in and living life by our values, not by those that we have taken on without question. What about resisting seeking advice and approval from others; relying on your own guidance and approval. How about doing what feels true and right for us, not what we have learned to be 'right' from our families or societies. What about questioning every single belief we have and then choosing our own?

When I studied and attained a doctorate, I felt like I was 'getting it right'. I was earning good money and I had become a 'doctor'. My parents were proud and I was miserable. I felt like a square peg in a round hole. I hated trying to be *professional* and *sensible*. Yet I ignored my inner guidance system because I had been deeply programmed to equate getting it right with career success and stability. *Getting it right* did not involve quitting a stable and respected job. Every time a stranger on a train or a plane asked me what I did, I could feel the lack of alignment in the body. I could *feel* the fact that I wasn't *lit up* with my answer. I knew I was meant to be doing something different. The universe sent me some ridiculous life events which showed me the glory of leaving a job and an environment which wasn't fully aligned with my spirit. I am so grateful for all of it.

Now I do what *lights me the f up* in body, mind and soul. There is nothing I would rather be doing (even being in a famous

289

rock band). I listened to my inner guidance system and took my time creating a job that is perfectly right for me, which I adore, which doesn't feel like 'work'. I have a dream team of people around me now, helping me spread the love and the joy. There are times I could still be more 'in alignment'; as I've said, this work is never ending.

How could *you* be more trusting with regards to *your inner knowing*? Allowing your body and soul to lead the way, trusting that **you cannot get it wrong** when you listen to *you*; when you block out the other voices and tune in to *your* voice. Listening carefully for the moments of joy and pleasure, those moments when you feel good in your body. Take this information or 'data' seriously; don't comply with a societal notion that this is frivolous somehow. Instead, view these signals as sacred and of paramount importance. Our bodies are trying to guide us. We just need to create enough space and time to listen to what they have to say to us. It's easy when you allow it. Once you start living like this, you can't go back!

What about trusting the journey and forgetting about the destination. I know that sounds *horrifically cheesy* but it is true. We can focus so much on getting our lives *right* that we completely miss the joy and pleasure that we are striving so relentlessly to create. We fear we are not enough, and we try so hard to prove this wrong by creating a life we think we *should* have, always focusing on 'what next'? We tragically miss out on our lives, on the present moment, where the preciousness, beauty and power reside.

'I will feel enough when I own a house, or when I'm not single anymore, or when I'm a mum, or when I'm earning over *x* amount or when I've created the most amazing piece of art, or when I've got that promotion, or when my house is tidy.'

It's time to stop looking outwardly for approval and to look inward, to our beautiful inner guidance system and trust that we are the only ones with the answers and with the love that we are forever searching for.

How to get clear on your values?

First question to ask yourself? When do you feel like the truest version of yourself? When do you feel like the least true version of yourself?

Write down the things that are important to you in life; it could be family, friends, fun, job, security, sex, music, money, travel, adventure, respect, success, religion, love, faith, humour, excellence.

Write them down on wee pieces of paper. Choose the one that shouts out to you the most. Put it at the top. Then work your way down. Do not worry about what you should say! You cannot get this wrong!

This exercise can be helpful to get to know yourself better and to aid you in living your life from a place guided by your inner wisdom and not by the conditioned beliefs that you have learned.

If you don't wanna do this, perfect! I didn't do it either! You can find *your* way and trust your own journey towards connecting more powerfully with your inner guidance system.

If this exercise feels aligned and right for you then go for it!

I want to leave you with an invitation. What would you do if KNEW you could not fail? If you knew you were supported?

If you knew you couldn't get it wrong and felt totally free, what would you do?

The rich tapestry of life and a little 'goodbye for now'

I'm so grateful for the highs and the lows and the bits in between. I've nearly finished this book and am pondering on what to leave you with.

As I mentioned, we've just bought a campervan. It's beautiful, a lifelong dream of mine. We collected it yesterday on Finlay's birthday. I got all romantic about the beauty of the synchronicity; on how it was ready for collection on his birthday. Yet the day, when it came around, was utterly shit. Neil and I were tense and cranky. Isaac probably picked up on this and was much more grumpy than usual, too. Loads of annoying stuff happened. The final icing on the cake after a day of frustrating events unfolding was getting ID'd for wine that I *really* wanted and I'm 40!

The hard days are different now, though, because I allow them. It's hard to believe that the heaviness will pass when you are in the middle of it, weighed down, but it always does.

I've just come up to bed having heard Isaac's little noises on the monitor. He wanted a cuddle, what a treat. I often smile in bed snuggling him tightly and thank the universe. I have everything I need in our little life. I'm so lucky. I was feeling anxious about his health this evening; manageably so but nevertheless fearful of him basically not being alive when I came up from watching TV. It's so much better these days. It used to be terrible. But it's still there, the dread and the fear. It's often worse around anniversaries and birthdays. It's not really fear about Isaac, it's sadness around Finn, I think. Isaac just fell asleep whilst we cuddled so I slowly extracted my body from his (you may know that move!) and reached out my hand to where Finn's cot used to be and stroked my own hand as though his hand was still there. It was a relief to cry. I miss him, I wish I could stroke his hand and celebrate his birthday. I wish he were here physically. Yet I do feel it was all meant to be. It's confusing.

I spread a lot of love in Finn's honour and I know I'm gifted at what I do. I ignite passion, belief, and action in people, and I'll be committed to spreading healing and love until the day I die. All thanks to him. Yet my heart is sore and it's all too big to understand sometimes.

I do wish everything would melt away sometimes and it could just be me and Finn, my precious little firstborn. I would hold him and kiss him and tell him of my love for him. He knows it all anyway, I know.

He taught me my biggest lessons in life so far:

Love is all that matters.

Life is fleeting.

Magic exists.

Because of him, I'm able to be brave because I'm so connected to my vision and purpose.

I have learnt that apathy is the enemy, *not* anxiety.

He has inspired me beyond belief to live my life from a place of trust and love and to make my life as beautiful and wholehearted as possible.

I hope this book has done the same for you x

The end

A wee exercise

I invite you at this point to play a song called Immunity by Jon Hopkins.

Either just enjoy, breathe and consider how the main messages you took from the book relate to your life

Or

Allow yourself to visualise the life you want to look back on when you are near the end of your life. (What matters to you, what do you want? How would your life change if you showed up as your best self. What would the impact be on yourself and those around you?)

Kyra
Goapele – Closer
Kendrick Lamar – Bitch, don't
kill my vibe
Alice Smith – I put a spell on you

Eliott
Yes – To Be Alive
Keane – Won't be Broken
Sigur Ros - Hoppipolla

Naomi
Ride – Vapour Trail
PJ Harvey – Rid of me
Back to the Planet - Daydream

Faten
Celine Dion – I'm Alive
Fairouz – My home
Majjda El Roumi - Words

Nadia
The Olympics – The Same Old
Thing
Joni Mitchell – Big Yellow Taxi
Joy Oladokun – Look Up

A few other songs I adore

Sufjan Stevens – Mercury

The O'Jays – Love Train (I
regularly listen to this and
imagine the love I'm commited to
spreading in my lifetime!)

Edward Sharpe & The Magnetic
Zeros – Home (this was our first
dance song)

Bombay Bicycle Club – Shuffle

Sigur Ros- everything by Sigur
Ros

Yo La Tengo - Shaker

Fourtet – Unspoken

Bon Iver – Everything by Bon
Iver

Ciara – Level Up

The Beach Boys – Good
Vibrations

Kate Bush – Cloudbusting

LCD Soundsystem – All My
Friends

Dona Onete – Jamburana

Lizzo – Eveything by Lizzo

Sister Nancy – Bam Bam

———————————————

Acknowledgements

Thank you to all the guest chapter authors for being glorious. Thank you for sharing your hearts so bravely and vulnerably. I will be forever grateful.

Thank you Nadia. This journey with you has been so connecting, meaningful and helpful. You are responsible for so much of the magic in the book. I can't wait to work together again soon. Thank you thank you thank you.

To my coaches, mentors and teachers, Corey Thomas!! Who first said "what if you told a story that you couldn't get this wrong", it all changed in that moment. To Kit and Rosie Volcano, to Riyah Thor, to Jambo Truong who guided me to write the book! Thank you thank you thank you.

Thank you Susan, my messenger besty, for your time and perspective!

Thank you to my parents for being so encouraging of the book – and for allowing me to talk openly about our family. How I love you both!

Thank you to my beautiful in-laws. I'm so grateful for your enthusiasm and support of my book and my career! And those vegan brownies and chips!

Thank you Isaac and Finlay, my babes, my guiding lights. I adore you both.

Thank you to my beautiful partner, friend, lover, mischief maker, Neil. You go above and beyond to support me in all my joy-spreading endeavours. I am deeply grateful for this. Thank you for embracing the transformational work so much. I adore you.

Where to find me

Instagram - **@drsarahmadigan**

Facebook - **https://www.facebook.com/drsarahmadigan**

My private online community you can request to join –

https://www.facebook.com/groups/1301905349979978

Email – **drsarahmadigan@gmail.com**

Website – **www.drsarahmadigan.com**

I'd **love** to hear from you.

Printed in Great Britain
by Amazon